to ... the
... ...tional
Portrait gallery or the Head of
a Department in the Victoria
and Albert Museum! And then
the whole time I have to keep
in mind the question of National
service — dreaded thought.

So you can see that life gets more
not less complicated. I hope the coming the
years will see either my artistic or my historical
interests get the better of me or perhaps I might
reach a compromise. I am still madly
interested in designing for the theatre and in
the history of Costume — neither of which seem
to fit in anywhere at the present. So you will
gather that my varied interests are leading
to complications.

I so hope the present 6th Form
is living up to the old standards and would
wish them luck in their examination results.
Hoping that you too are in the best of health
and enjoying a pleasant holiday.

Yours Sincerely

R. Stoney

ROY STRONG

ROY STRONG

SELF-PORTRAIT AS A YOUNG MAN

Bodleian Library
UNIVERSITY OF OXFORD

First published in 2013 by the Bodleian
Broad Street
Oxford OX1 3BG
www.bodleianbookshop.co.uk

ISBN   978 1 85124 282 5

Thanks are due to the following for permission to reproduce images in this book:

Peter C. Amsden ARPS ABIPP: p. 224
Cecil Beaton/Vogue © The Condé Nast Publications Ltd: front cover, p. 272
Michael Borrie: p. 151
The Ernestine Carter Collection/Fashion Museum, Bath and North East Somerset
    Council: p. 231
Lucinda Douglas-Menzies/National Portrait Gallery, London: p. 210
Copyright © John French/Victoria and Albert Museum, London: p. 228
© Paul Joyce/National Portrait Gallery, London: p. 140 (top)
© Roger Mayne/National Portrait Gallery, London: p. 184
Jonathan Myles-Lea: pp. 52, 239
© National Portrait Gallery, London: pp. 140 (below left), 180
Bern Schwartz and © Bernard Lee Schwartz Foundation: p. 104
The Weiss Gallery, London: p. 200
Diederike van Dorsten-Timmerman: p. 157

Photograph of Francis Wormald on p. 140 from *Proceedings of the British Academy*,
vol. LXI, 1976

Quotation from David Piper's unpublished account on p. 178
© National Portrait Gallery, London

Every effort has been made to obtain permission to use material
which is in copyright. The publishers apologise for any omissions
and would welcome these being brought to their attention.

Cover design by Dot Little
Designed and typeset by illuminati, Grosmont, in 10.5 on 16 ITC Bodoni Twelve
Printed and bound by MPG Books Group Ltd on Arctic Matt G. Print 115 gsm

British Library Catalogue in Publishing Data
A CIP record of this publication is available from the British Library

CONTENTS

To Antonia Fraser
who has always been curious as to whence I sprang

ACKNOWLEDGEMENTS

Tᴴɪs book is a monument to memory and also to what archives I have from that remote period of my life. Nonetheless, a number of people have helped me on my way. To the Director of the National Portrait Gallery I owe access to material in their archives from 1959 to 1967, including Sir David Piper's fragmentary autobiography. Mark Weiss quite late in the writing of this book sent me a letter I had written to David Piper in 1959. Brian Allen provided me with vital material in typescript concerning the early days of the Mellon Centre for British Art. My eldest brother Derek read and commented on the first chapter, which inevitably could only be one person's view of the same circumstances. Various friends and institutions have assisted in the task of putting together the pictures or have answered queries, among them Diederike van Dorsten-Timmerman, Rosemary Irvine, Michael Borrie, the British Academy, the National Portrait Gallery, *Country Life*, the Victoria and Albert Museum, the Fashion Museum Bath, Bantam Press and Sotheby's.

The relationship with the Bodleian Library and its Publishing Office has been an exceptionally happy one. They found me one of the best editors I have had in my long writing career, Johanna Stephenson. She has been a joy to work with. Then there has been the additional bonus of the critical eyes and probing minds of Dr Samuel Fanous, Publisher, and Dr Chris Fletcher, Keeper of Special Collections at the Library and now one of my literary executors. Autobiography, if it is to be any good, must be an act at times of quite painful and honest disclosure. They gave me the confidence of a younger, less reticent generation to overcome any lingering inhibitions.

Roy Strong

PREFACE

THE ORIGINS of the present book lie in the decision that all my papers should pass on my demise to the Bodleian Library, Oxford. In reviewing that decision, it became clear to me that what was missing was any early material from years when I could hardly have been expected to think in archival terms. There were family photographs, little appointment diaries going back to the 1950s and, much to my surprise, two sets of letters to friends running from 1953 and 1956 respectively. But the urge to write also came out of a conversation I had years ago with the distinguished historian Sir David Cannadine, who tried to persuade me to write the history of the meritocrats, those who harvested the opportunities offered by the 1944 Education Act and climbed both the educational and the social ladder and reached the top. It was a short-lived era, barely twenty-five years, cut short by the introduction of the comprehensive system in the mid-1960s. This is not the book he wanted me to write, but one person's journey through that terrain.

To it I add an observation by one of my former editors, Jörg Hensgen, who once noted that everything I cared about and represented had been formulated at a very early age and that I had never wavered from them. The text that follows probably bears that out and charts where most of it started. No one can quite escape their generation and the circumstance into which they were born, in my case as a child in an island at war seemingly against the world, with our whole civilization and culture under threat.

This is a work which draws on what papers I have from that period and also on memory. It ends with my appointment at the age of thirty-one as the youngest-ever Director of the National Portrait Gallery. To an extent, but not wholly, what happened thereafter can be followed in *The Roy Strong Diaries* (1997).

THE ARCHIVE ROOM

M Y WIFE DIED on the afternoon of 10 October 2003. For those who have undergone such a trauma I have no need to spell out the anguish of the heart. Nor will I, for this book tells another, happier story, that of a young man from nowhere who went somewhere. But why, you may well ask, begin such a memoir in a space called the Archive Room?

This room has a particular history. It is one that owed its existence to my wife, the designer Julia Trevelyan Oman, who in 1978 received an inheritance from her aunt, the biographer Carola Oman, Lady Lenanton. Four years previously, and two years on from our marriage, we had purchased a house called The Laskett in the village of Much Birch in Herefordshire. This was an unprepossessing red sandstone box which brought with it almost four acres of land which was soon to kindle our *furor hortensis*; but that belongs to another story. The house itself was to be our permanent home where we intended to end our days and so it called for workspaces for both of us. At the back of the house was a tumbledown stable block, which sounds grander than it really was, for it was little more than somewhere to house a horse and a small carriage. That Julia had transformed into her studio block. At that date she was at the apogee of her career, having designed two major productions for the Royal Opera House, the opera *La Bohème* in 1974 and two years later the ballet *A Month in the Country*. The Lenanton bequest, however, enabled us not only to add a large drawing room but to join the main house to the studio block.

The result included a large studio room rapidly colonized by my wife's kleptomaniac instincts. Photographs record this extraordinary explosion of things. The walls were lined with pinboards onto which she mounted collages of items which triggered her memory and imagination: pieces of wallpaper and fabric, tassels, old labels, corn dollies, sprays of dried flowers, odd pieces of old porcelain, postcards – anything, in fact. Shelves groaned beneath her accumulation of biscuit and sweet tins, custard cups, bottles, shells, stones, the bric-a-brac of a lifetime, each and every one etched in her mind with an association. The interior space was jammed with tables and plan chests on which sat architectural drawing boards, boxes filled with crayons, pastels, coloured pencils and inks, pencil sharpeners, pens, paperclips, rubbers, the myriad items that any artist calls to be readily within reach at the moment of creation. Amidst this seeming chaos there was always a box lined with something warm ready to receive a cat, which would curl up to sleep within stroking distance. Julia gutted every single newspaper or magazine that entered the house and boxes were stuffed with reference material under period or theme. This was a practical working room lit by fluorescent tubes. Few were ever allowed into this sacred space. It was a world of its own within a world.

During Julia's last weeks (she died of pancreatic cancer in four) she said to me, 'You will come and work here won't you?' What reply could I give other than in the affirmative? But after the event I was paralysed every time I ventured into it. I stood there transfixed, as though to touch or move a single item was an act of desecration. And then, about six months later, came the turning point. One of Julia's greatest friends was David Walker, himself a distinguished designer in the theatre, hugely lovable, perceptive and camp. I told him one day of my paralysis. I could not work there as it was, I just could not. 'Of course you can't', he said. 'You're sitting in the middle of someone else's mind. How could you?' That was the moment of release. I suddenly realized that I could not spend the rest of my life like some male Miss Havisham.

And so the great dismantling began. I would get up at about 6 a.m. during the summer months of 2004, go over to the studio block and start working my way through the piles of stuff. When I record that in the long run some 120 skips left The Laskett over the following two years, it will give some idea of the scale of the sorting out and reframing of my life. That excavation turned out to be an extraordinary voyage of discovery, for buried amidst this morass of material was much of importance, which in turn dictated that the studio should become the Archive Room. Early on the Oman family papers came to light, among them such treasures as the letters of Sir Charles (1860–1946) to his wife when he was MP for the University of Oxford. He was a man of huge ability, Fellow of All Souls, Chichele Professor of Modern History. Where should the papers go? I consulted an old friend, Michael Borrie, who had been Keeper of Manuscripts in the British Library, and thanks to his guidance they found their way to their natural home, the Bodleian Library, Oxford.

The room began to take on a life of its own. This was to be, at least in part, a shrine to a vanished intellectual dynasty, the Omans, and so up onto its walls went the family portraits and their books into the bookcases. Then there was the fate of my wife's vast archive of theatre design, some 20,000 items. That I had decided already should go to the University of Bristol Theatre Collection: they had honoured her with a D.Litt., a rare distinction in her profession. Not long after, a grant was obtained and all of it was catalogued and put online.

That was the Omans sorted and taken care of. But the reader may well ask at this juncture what about the Strongs? Good question. I was acutely conscious throughout my marriage that I had married into a family that was aware of itself and its connections. When we went to a concert at Chequers Julia wrote to the then prime minister saying what pleasure it had given her to sit beneath the portrait of her ancestor Sir Walter Raleigh! In any marriage there is a link between two families, in my case a humble one with a very different background. There were no archival papers except my own, a substantial personal archive accumulated over half a century. Where should that go? The Keeper of Western Manuscripts at the Bodleian, Dr Chris Fletcher, had already cast a predatory eye in its direction and so the deed was done. On my death it, too, is to join the biographical collections of the Bodleian Library.

The end of life is so much clearing up and seeing that those left do not have a ghastly time sorting things out. But dealing with such matters inevitably leads one to take stock. Suddenly I was aware that there was a significant gap in my archive that I alone could rectify. I first became national news in 1967 when, at the age of thirty-one, I was appointed Director of the National Portrait Gallery. Thereafter there is a torrent of material; but what about the three decades before? Who was this young lion and whence did he spring? What was his background – and who, indeed, were the Strongs? Some answers are contained in my archive, in three volumes into which I mounted what material I had on my family; but inevitably much, much more is locked within my memory.

This memoir is the consequence of asking these questions. It is a story that opens in a 1920s' suburban street in North London and the birth of a child. But, I should add before embarking on that saga, in the middle of the Archive Room now stands a Victorian partner's desk and, yes, I can happily work there just as my wife had wished.

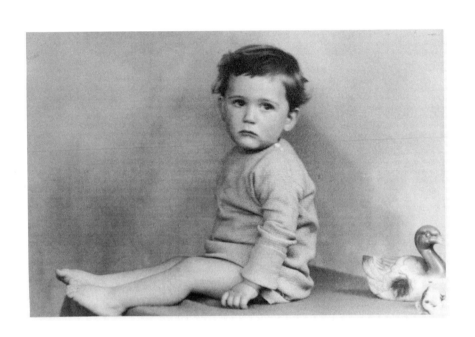

ONE

HARD TIMES

1935 to 1945

MY ARRIVAL in the world is visually signalled by a studio photograph of me aged eighteen months. I do not look happy. Here, however, is a child blessed with an abundant head of hair, which, I am glad to record, I still have in my late seventies. To one side there is a celluloid duck, not a studio prop for I remember it well, bobbing in the bathwater. This was me in the year of the coronation of George VI, a troubled infant staring out at what was already a troubled world heading fast towards cataclysm. This is the infant who was to be Director of the National Portrait Gallery at thirty-one and of the Victoria and Albert Museum at thirty-eight. The beginnings were not, however, propitious.

I was born at about five o'clock on the morning of 23 August 1935, the third child of George Edward Clement Strong and Mabel Ada Smart. I was a large child, over 8 lb in weight. A doctor must have been present because a reddish hand-mark on my left chest betokens that the birth of this particular infant called for a little manual assistance. Two brothers had preceded me, Derek Clement in 1929, a year on from my parents' marriage, and Brian Arthur in 1933.

My arrival was in a sense a disappointment, for I had been destined to be the daughter my mother longed for. Years later I read that medical research had shown that many boys born in such circumstances either were or had an inclination to be homosexual. In the social context into which I was born the notion that a child could have such a propensity did not exist and I was not to know what being homosexual entailed until I was into my early twenties. But I can see now, in retrospect, certain aspects of my character would square with it in some people's eyes.

The birth took place in the upstairs front bedroom of the 1920s' terraced house which had been built only a few years before on what until then had been orchard land. If I remember rightly it cost about £800, for which my father had a mortgage whose monthly payment was to become a permanent fixation. Number 23 Colne Road, Winchmore Hill, was to dominate and blight my life until, in 1964, I at last escaped. But all that lay in the future in the year of my birth.

The house was a clone of millions of others built between the wars. As you faced it from the pavement there was a wooden gate opening onto a straight crazy paving path to the front doorstep. To the left there was a containing ribbon of brick from which arose posts supporting swags of iron chaining (confiscated in 1940 for the war effort). The front garden had hedges on all three sides, two of golden and one of green privet. The golden hedges were low and clipped straight but the green one was trained into architecture of sorts. That hedge witnessed my earliest encounter with the art of topiary (to the revival of which I later

Suburban icon: 23 Colne Road before the War.

contributed). To the left of the path there was a narrow flowerbed, which in summer was edged in true Victorian style with alternating white alyssum and blue lobelia, behind which there would be a planting of annuals such as antirrhinums. This border and the hedges held in a patch of greensward which stretched under the bay window of the house. The lower level of the bay was brick, while above the ground-floor window there was a canopy of tiles giving onto pebble-dashed walls. The house was painted green and cream and in summer there was a canvas curtain to protect the front door paint from blistering. Only in the 1950s did the painting scheme change when, in the spirit of the Festival of Britain, a contrasting bright colour was applied to the front door. The doorstep, again a lingering from an earlier age, was cleaned and polished with a substance called 'Red Cardinal' and, again in summer, hanging baskets were suspended from the porch. These inevitably had to be watered and were a constant source of bickering between my parents as water and soil were spattered all over the spotless step.

Pushing open that door revealed, to the right, a hallstand for hats, coats, umbrellas and walking sticks, still in use in the thirties. A little further on, to the left, a door opened into the sitting room, invariably referred to as the 'front room', and, further on again but with a slight bay to the left, a second door led to what was meant to be the family dining room, with a door opening onto the garden. All the rooms were wallpapered up to a picture rail in vaguely Art Deco patterns. Fireplaces were surrounded with two-tier mantelpieces with, in the front room, a clock as its centrepiece flanked by framed photographs of my father and mother in their prime. That indentation reduced the size of the dining room in the interests of a larger kitchen, although in today's terms it remained pathetically small. I have little memory as to what these rooms looked like before the war, although they must have contained the same furniture: a draw-leaf dining table with bulbous legs, sideboard and dining chairs in a vaguely Old English style and a three-piece suite with hard wooden arms upholstered in an Art Deco tapestry fabric. There were two pictures, both reproductions, one by Millet entitled *Between Two Fires*, in which two women in vaguely

Dutch seventeenth-century dress attract the attention of a gentleman in black and wearing the hat of a Puritan, seated at a table, the other Millais's *The Boyhood of Raleigh*, in which an old tar gestures with one arm out to sea as he entrances two young boys with tales of maritime adventure. Both pictures were the product of painters re-imagining the past. Upstairs there was a landing, off which opened a separate bathroom and lavatory, two bedrooms capable of accommodating double beds, both with fireplaces, and the so-called 'box room', a small room over the porch of the house. The room in which I was born had a burr walnut bedroom suite comprising bed, wardrobe, chest of drawers and a dressing table which sat in the bay window.

Snaps taken with a Box Brownie camera record the back garden during those years leading up to the war as a long rectangle divided into three sections: a terrace with the inevitable crazy paving, a bed at its centre and, outside the back door, a coal and coke bunker; next, a path with rose arches leading straight from that door to the back gate, a rectangle of lawn with flanking flowerbeds filled with flowers typical of the period such as Russell lupins, fencing topped by trellis, and espaliered William pear trees; and finally a garage housing a car, its garden aspect garlanded with the rose Paul's Scarlet. Near the house there was a plum tree and close to the back gate two rowan trees whose scarlet berries enlivened the autumn. One of my father's redeeming features was his love of the garden (which I was later to inherit), although that, too, became a source of marital division as the rose arches were demolished in response to my mother's complaints. Not adding to marital harmony either was the fact that the garden was 'his' and on no account was she to touch it or pluck as much as a single bloom.

What I have described so far is a scene that could be duplicated a million times across the country in those years. For the vast majority, as was the case with my parents, it was a step up from the previous generation. The house had electric light, an indoor bathroom and lavatory, a gas stove for cooking and a boiler with which to heat water. This, certainly in the case of my mother, was a huge advance on the home of her childhood, 48 Farrant Avenue, Wood Green, where Grandma Smart – known to us as Nan Nan – still lived. There cooking continued to be done on a solid fuel range, the house was lit by gas, the lavatory was outside, there was but one cold tap in the kitchen, and a bath meant a tub in front of the range or a visit to the local municipal ones. Chamber pots were de rigueur, even in my parents' house. But looked at from afar, Colne Road was a great improvement on what the previous generation expected. And, up until the outbreak of war, a domestic could from time to time be afforded to help with the housework.

The road itself needs to be set in context. It was situated at one of those junctions in suburbia where social gradations could be measured by the nature of the property. The earliest houses were a pair of semi-detached Victorian cottages opposite, built some time in the 1870s. Every other house was later but all ranging in date from the 1920s and 1930s and in those bastardized vernacular styles which Osbert Lancaster was so brilliantly to lampoon. At one end there were large semi-detached ones, to one of which the singer Sir Cliff Richard owed his origins. At the other there was a fair amount of Mock Tudor with beams and leaded windows. Then there were short terraces with a semi-detached at either end, variations in wood and stucco and brick but always with a sense that some were classier than others, differentiations registered by subtle differences like the addition of a bow window, a porch with leaded lights and, above all, space for a garage to one side.

The social mix was white collar: teachers, small businessmen, shop-keepers and office staff who commuted daily into the inner city. This was the world of 'keeping up appearances', of front gardens kept in immaculate order, the lawns mown, the beds filled with annuals each summer and the containing hedges of privet neatly clipped. It was a road lined with those quintessential trees of the era, the laburnum and the flowering cherry. There was little commerce between those who lived there beyond a salutation, but there was a strong corporate feeling as to which rung of the social ladder they occupied. When a house opposite was purchased by a taxi driver who parked his vehicle outside, it was clear that a social order had been irrecoverably breached.

But then other prejudices spring to mind. Anti-Semitism was certainly present and although my father, when reduced to penury in 1939, would clean the car of a Mr Freeman who lived around the corner, there were always mutterings as to his ethnic origins. There were suspicions, too, about the Italian jeweller who lived at the semi-detached end of our particular terrace. Catholics were also suspect. I was not encouraged to make friends with a boy opposite, whose family was Catholic and went to mass at St Monica's Church in Palmers Green – although I was taken to see the crib in the church each Christmas and was hugely attracted from the start to this mysterious place with its many images and flickering candles. Anyone black was looked upon with a kind of horror. A black young person once came to the door for my middle brother and extended his hand to my mother (who had a coat in the now unmentionable shade of 'nigger brown'), which she had no option other than to shake. She was shattered by the event.

Both house and road need equally to be set within the broader context of Winchmore Hill, a district of the London borough of Enfield. A wide road called Green Lanes (any greenery had long gone) ran from this former market town into the city via Bush Hill Park, Winchmore Hill, Palmers Green and Wood Green, where it was possible to board the Piccadilly Line to Central London. That route was to determine my movements for over two decades of my life. Colne Road was on the fringes of Winchmore Hill and quickly tipped over towards Bush Hill Park and then on to the working-class district of Edmonton. In the other direction the land rose towards what had been the old village, which still had traces of its rural past and where, along Broad Walk, there were substantial detached houses that had produced Rod Stewart, Ted Ray and Frank Ifield.

In one of these houses lived Arthur Rowley, head of a building firm, who was a friend of my father's – indeed, his only friend. I never discovered when this friendship began but there were jokes that my father had been his batman in the war. This was an unequal friendship of a curious kind. Arthur had married someone called Maureen Couchman (there were mutterings about her ethnic origins too), who told my father that smoke must have got into his eyes when he married my mother, a remark which he cheerfully related to her. The Rowleys' car would from time to time stop outside our house. Mrs Rowley would stay put while her husband came in to indulge in a desultory conversation with my father and then leave. Father was a kind of 'bought' sycophantic friend whom Arthur Rowley would take to Yarmouth from time to time for a holiday.

Something would lead me to believe that some kind of allowance came to father from Arthur, although I had no way of knowing that until late in life when, as I was in the process of writing this memoir, my eldest brother revealed that that was indeed the case. When poverty hit my father with the outbreak of war, Arthur had lent him a sum of money, which my father paid back in instalments. Although they fell out from time to time, Arthur was also to make a small allowance to my father in his penniless old age. I knew nothing of this. If I had – and had also known my father before 1939 – I would have viewed him in a very different way from how I have described him here.

———

At this point it might be reasonable to ask who were the Strongs? The answer to that is nothing very much. I owe the volition to research the family history to my Canadian cousin, Laurie, the only other successful member of the family (he was a champion tennis player and ended up as President of Unilever in Canada, to which he emigrated), whose many daughters asked him about their origins. This set my eldest brother, Derek, off on the quest.

Our history cannot be taken back further than my great-great-grand-father, William Strong (1809–89), who was born in Reading and died in Winkfield, both in Berkshire. In 1865 he is described as 'farmer' but by 1889, perhaps as a consequence of the great agricultural depression, was classed as a 'jobbing labourer'. William was twenty-seven when, on St Valentine's Day 1836, he married a soldier's daughter, Anne Rose (1815–82), and together they had four children, William, Henry, George and James. Anne was literate as she signed her name on the wedding certificate, whereas William made his mark. My great-grandfather William Edward Strong (1838–1921), born at Winkfield, was described in 1862 as 'master draper', seemingly a step up from his father, but by

1892 had become a 'Grocer's Warehouseman'. By then he had migrated to 9 Cromwell Road, Swindon, where he died in 1921 having fractured his skull while unloading a delivery of sugar at the age of eighty-three. He had moved there from Lechlade where, in 1865, he had married Mary Matilda Tytherleigh (born 1843), recorded on that occasion as a dressmaker from Highworth, Wiltshire. Mary Matilda came from a family of grocers and her father, Charles Large Tytherleigh, had married a yeoman's daughter. William Edward and Mary Matilda had ten children; their second son, Alfred Augustus (1867-1935), was my grandfather.

Born at Lechlade, Alfred Augustus was listed as a compositor in 1892 and died at the age of sixty-eight in the year I was born; he was buried in Tottenham Cemetery. On 6 November 1892 he married my paternal grandmother, Rachel Peake (1864-1947), daughter of James Peake, a labourer, and Ann Maria Blackburn, daughter of another labourer. At the time of her marriage Rachel was listed as living at 25 Munster Square, St Pancras, while her future husband lived in Osnaberg Street. Rachel came from Suffolk farming stock. She was a widow for the last twelve years of her life, taken in by one of her sons, Uncle Charlie; I was eleven when she died. Photographs of her record a powerful matriarch, the dominant presence in any family group. Her husband was a depressed figure by her side, his features as downturned as his moustache and body. She had five children in all, four boys, Reginald (Reg), George, William (Will) and Charles (Charlie), and one daughter, Matilda (Tilly). The last told me that her mother had no time for her, but only for her boys. Of the four boys Will was the most successful, having a flair for languages and becoming fluent in French. He must have been a monument to self-improvement during a period when opportunities

My father in his heyday, about 1920.

to rise from that area of society were few; he became a mainstay of Lazard's Bank. Wisely, he removed himself from the somewhat baleful influence of his brothers and there was a final parting of the ways when they indulged in a card party after their mother's funeral. He never spoke to them again.

Alas, I have no memory of my father before the war. A scattering of snaps and photographs suggest a very different man from the one I remember: there was a smile on his face and he presented a dapper appearance, often wearing plus twos, caught astride a bicycle or standing by his car. He also exuded an aura of prosperity. Born in 1895, he was a Victorian: there are quintessential studio photographs of the period of him in knickerbocker suits. The First World War broke out three or four years after he would have left school and conceivably joined the firm in which he was to spend most of his subsequent working life, Ayres & Smith the hatters, situated in Soho's Lexington Street.

What I do know is that he was old enough to be called up towards the end of the conflict. Like so many people who have experienced war, he would never talk about it. The only glimpse of its impact on him was the mandatory 'You've seen nothing yet, my boy.' Apparently he was meant to have been shipped to France, where he would certainly have been killed, but the action called for troops on the North Italian front. There's a photo of him in army uniform, with slicked-back, well-pomaded hair, and another with a group of what may be Italian troops, *Alpini.* His job after the war, by which time he would have been in his mid-twenties, was to travel the South Coast selling both men's and ladies' hats for Ayres & Smith. Every man and woman wore a hat at this period – indeed, it was inconceivable not to. Presumably my father's wages were topped up by commission on what he sold. Occasional flashes of what had once been a jokey charm were turned on later in life, giving me a glimpse of the earlier man.

On the outbreak of the Second World War in 1939 his world collapsed. His employer's firm was turned over to making military headgear and his income was reduced to five pounds a week, out of which he was expected to keep a family of five besides paying the household bills, the mortgage and the rates. Something must have snapped, for in effect he nose-dived into poverty. The solitary domestic helper went, as did the car, the telephone and the piano. My mother was goaded by him: 'Mabel, when are you going to get your war job?' I was never to know the successful younger man, only the diminished older one, someone who had shrunk back into himself. And when peace came the old days never returned, for the world of men's hats had evaporated. They simply did not wear them any more.

In those years and into the decades after 1945 the pattern of my father's life never changed. Each morning he would leave the house at eight o'clock on the dot, carrying a cardboard box containing his samples. The day must have been a weary round of those department stores in London that boasted a hat department, attempting to woo the buyers. His return in the early evening always signalled the descent of a pall over the house. Having hung up his hat and coat he would go upstairs, take his jacket off and put on slippers and a pink woollen dressing gown, which he wore until it was in rags. A bottle of whisky was secreted under the stairs, more often than not his first port of call. Then he would take up a commanding position in the sitting room, to the right of the fireplace on an upright armchair, the carver from the dining room set. In the bay was his bureau with the flap down; on this sat the radio, over which he had total control. There he would sit, sipping, smoking and progressively nodding off.

He became a hypochondriac. No one but no one could ever be as ill as he was. Year after year he would inform us that he would never survive the winter, lamenting, 'I'll never make old bones.' Needless to say, he died in his ninetieth year. That is not to say that there was nothing wrong with him. He suffered from a hernia, but would never have an operation to right it, and also from asthma, for the relief of which he relied on a patent medicine called Potter's Asthma Remedy, a filthy powder which, when ignited, gave off a foul inhalant. Also, whenever it took his fancy and despite any circumstance, he would suddenly arise and go to bed, announcing that he was ill. Up and down the stairs my mother toiled in response to his every whim. He would never on any account agree to an injection. With the advent of the National Health Service in 1948 a golden age beckoned for him. Up until then going to the doctor had to be paid for; now it was free, so round to Dr Curnow's surgery he went. The house sank beneath the pills and potions he could now get for nothing or, when it came in, for a modest prescription fee. The extraordinary fact was that most of them he never took: I recall an upper cupboard in the kitchen after he died piled high with medication sunk beneath layers of dust.

My mother always referred to him as 'Your father'; when addressing her he invariably referred to 'Your children', as though he had had nothing to do with the creative process. Father never read a book. Indeed, there were no books in the house apart from some kind of medical dictionary, which only convinced him that he had everything in it, and a multi-volume series on how to be successful in life, which he patently had not been. These must have arrived via some doorstep salesman and remained unread on a shelf in a glass-fronted cabinet. The only newspaper he read was the *Evening News* – but that was for the crossword. His one hobby was fishing, which must have dated back to childhood visits to his mother's family in East Anglia; it was the Norfolk Broads to which he most responded. In the summer, however, off he would go with his fishing rod and tackle by Green Line Bus to a stretch of the River Lea at Picketts Lock near Edmonton in Hertfordshire.

My father had no concept of being a parent, no interest in what happened to any of us. Of the three there was a flickering towards Brian as he was a sportsman. But Brian was also wayward, could be violent and early on became a compulsive liar and, eventually, a criminal. His physical force was such that my mother found it difficult to control him and when he had done something horrific vainly implored my father to exert his authority over the boy. Nor did my father want to know anything about our education. In my case he only went once to a parents' meeting at the school. I recall the devastating effect on me when, with a good school report, I pressed it open proudly into his hands so that he could read it. It was immediately slammed shut and pushed back into my face. On another occasion I had spent a term making him a Christmas present, to which he almost immediately took the scissors.

Father died in 1984. I have long been in the habit of writing as it were a personal obituary when someone I know dies. That on my father was perhaps the most impassioned that I have ever penned. Two paragraphs in particular capture my sense of utter alienation:

> For a time I hated him. I use that word deliberately. As I grew up I suddenly saw him for what he was, and for what he had done to my mother and to all of us. I hated him for that. In one's teens it was all bottled up. How could it have been otherwise? From time to time it would explode in violent rages when I had endured some awful humiliation. I have never but never felt anger, rage and resentment so deeply, so bitterly, as I did in my early teens.
>
> I blamed him too for what I had become: 'Mother's boy'. For years as I grew into manhood I took his place. I went everywhere with her even into my early twenties. It was all so wrong, and when I achieved the break, my mother never quite recovered from it. On my marriage it was total. But it should never, never have been allowed to happen in the first place.

There let it rest.

So much for the paternal inheritance; but what of the maternal? That is very much a parallel tale of a drift to the metropolis of country folk in the late Victorian period. My mother's grandfather was Walter Smart (1833–1913), son of a John Smart, a carpenter. That much comes from the marriage certificate, dated December 1858, when he married Harriet Lea (1830–1900) at St James's Church in Shoreditch. He was a postman of 69 Freegrove Road, Holloway, and she a farmer's daughter. They had two children, a daughter, Amelia (1860–1919), and a son, Charles Alfred Smart (1867–1948), my maternal grandfather. Charles had some sort of clerical post in the Port of London Authority but ceased work early on grounds of ill-health. I remember him well: a gentle, diminished soul, his fate similar, I would guess, to grandfather Strong's, having married an equally uncompromising and dominant woman. My mother adored her father; indeed, he warned her against marrying George Strong but that went unheeded. Grandpa Smart died of cancer in 1948, aged eighty-one. I remember my mother returning from that event and sitting down, grief-stricken. He was a child of his period, devoted to self-improvement; a small batch of his papers, including notes on things like windmills, were passed to me on his death. Poor man, my memory of him is of someone obliterated by his wife, a silent being sitting in a chair by the range. My mother told me that his eyes were weak and that he had therefore prepared himself for what he believed to be inevitable blindness by teaching himself Braille.

Grandma Smart – Nan Nan – was one Emily Hearn (1876–1968), who was to outlive her husband by twenty years and die at ninety-two. She was born at Goose Green, Great Torrington in Devon, into a Methodist family. Her father, John Hearn, was a cabinetmaker and her mother, Elizabeth Rew, a glovemaker. Family tradition has it that the Rews

My somewhat shy mother in 1922.

were glovemakers based in Taunton, of Huguenot descent. John and Elizabeth were married on 1 February 1875 and their daughter, my grandmother, was born a year later. At some date the Hearns must have moved to London, for they, too, were in the Holloway area in Blackstock Road, within walking distance of Freegrove Road. There are small oval photographs of them, John a handsome, kind-eyed, bearded man, Elizabeth tight-lipped and determined.

On 10 July 1895 Charles and Emily, my maternal grandparents, married. They were to produce four children: Sydney Charles, Reginald, Elsie Emily and Mabel Ada (1903–1990), my mother. Of that *galère* of aunts and uncles Reginald can be discounted as he removed himself from the orbit of the family after marriage and died young. Sydney, not the world's brightest, married Elsie Snewin and followed their only daughter, Vera, to New Zealand not long after the war. Aunt Elsie, however, is another matter. She married Leonard Bryer, who worked in a firm of stockbrokers. She was bright, quick and a monument to social mobility, moving up a rank into a world of middle-class comfort and aspiration in Purley, Surrey. She opened my eyes to the possibilities of becoming 'a better class of person' by her assurance, modulated voice and appearance.

Once again there are the usual stilted studio portrait photographs of my mother as a baby, taken not long after her birth. Elsie stands pert and upright, the two boys loll somewhat gormlessly nearby. I can follow my mother's early years through photographs, a shy, awkward, not very intelligent young woman but smiling and happy. She, like my father, must have left school at fourteen but how she filled those intervening years until she married my father in 1928, when she would have been twenty-five, I know not. There were holidays on the East Coast and it was on one of those that she encountered my father, who was eight years her senior – indeed, like me, he married late, being thirty-three. Decades later and in the aftermath of having eloped and married my own wife, much to my mother's disapproval, Aunt Elsie told me that my parents' engagement had been broken off and that she had been used as the intermediary to heal the breach. On 21 July 1928 they were married in Hornsey Parish Church, my father in full morning attire and top

The wedding, 1928: Uncle Reg, my father, my mother and Aunt Elsie Bryer.

hat and my mother in a short-skirted wedding dress and a lace bonnet resembling a nightcap. Aunt Elsie, likewise in a matching short skirt but wearing a large broad-brimmed hat, appeared in the role of matron of honour; my father's brother, Reg, was best man.

There must have been some years, perhaps a decade, when the marriage worked and the house was not as I remember, run on the basic principle of 'Whatever you do, don't tell your father.' Looking back, I can see a marriage which, by the time I became aware of relationships, had become loveless. By the early 1940s they were two people yoked together in unending unhappiness. What can be said in my father's favour was that he was never violent, either to my mother or to any of us children, which at that period at least was something to be grateful for. But I hated the way he set out to demean my mother. He could not bear seeing her read: why wasn't she scrubbing the floor or cooking or doing some other menial task around the house? Every evening her role was to see that his supper was prepared and ready on the dot. We had already been fed earlier at 'tea'. What was left of the meat ration which had not been swallowed up to provide the Sunday lunch roast joint was consumed by him in steaks and chops through the week. We looked on unquestioningly.

Father ate at the kitchen table as my mother ministered to him. Once he was settled and provided for, she returned to the communal living room. From time to time the air would be rent with a shout of 'Mabel! Mabel!' as though he had been struck by lightning. Out she would rush to find that she had failed to put the mustard on the table. It would not occur to him to get up and fetch it himself from the nearby larder cupboard. If she dropped anything there was a drama, with him screaming: 'Mabel, Mabel! What have you broken now?' He got pleasure from goading her in front of others, drawing attention to this or that deficiency. He was never kind to her; I never once saw them exchange an affectionate gesture or word to one another. Christmas and birthdays were reduced to a financial transaction, the amount carefully written in a notebook stored in his bureau. Not once do I remember him returning with some small thing for her, such as a bunch of flowers. The garden was his: she touched it at her peril.

I was too young to know what any of this was about: it was just how things were, and of course I had no experience of any other family life with which to compare my own. When I did eventually have friends with parents whose relationship I might describe as normal, it began to cross my mind that it all should have been very different. I noticed, for instance, how other mothers kissed their children as they saw them off to school and, as an index of relationships, I remember asking Mother if she would do the same. Any such spontaneous expression of affection was absent from our house. Life for her in a loveless marriage must at times have resembled a life sentence and one of my most vivid memories was of her sitting alone in the kitchen, weeping. But she was penniless and the only object of any value which might have paid for a divorce was her diamond engagement ring. But divorce then was one of the ultimate disgraces and carried with it a huge social stigma.

When my mother died on 6 March 1990, I reflected on her life:

> She led such a circumscribed life as she made virtually no friends, really none at all. ... One great oddity was that she could never bring herself to say the words 'Thank you' if you gave her a gift. I never did discover what that was about. She was possessive of her children on a scale which, in the end, was self-defeating. That house was one of unhappiness, bitterness and resentment. I wish that I could think of it in any other way, everyone turned in on themselves, snapping and sniping. There was no common ground between any of the five members of the family other than blood, all of them different in terms of temperament, intellect and emotional response. Life for her was a failure. She'd married the wrong man, she couldn't cook, had no real interests, no initiative or sense of inquiry or delight in things apart from children. She had loved her father and learnt one thing from him: that education was what, in the case of her three boys, she must fight for. That she did and I owe her an enormous debt, for she did it at a price, years of taking every and any kind of job, clerical, library assistant, shop assistant, anything to get those extra pounds which meant at least that I could go on.

I had married in 1971, precipitating the break: 'she had created a slow death in our relationship from the moment that I married Julia, whom she rejected. I can remember then throwing myself on the bed, sobbing my heart out. That was the first withering.' Others followed as my flawed brother wreaked havoc on us all. After Father died it left them together in a house which for me, as I had found happiness, seemed to epitomize the exact opposite.

———

If my father's life followed one unending fixed pattern, so did my mother's. Mercifully, she loved children and being a mother to them. The downside was that she would have preferred it if none of us had ever grown up. Money was unbelievably tight, down to counting pennies. She scraped by thanks to a succession of piteously paid jobs. The first was assisting in a postal lending library; after the war for a time she collected money from those who bought on long-term credit – the 'never-never' – and later she served in a small jeweller's and watchmaker's shop. My mother seemed to shop every day. Between-the-wars developments such as ours invariably had some kind of village heartland. In our case it was Bush Hill Parade, a ten-minute walk away. There was a baker's shop, a haberdashery, a sweet shop, a greengrocer, a fishmonger, a post office, a chemist, a small branch library and a small park. The shop that dominated our lives, however, was William's, one half of which was a butcher's shop, the other a grocer's. One queued for everything. In the grocer's shop you queued up at one counter for dairy products and then promptly crossed to the opposite side and joined a second queue for other comestibles. Items like lavatory paper were asked for in hushed tones and delivered over the counter wrapped in newspaper so as to be invisible. Food rationing after the war was at times sharper than during it, and did not finally come to an end until 1954. Ration books were an

The three Strong brothers, Derek, Brian and myself, 1938.

everyday fact of life. Suburban life lived on rumour: the news that the butcher had offal or that the greengrocer had oranges sparked a rush to the shops to join the queue. At William's, shoppers were rewarded with a 'divi' in the form of stamps which slowly accrued towards some modest reward.

The rhythm of life at 23 Colne Road never changed much. Derek, my eldest brother, returned from being evacuated in 1941. Although missing some of his secondary schooling, he gained entry to an old foundation grammar school, Latymer. Most of his life was swallowed up by the Army Cadet Force and then National Service, first in Northern Ireland and then in Greece. My father arranged a job for him at Barclays

Serving king and country: Derek about 1950.

Bank, where he was to spend the rest of his working career. He was to marry happily, have children and grandchildren and indeed create a family life of the type which had been so singularly missing from his parents' home. I have known few other people who have had such a strong sense of responsibility and caring.

Brian's life was to be a very different one. Barely a couple of years my senior, he was to fail the Eleven Plus and proceed from secondary school to technical college. My mother wanted him to resit the examination but by brute force he prevented her from going to see the head teacher. He was later bitterly to regret that action, which prefaced a life of deceit and brought misery on the family and on me in particular.

Brian was to be a running sore in my life until in August 1997 he at last died. I learnt of his death when I was staying with friends in Italy,

Wayward brother: Brian about 1950.

and once again put pen to paper to reconcile myself with a terrible
story:

> It was like when my father died, only worse. It was like a weight, a
> curse, a threat taken away from me. There was nothing I could do
> and I felt nothing, just that a chapter was finally closed which had
> in fact closed with me fifteen years ago. Why is it that everything to
> do with the Strong family always had to be so unutterably awful, so
> humiliating, so haunting? Why aren't there those normal relation-
> ships of love and joy, turbulence and tranquillity? I can't answer
> that ... my last memory of him was of virtually drawing a knife on
> me in the kitchen ... There's a streak in the family which I've found
> disturbing. He was the only one out of the three of us that my father
> had any time for. Brian was sporty with hair tinged red. But he was
> violent even as a child. He was never disciplined or controlled. He
> exerted brute force. He was secretive and, worse, a compulsive liar.

But he was bright. He needed a man to control him but my father opted out. Mother always caved in.

Over the years everything went from the house to bale him out until it was virtually emptied – even her engagement ring and a second mortgage. Everything for Brian was a quick fix, car dealing and God knows what else. Much was concealed from me ... There were at least two jail sentences and he was extradited from the USA for attempting to smuggle drugs. His marriage [like me he did not tell our mother until after the event] was a disaster. Yet there was one good side. He taught maths and physics privately and was apparently a good teacher. But oh what a liar! He would lie that he was working when in fact he was a full-time student somewhere. God knows why. He even induced me to obtaining a bank loan to bale him out. And he was always right.

... Early on I sensed that I had to draw back. But he persecuted me. I have the letters, ones from someone mentally unbalanced, deranged. And then he started to ring me up, threatening – ring and ring and ring – it was terrible. Julia was shattered, so we changed the telephone number. Eventually I found out that the allowance I made to my mother was taken by him and so I re-directed it via Derek. ... He returned to Colne Road and as long as he was there I never went again. It was so terrible, so traumatic what he did that I went to see both a priest, Gerard Irvine [for whom see Chapter 3], and a lawyer, John Underwood, to seek guidance. I was guilt-ridden. Gerard looked at me and said, 'You must never go again'. So I never did see my mother for the last seven years of her life. That too haunts my inner recesses but even she in the end was corrupted by him...

Even at my apogee there was always this dark figure hovering, waiting to pounce, grinding, relentless, bent. Looking back, the whole of my life has been fleeing that family, struggling to detach myself, get as far away as possible and make a life and home full of the old-fashioned virtues I was never surrounded with as a child.

That was what I wrote on Brian's death. I reread it with a sense of horror, one which will only be shared by readers who have had a family destroyed by the actions of one of its members. As my star rose, Brian's plummeted of his own making, and in 1977 proceedings were brought against him for bankruptcy. This was followed by a warrant for his arrest for contempt of court. It was then that his pursuance of me entered its darkest and unbalanced phase with a stream of letters claiming that I owed him money for everything from arranging for me to go on to the sixth form at the grammar school to coping with my mother on the day I told her that I had married my wife. Much, I know, was concealed from me, including a civil court action in 1985 involving a woman with whom he lived – which he lost.

Looking back, and perhaps this is to salve my conscience, Derek telephoned me in March 1990 telling me that my mother had been taken into Enfield Hospital and that I should come quickly. I dropped everything, ready to leave at once. The phone rang again and I was told that it was too late.

My mother's will was quite specific: that the house was to be sold and the proceeds split equally between her three sons. I had already made it clear that I did not want a penny of it. By then my eldest brother and I had already gone through two mortgages to bale out Brian. It was clear that he would not move out of the house and that if we made any attempt to send in the bailiffs he would go to the papers claiming that I had thrown him onto the streets. It was my saintly brother Derek who dealt with all of this, resulting in an accommodation that Brian should stay in the house until his demise. He died intestate and once again Derek cleared up the mess.

But all those dramas lay ahead in the post-war years. My mother had to feed and clothe three hungry boys. Every Sunday morning there was the ritual of pastry-making with flour, margarine and lard. Enough tarts and pies had to be made to provide some kind of pudding through the week. As the seasons unfolded, these were filled with rhubarb, gooseberries and apples. From time to time she would make a suet pudding, boiled wrapped in a cloth and served with golden syrup. Brian once remarked that her headstone should be a tin-opener, and there was a degree of truth in that. Although she would sit looking at women's magazines filled with recipes, she never actually cooked one. With the gas stove came something called *The Radiation Cook Book*, which she also never used. How I shudder to think of what I consumed in the way of tinned cling peaches dripping with sugar-stuffed syrup and topped with Carnation Evaporated Milk. Potatoes were always boiled, peas tinned and any actual vegetable cooked to a mush. Vast quantities of bread and margarine were consumed with home-made jam, virtually always plum. I can see her now, standing there in her apron, holding the loaf close to her breast and sawing off a hunk of bread. The only meal that vaguely approached normality was Sunday lunch, almost invariably a half-leg of lamb around which potatoes were roasted. Gravy was made in the baking tin by adding water and Bisto gravy powder, which had two waifs on the packet inhaling the smell of it. Lamb was always accompanied by onion sauce, the onion pre-boiled and added to – or rather drowned in – lumpy white sauce. But in those days of rationing, with one egg a week, you were lucky to have what was placed on the table and often had to be quick off the mark before someone else snatched it.

Breakfast was always Shredded Wheat or Quaker Oats with milk, which was delivered daily (Derek for a time assisted the milkman for some pittance); and then there was tea. The main meal of the day from the age of five onwards would have been at school, so tea was the last meal before bedtime: bread and jam, cake, ghastly wartime fairy and rock cakes, which, as things became easier, were to be supplemented from the baker's with Battenberg, bright yellow and pink sponge squares wrapped in marzipan, hot cross buns and pieces of what was called 'slab cake', sections cut from a large rectangular cake. Reading this now, I am hardly surprised that the household seemed to be permanently afflicted with constipation. The idea that fresh fruit and vegetables were an essential part of a good diet did not exist. Salad of sorts only appeared in the summer, when lettuce and tomatoes were harvested from the garden.

What little hot water we had was supplied by a boiler in the corner of the kitchen, lit by my father first thing every morning and fed with coke. Only once a week was this kept going for any length of time as, one by one, we had a weekly bath. Mondays was always wash day with an old-fashioned boiler, my mother bent over a washing board in the butler sink, with a mountain of dirty shirts, socks and underpants – not to mention sheets and pillowcases. Everything was put through the hand mangle and hung out on a line in the garden in the hope that it would dry in time to be ironed that evening. For this operation layers of old blanket and sheeting were spread across the kitchen table and the clean laundry ironed piece by piece with flat irons heated on the cooker.

The cost of fuel was crippling, so the only proper fire in the house was in the front room; here we gathered every evening to listen to the radio while my mother knitted or did mending. The fire was banished by the Clean Air Act of 1956 and replaced by an electric fire. Our bedrooms were like refrigerators. Derek was lucky in that he had his own, the tiny box room. I had to share a double bed with Brian until, as we reached puberty, two old Victorian iron bedsteads came our way. The floor was covered with a linoleum square in shades of unutterable green. To the left of the chimneypiece a hanging cupboard of sorts was improvised, while to the right stood what was referred to as the 'Green Thing', a chest of drawers from which the latter had mostly gone, leaving shelf-like enclosures allotted either to Brian or myself. A curtain hung before it. There were unlined curtains at the windows, which looked down on the garden. Two actions dominated life in that room. One was the question of whose turn it was to leap out of bed and turn the light off, the other the ritual of scraping the ice off the windows in the winter. 1947 was the coldest winter of the century. And always but always there was the ritual of the hot-water bottle, covered in a knitted bag and placed in the bed earlier in the evening. I used to hug it with fervour.

But what of the war? My father was too old to be called up. The family had its last corporate holiday ever in August 1939, at Caister in Norfolk. My brothers were evacuated to the country, to Norfolk, while I went with my mother to the South Coast, where we were billeted in a policeman's house. That much I remember – and the beaches with their barbed wire. Why we were evacuated to where the enemy could have landed I know not. Later we went to a cottage near Diss, which had no electricity and was lit by oil lamps. And then we returned to London. I was evacuated once more, in 1944 when the 'doodlebugs' were launched on the metropolis. This time it was to Pontypool in Wales. Now, when I travel to Hereford via Newport I pass through that railway station and recall the six weeks of misery I endured, crying myself to sleep every night. But on that journey I saw my first castle, hard by the railway station at Newport, and that excited me.

During the war our house took on a guise that lasted until 1945. All the windows had brown sticky paper criss-crossed on to them to avert shards of glass shooting in every direction during bombing. Windows were draped in blackout curtaining, for not a ray of light was to be shed to the outside world – which was wrapped in darkness as there was no street lighting. One neighbour had gone to the war, so we stored his furniture in the upstairs bedroom for the duration. An Anderson shelter was placed in the room below, previously the dining room, and here a bed for me was sited. Nearly all our furniture was crammed into the front room, the sofa jammed into the bay window, the dining table in the centre, covered with a cloth and surrounded by chairs. In the garden outside, grass and flowers were replaced by rows of vegetables: potatoes, cabbages, curly kale, tomatoes, lettuces and runner beans. At the bottom of the back garden, up against the wooden garage, a pen was built to house chickens and later ducks, all welcomed in the straitened circumstance of rationing.

Nearer the house was the Anderson shelter proper. When the siren sounded I recall being seized hold of, wrapped in a blanket and carried outside into this dugout. My father joined other neighbours fire-watching. We could hear the aeroplanes above and the bombs falling. One day I recall that we went to a neighbour's house to study the bomb crater in his back garden, while several houses in an adjoining road had vanished. Then, of course, I carried a gas mask with me everywhere. The knitted balaclava was worn not only for warmth but because it helped cut out the sound of the aircraft. As I walked to school I was told that if the siren sounded I was to ring the doorbell of the nearest house and be taken in until the all-clear. At the infant school, when the raids came we were marched to the cloakrooms where we sat in long lines, knitting. For nearly everyone that meant making scarves, one boy knitting one which encircled the room. Any scrap of silver paper was assiduously collected and delivered to school as part of the war effort. Our clothes bore the Utility sign and could only be purchased with coupons – everything was 'make do and mend'.

It was upmarket Aunt Elsie who first spotted that something was wrong with my eyesight. Up to Moorfields Eye Hospital I was taken. There it was discovered that I was long-sighted with an astigmatism in my right eye, and that meant wearing glasses. As we have already seen, the earliest photographs show me without them, a sad-faced child with a huge head looking unhappily to camera. By the age of six, there I am with owl-like wire glasses, bat ears and my hair falling over my forehead, staring out from a school photograph. I recall the agony of the annual eye test, when drops were put into my eyes which temporarily blinded me and I would be led to a chair to wait my turn to see the oculist, feeling very vulnerable.

This was the period when I went to Raglan Primary School in Bush Hill Park, within walking distance of home. As a school it had a good reputation for 'grounding', by which was meant the basics of reading, writing and arithmetic. Over it presided the formidable – if physically repellent – Miss Dean, who rightly prided herself on just that, and I quickly learnt to read and write.

Colne Road was not a house with books to explore. My mother loved to read, her favourite author being Pearl S. Buck, and she read to me – not children's classics like Beatrix Potter but 'Bumper Story Books' and the adventures of Rupert Bear. But I had already taken to paint,

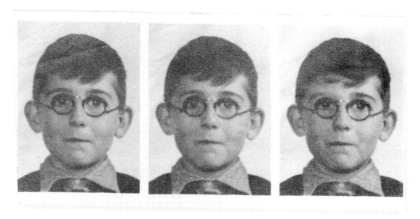

Wartime waif: myself aged six, 1941.

paper and brushes rather than the written word, so I can truthfully say
that my earliest impressions and excitements were always about things
visual. That must have begun very early, certainly by five, and was
perhaps the consequence of being a solitary child during the war years.
There were children's colouring books and that mysterious genre known
as 'magical' painting books, the application of water to the seemingly
white paper turning it into colour. During the war years there were only
two accessible vehicles for escape into other worlds. One was the radio,
over which my father presided, and the other the cinema.

There were three picture houses – for we always talked of 'going
to the pictures' – within striking distance. The cheapest seats were
one shilling and ninepence. Nearly all the films of which I retain a
vivid memory were costume dramas. Many came out of Gainsborough
Studios and were prefaced by an oval framing a seated lady attired close
to Gainsborough's portrait of Mrs Siddons in the National Gallery,
who slowly turned her head and graciously bowed towards us. *The*

Man in Grey (1943) and *The Wicked Lady* (1945) stick in my mind, the latter notorious for the plunging Restoration necklines worn by Margaret Lockwood. Earlier films came round again: Korda's *The Scarlet Pimpernel* (1934), with Leslie Howard and Merle Oberon wearing ravishing costumes by Oliver Messel, and *The Hamilton Woman* (1941), with Laurence Olivier and Vivien Leigh. Who could ever forget the opening sequence of that, with Emma as a bedraggled old crone taunted by someone and then lifting head into the light and saying 'I was Lady Hamilton' before dissolving into young Emma in all her beauty, running through the splendours of the palace in Naples? These films enticed me into other ages far distant from the drab impoverishment of the war years. Thus history threw open its door to me, through which I was shortly to enter when, in 1946, I passed the Eleven Plus and proceeded to Edmonton County Grammar School.

In retrospect mine was a far from happy childhood but that could only be appreciated later in life, when I had experienced true happiness. Decades later I agreed to give a lecture on happiness at the University of Birmingham, endowed by some good citizen who had gone off to the United States, made his pile and financed this annual event. The topic was fixed. When it came to actually writing it I was paralysed until I realized that personal honesty was what was called for. When I delivered the lecture, I stared at the audience and uttered these words 'Can I now give thanks for unhappiness?', adding that it led me to find refuge in distant worlds of the mind and the imagination. In a sense and in retrospect that can be seen to have been the consequence of being born into a dysfunctional family where any form of communication between its members was lacking, along with any normal demonstrative emotional bonds. At a very early age I had learnt that my future was to reside in forging bonds of a very different kind, those that came through learning and the arts.

What I can write is that there was always love and affection from my mother, although that came, as I was to learn later, at a price. There was always food to eat and there was always a firm moral structure. Even my father never demurred from that, with commonplace phrases like 'If you have a pound, you can't spend a pound and a farthing' or 'Never a borrower nor a lender be'. To be in debt or live beyond one's means was seen as beyond the pale. Obedience was demanded and bad language of any kind reprimanded. Above all, there was in the case of my mother an aspiration to something better for her children and a firm belief that that could be achieved through education. And it was education that was in one sense to give me the family I never had.

The sense of the beleaguered nation must also have left its mark and was to continue into the post-war years. My earliest awareness of anything to do with things cultural was of an England under threat. That has coloured my entire creative life, a deep and instinctual feeling for England, the inviolate island and its civilization. The circumstance was there almost from my birth and its natural outcome was to find its fullest expression in my directorate of the Victoria and Albert Museum, which was devoted to the nation's heritage in the form of its great houses, churches and gardens as well as both its historic and its contemporary creativity in terms of design and craftsmanship.

TWO

A WINDOW OPENS

1946 to 1953

I PAINTED a self-portrait of myself in 1948. The image has a certain fascination as a kind of pre-Hockney icon staring out at the viewer. The hair is brown, articulated solely by a low parting on the left. This was the Brylcreem era, when men's hair was smarmed down still in the between-the-wars mode. My ears stick out either side, supporting round tortoiseshell glasses linked by a gold bridge across the nose. The eyes are grey-blue and my lips are small and tightly sealed. The shirt is striped in shades of soft brown and the tie is a vivid blue with white stripes, its knot pushed into prominence by some form of gold tie clip which drew together the two sides of the collar. This is me at the age of thirteen.

———

I cannot recall what prompted this facial self-analysis – unusual, I would have thought, in someone so young. I would have been in Form 3, with

four more school years ahead of me. Were these the first stirrings of a
desire for self-fashioning, which was certainly there later? Who knows.
These were years which had austerity as their backcloth. The decade
after the war was an era dominated by rationing, coupons, smog, coal
fires, queues, dried egg, the black market, the spiv, the 'pictures' (with
Kind Hearts and Coronets and *Passport to Pimlico* to make us laugh and
Scott of the Antarctic to instil in us the stiff upper lip), of trolley buses,
of the balaclava worn during the icy winter of 1947 (which notched up
the coldest day of the century), of the football pools (which my father
did, to no avail) and flaking paint everywhere. The drabness of it all
seemed never ending. There was an ethos of weariness and resignation.
And, to make matters worse, we had supposedly won the war.

But I had a huge advantage over those who had been adult before 1939
because I had known nothing different. I had been born into depriva-
tion and austerity, so the reopening of the museums and galleries and
the renaissance in the theatre came as magic to me. I recall the first
exhibition that my mother took me to in 1946 at the Victoria and Albert
Museum. It was of French tapestries, ones that today the French would
never allow to travel. I was thrilled to see these extraordinary objects
draped across the museum's walls. In my case this was the overture to
the long series of exhibitions that awakened my passion for the visual
arts during the late 1940s and early 1950s. Those at the V&A included
rococo wood sculpture from Bavaria and treasures from Denmark.
Then we benefited from the Continental museums and galleries being
in a post-war state of disarray: both the Kunsthistorisches Museum in
Vienna and the Alte Pinakothek in Munich sent their best pieces to the
National Gallery and what is now Tate Britain. Side by side with these
began the great series of winter exhibitions at the Royal Academy,

whose organizers managed to prise open the doors of country houses and exhibit pictures never before seen in public. There were memorable exhibitions of Dutch and Flemish art. By the time I was fourteen my idea of bliss was to travel to South Kensington with my school friend James Platt, both of us with a packet of sandwiches. He went to the Science Museum and I went to explore the V&A, and in particular the Costume Court. I took with me a sketchbook to draw what I saw.

Then there was the theatre. The Wood Green Empire was a Stoll theatre designed by the maestro Frank Matcham, whose most famous work, the Coliseum, is now the London home of English National Opera and Ballet. The Empire opened in 1912 and died in 1962, having been converted in 1955 into a studio for the very art that killed it off: television. It was a receiving house on the variety circuit; but variety was regarded as very 'lower class' and there was no question of going to that. However, from time to time the Empire lifted itself and to it came the Carl Rosa Opera Company, the International Ballet Company and the D'Oyly Carte Opera Company with its repertory of Gilbert and Sullivan plus the incomparable Martyn Green. To the Empire also came touring versions of musicals of the ilk of Vivian Ellis's *Bless the Bride* and Ivor Novello's *The Dancing Years*. On one occasion we were given seats at the Palace Theatre to see Novello's post-war revival of Ruritania, *King's Rhapsody*, a monument to escapism with the maestro displaying his famous profile. But it was to the Wood Green Empire that I owed some of my earliest experiences of the magic of the theatre. Tickets were cheap, a seat in the gallery costing little more than a ticket to the cinema.

My first experience of ballet was Mona Inglesby's International Ballet, when it came to the Wood Green Empire around 1950. Decades later I took part in a radio programme about *Swan Lake* and was asked when I saw my first ballet. The reply was all those years ago, when the Prince was danced by a very young Maurice Béjart. Not long after, through the post came the gift of a book, *Ballet in the Blitz*, which told the story of that company. Its founder had been touched to hear that performances by her company had first ignited my passion for dance. She had formed the company, which has since been virtually written out of ballet history, in 1940 and took it on the road through the war years. It folded in 1953, one of the early casualties of television.

Critics tended to be dismissive of the International Ballet but it must have introduced countless numbers of people all over the country – like me – to the dance. I was so hypnotized that I went to see them the week that they were in repertory three times, also taking in *The Sleeping Beauty* and *Coppelia*. What has emerged since is this company's significant role in preserving the choreographic traditions of the Imperial Maryinski Ballet in St Petersburg. Mona Inglesby had engaged Nicolai Sergeyev, its Régisseur Général, who had brought the company's notation records with him out of Russia. After the company folded that precious set of documents was offered to both the Royal Ballet and the Kirov, the Maryinski's successor, both of which turned it down. The records subsequently passed to the Harvard Theatre Collection whither, in the year 2000, the Russians made their way in order to restage the original choreography of *The Sleeping Beauty*.

It was, however, the great production of that ballet at Covent Garden in 1946 on which I had set my sights. Although I have sold much of my library, a handful of books linger on the shelves, representing certain moments in my life. One of these is a nothing book really, published in 1949, when I was fourteen: *Souvenirs de Ballet*, edited by

Duncan Melvin with contributions from the ilk of the ballet historian Cyril W. Beaumont and the designers James Bailey and Roger Furse. It opened with an article on the Royal Ballet's founding choreographer, Frederick Ashton (with whom my wife worked thrice), with a portrait of him *en profile* gazing towards a looking glass into which had been tucked a postcard of Queen Alexandra. There was also an article on the person whose work fascinated me most, Oliver Messel, whose designs for *The Sleeping Beauty* left such a mesmeric effect on more than one generation of ballet-goers – so much so that no production designed to replace his has succeeded, leading Monica Mason, a later Director of the company, to reinstate them in 2006 (my article on the designs is still part of the programme). I pored over the black-and-white half-tone images knowing that this was what I wanted most to do with my life.

It must have been about 1951 that a brother kindly purchased a seat for me at the back of the amphitheatre at Covent Garden, where I saw Messel's production for the very first time. I was spellbound by its ethereal transparency, its settings seemingly designed in the manner of Bibbiena through the prism of an English watercolourist of the Romantic age. Years later, in 1983, I took on loan at the V&A (and later purchased) Messel's archive and we staged an exhibition (at which press interest inevitably focused on whether Princess Margaret and Snowdon would even speak to each other). I took the opportunity to write a tribute to Messel in the catalogue:

> Why was his work so hypnotic? He was, of course, a romantic of the Rex Whistler generation and after the starvation of the war years he swept his audiences away with his painterly stage visions, which belonged so closely to the English watercolour tradition. His effects always reminded me of Prospero's famous words: 'like an

insubstantial pageant faded', because Messel's work always had that slightly unreal, transparent, bleached-out effect, as though we were being presented with an hallucination from an earlier century.

(from Oliver Messel: An Exhibition held at the Victoria and Albert Museum, ed. R. Pinkham, London 1983)

It was the early 1950s that in effect formed my artistic imagination, those vital years between about fourteen and eighteen when a highly visual young person looks around himself for the first time. Although I was to become a writer and have the honour of being made a Fellow of the Royal Society of Literature, writing was never my primary talent. That lay, looking back dispassionately, in an emerging ability to draw, paint and design. It was during these years that an aesthetic pantheon was formed, which was to remain with me and resurface in one form or another over the future decades. One side of that pantheon was to be locked in the Elizabethan age (to which we will come later) but the other was formed earlier by the work of those artists who, along with Messel, seized my youthful imagination. Without exception they belonged to that group in whose work we witness English mid-century Romanticism.

John Piper was the painter for whose work I held an unwavering passion. For years I cherished a postcard of his painting *St Mary le Port, Bristol* (1940), which was in what was then called the Tate Gallery. Rich in browns, ochres and russets, this was an icon for me: the desecration of a medieval church by enemy bombing. It is difficult now to recapture the extraordinary potency of a colour card during those post-war years. Each one was treasured and placed to be contemplated. Piper's painting, along with a 'Rainbow Portrait' of Elizabeth I, acted as a mascots, code images for England. This was the era of the King Penguins and Penguin

Modern Painters and I devoured both volumes devoted to Piper, one his record of the churches of the Romney Marshes, the other of works including his wartime records of Windsor Castle, which years later the Queen Mother was to show me at Clarence House. John was to enter my life through my wife and to become a friend. I wrote a tribute to him in *The Times* on the occasion of his eightieth birthday, recalling his inspiration; next to that cutting in a scrapbook is mounted a card from him which reads: 'much the nicest thing to happen to me yet in relation to my 80th'.

It was in 1950 that I first saw the work of someone else who was to become an icon in my life and also a friend, Sir Cecil Beaton. I was too young to have seen his famous 1945 production of Oscar Wilde's *Lady Windermere's Fan*, which had been part of the post-war neo-Edwardian revival, although I was familiar with that production through his photographs. What I saw at the Haymarket Theatre were Beaton's sets and costumes for *The Second Mrs Tanqueray*, in which Eileen Herlie played the principal role. Twenty-six years later I was to recall the impact of that on me in an introduction to an exhibition of Beaton's work at the Parkin Gallery. By then Cecil had had his stroke and was in need of money, which precipitated the exhibition. This is what I wrote:

> I still remember the impact of those sumptuous sets and costumes, the magic Beaton touch bringing Edwardian opulence to the greyness of post-war London: rich, swagged draperies, huge potted palms, trailing, heavily fringed tablecloths and an explosion of bijouterie. Every costume caused a gasp in a world just embracing the extravagance of the New Look. Then and ever since one has recognized that the art of Cecil Beaton stood for something important – Style.

When I was a teenager it was Beaton's portraits of the Sitwells that caught my eye: Edith as a medieval tomb effigy, plucking a harp against a vast tapestry, or the three siblings *en profile*, with massive use made of tin foil. Add to them Diana Cooper as the Madonna in *The Miracle* and the future Queen Mother in her Winterhalter crinoline. I was keenly aware even at that age that these were stage-managed images – and I persuaded my mother to pose, clutching a rose from the garden, in my attempt at a Beatonesque portrait. Alas, my wand failed to exert its magic! Cecil Beaton was to enter my life in person in 1967 (see the Epilogue) and to change it forever. He was to open a whole new world to me, the *beau monde* as it reconfigured itself in the post-war era for one last fling before being killed off by inflation in the 1970s and the advent of celebrity culture.

Perhaps a stranger and rather forgotten figure whose work haunted my imagination during these formative years was the painter and theatre designer Leslie Hurry, a reclusive, shy and tortured being whom I briefly met in 1979 in London's Mercury Gallery. But in the 1940s and early 1950s his surrealist designs for Robert Helpmann's *Hamlet* (1942), which I only saw decades later when Nureyev danced it, and *Swan Lake* (1943) for the future Royal Ballet were to be landmarks. Just as my paintings were attempts at a version of Piper's style, so my costume designs often attempted to mimic the nervous sinuosity of Hurry.

We can round off the pantheon with Rex Whistler, tragically a victim of the war, whose prolific graphic work was still to be seen everywhere in the early 1950s, a capriccio world of Gothick gazebos and classical urns swagged and wreathed, of decorative cartouches and swooning romantic poets, all observed with a tongue-in-cheek slight whimsicality. Whistler, Beaton and Messel all belonged, although unknown to me at the time, to the same group. It is interesting that they appealed to me so much and possibly explains why I got on with that generation which was to be swept away in the tide of the 1960s. I have never ceased to cherish them.

My first encounter with opera was a Carl Rosa production of *La Bohème*. That company, founded in 1873, took opera the length and breadth of England in an era long before Sadler's Wells or Glyndebourne took to the road. I owe this to my father, who had an obsession with that opera and also with Lehar's *The Merry Widow*, to both of which I was taken in the early 1950s. Although I did not respond as strongly to opera as I had to the ballet, these two must have made quite an impression as I returned alone for the Saturday matinée performance of *Madam Butterfly*, which reduced me to tears sitting amidst the orange peel in the gallery.

All of this and my obsession with history generated a strong desire to enter into imaginary worlds away from the reality of the present. Much of it may go back to a gift one Christmas of a Pollock's toy theatre play. I still have the theatres I treasured during those years, the Adelphi and the Britannia, together with boxes of scenery and cut-out figures of several plays, *The Silver Palace*, *The Miller and His Men*, *Douglas* and *The Brigand* among them. Through them I was able to relive the Regency and Victorian theatre with its preoccupation with spectacle and melodrama. Pollock's had migrated from Hoxton to the Adelphi in the post-war period and a toy theatre renaissance ensued, with plays like *The High Toby* by J.B. Priestley (impossible to perform!) with scenery and figures by Doris Zinkeisen, and Roger Furse's designs for Olivier's film version of *Hamlet* adapted to the format. The plates with old plays were still available, sometimes reprinted, and I would

Gateway to the imagination: my Pollock's toy theatre.

spend hours colouring, mounting and cutting them out, followed by the joy of staging a production. The only two plays I attempted to stage were *The Brigand* by Planché, first staged at Drury Lane in 1829, and John Home's *Douglas*, which went back as far as 1753 but enjoyed a renaissance with Master Betty, the blonde and beautiful wonderboy who made such a sensation as Young Norval in 1804. I still remember his opening lines, which I recited as I pushed the cut-out figure onto the tiny stage:

My name is Norval! On the Grampian hills
My father feeds his flocks; a frugal swain,
Whose constant cares were to increase his store,
And keep his only son, myself, at home.
(John Home, *Douglas*, act II, scene I)

I recall choosing this speech for the Radio 4 programme *With Great Pleasure* when I was Director of the National Portrait Gallery, when I had as readers Dorothy Reynolds (who wrote *Salad Days* with Julian Slade) and her husband, Angus McKay.

Looking back, I bless the bliss of those hours of delight spent with 'penny plain, tuppence coloured' printed sheets. They were an escape to a world away from the unchanging ordinariness of a suburban home and the unutterable greyness of the era. The toy theatre of Victorian melodrama, pantomime and arena spectacle introduced me to the practicalities of the stage, albeit of an old-fashioned kind, with its backcloths, cut cloths, ground rows, borders and side wings. It was a world of heroes and villains, of maids in distress, of sunlit, dreamy landscapes, Italianate palaces, threatening castles, glittering grottoes and amazing fairy-tale epiphanies. Inevitably it led to a fascination with the history of the theatre and I moved on to work my way through the works of W. MacQueen-Pope, who wrote the history of virtually every London theatre in a series of publications, almost a book a year, which in a way were clones of each other. The titles MacQueen-Pope chose say it all: *Haymarket: Theatre of Perfection*; *St James's: Theatre of Distinction*; *Gaiety: Theatre of Enchantment*.

That interest stimulated a journey back in time and I was surprised to find among the folder of work I have kept from those formative years a copy of one of Inigo Jones's designs for *The Masque of Oberon* (1611).

That in turn leads me to another book with which I did not part, on Purcell's *The Fairy Queen* as presented by the Sadler's Wells Ballet and the Covent Garden Opera in a production of 1946. The designer, the painter Michael Ayrton, had based his designs on those of Inigo Jones. As in the case of Messel's *Sleeping Beauty*, I must have seen it from aloft about 1950, thrilled to witness the transformation scenes, the various choreographed masque sequences and the final chinoiserie set behind which Apollo arose with a sunburst behind him. The Stuart court masques intrigued me at a very young age. I was to return to them in 1965 and, more significantly, in 1974, when, in collaboration with the American scholar Stephen Orgel, we produced the first complete two-volume catalogue of the Inigo Jones designs at Chatsworth.

Simultaneously I started working my way through some of the more recent playwrights, and it was during these years that I read the complete the plays of Noël Coward, George Bernard Shaw, Frederick Lonsdale and Oscar Wilde. I devoured these texts, but at the expense of reading the great novels which an educated person would have taken in their stride during their teenage years and to most of which I came much later, realizing the horrible gaps in my literary self-education.

What I have not so far mentioned is the repertory theatre, the Intimate at Palmers Green, next to St Monica's Catholic Church. In its heyday the Intimate had as its leads Michael Denison and Dulcie Gray, until they hit stardom, and to this theatre I owe some of my earliest exposure to Shakespeare and Sheridan.

Most of this was to be stored in my mind, and to some extent had to go into abeyance for quite a few years while I focused all my energies on succeeding in the world of academe. Years later someone remarked to me: 'All you've done, Roy, is to turn museums into theatres.' The remark had more than a degree of truth to it. My approach to any museum restaging or great exhibition was always in terms of the excitement of a first night; I aimed to transfer to the museum world that sense of glamour and revelation as the curtain went up.

———

But that is to anticipate, for the next seven years were to be dominated by schooling. Education in the area of London in which I was raised was a relatively new phenomenon. Latymer was the old grammar school, founded as long ago as 1624; everything else was recent. My education started, as I have said, at Raglan School in Bush Hill Park, which opened in 1928, the first to be founded by Edmonton's Education Committee. Four years later a separate infant school was added, which was where I began. From the infants, a few years on I crossed over a playground to the main school in preparation for the Eleven Plus examination for entry into a grammar school, upon which everything hung. I was eleven on 23 August 1946 so I sat the examination when I was still ten. I passed and so migrated to Edmonton County School in the September of that year, two years on from the Butler Education Act, which not only introduced the examination but established the tripartite system of schooling of grammar, technical and secondary schools.

Edmonton County School was situated on the Great Cambridge Road, a step or more on from my elementary school. An examination of a map of the area demonstrates that the road was the dividing line between the suburban world of Bush Hill Park and Winchmore Hill and the working-class district of Edmonton. That was reflected in the make-up of the pupils: I was acutely conscious that I came from what was, in that context, the upper end of the social spectrum. The school is now a specialist technology college but it had begun its life in 1919 as Edmonton Central School and from the outset it was co-educational. Initially it came under the Municipal Borough of Edmonton but in 1922 was taken over by Middlesex County Council, the authority that was to provide the county grant enabling me to go to university, and relabelled Edmonton County Secondary School. Only two years before I arrived, and as a direct consequence of the 1944 Butler Act, did it become Edmonton County Grammar School. Alas, its life was to be truncated twenty-three years later when it became a comprehensive.

Set into that framework, I can see why the institution had the energy and vision of youth, of contributing to a new order of things. The school motto was *Non nobis solum* ('Not for ourselves alone'), and the school song, which was sung to what I discovered years later was the tune of the Canadian National Anthem, ran as follows:

> O mother school, thou Alma Mater dear
> Thy brow is crowned with bays we wreath for thee
> Thy smile serene, thy friendly mien
> Has lured us, lures us still.
> Thy word of cheer, thy rod severe
> Hath strengthened heart and will.
> Thy faith divine, thy courage bold,
> To high endeavour shall thy children hold.
> To high endeavour shall thy children hold.
>
> May thoughts of thee inspire the coming years,
> Thy counsel free chase far all secret fears.
> May friends we've made stand by us still
> To hold us on our way.
> May fortune smile as we climb the Hill
> Towards the Closing Day.
> When comes the end, be still our friend

Then Alma Mater smile and say 'Well done'.
Grant every son and daughter God's 'Well done'.

Hopelessly politically incorrect in today's terms – we used to raise the roof with our rendering of it.

The building itself was designed by L.T. Curtis in a vaguely between-the-wars neo-Georgian style. There was a handsome central entrance in stone, with pilasters and swags of fruit, on either side of which stretched wings punctuated with symmetrical pavilions whose surface was articulated with pilasters and a pediment in brick and stone. It could accommodate six hundred of us and, although it was co-educational, it was a case of east is east and west is west and ne'er the twain shall meet, for the wing to the left was the domain of the girls and that to the right the boys. I never saw the inside of the girls' wing except when I was asked to go to the female teachers' common room; there was no question of male and female teachers sharing one. That separation of the sexes meant two playgrounds but it did not extend to the playing fields at the back, although, so far as I recall, girls and boys never used the area simultaneously. Both sexes came together in the school hall, a huge vaulted and panelled room with a stage at one end and folding doors on one side, which opened out into the space I hated most, the gymnasium. Day in and day out we marched in, the girls from one end and the boys from the other, to someone banging out 'English Country Garden' on a piano to morning assembly. We sat in rows, cross-legged on the floor, form one at the front and the sixth form at the back. A hymn would be sung from *Songs of Praise* and a prayer said, followed by a few cautionary words from the headmaster, Mr H.B. Champion, a grim figure guaranteed to strike terror into one's heart and whom one encountered teaching Scripture when he dilated upon the vengeful acts of Yahweh in a manner almost enough to put me off religion for the rest of my life. The hall was the setting for speech days, any dramatic or choral performances and, a rare instance when the sexes actually touched each other, dancing lessons, mainly confined to the waltz, barn dance and the valeta.

Scattered through the building there were framed reproductions of Old Master paintings in gilt frames. I was immediately attracted to these, paintings by Hobbema, Reynolds and de Hooch among them. On the first floor there was the seldom-visited library, the Botany laboratory, the Domestic Science Suite (for use by girls only) and the Art Room, a large studio-like space with a north light, on one of the walls of which I was eventually allowed to paint a mural depicting backstage at a theatre.

Discipline was absolute. Every teacher was addressed as 'Sir' or 'Miss' – most of the female staff were unmarried. Staff who had been to Oxbridge wore their gowns and a suit was de rigueur, except for the sports teacher, who wore white flannels and plimsolls. Classes numbered about thirty pupils and there was a division into A, B and C streams within any given year, based, I think, on potential ability. Each classroom was identical, with a blackboard along one wall, the teacher's desk and chair next to it in the centre, and then serried ranks of pupils' desks with lift-up lids that opened to reveal a space into which to place papers and textbooks. All writing was in ink using a steel-nibbed pen and an inkwell. The girls sat in two lines of desks on one side and the boys on the other. Everyone wore school uniform, the girls in navy gymslips and white blouses, the boys in grey flannel shorts, black shoes and grey woollen knee-socks, white shirts and school ties (black with gold stripes), a pullover if cold, and a navy blue blazer with the school arms on the breast pocket. And then there was the school cap with its peaked front.

Each class had its own form teacher and then, through the day, the teacher changed with the subject. On any member of staff entering the room we all stood to attention. Teachers in that era seemed to belong to a different race. Any misbehaviour, like talking in class, was sat upon immediately, in the case of the boys with a sharp smack of the cane on the hand. Other forms of punishment included writing out lines and periods of detention. Any pupil who uttered a swear word or insulted a member of staff was frogmarched to the washroom of the lavatories and the offending mouth was washed out with soap. I only witnessed one incidence of that. The rules included a ban on any form of jewellery, which was confiscated on sight. Sometimes girls mysteriously vanished, and in retrospect I can now conclude that they must have been discovered to have been pregnant; no reference was ever made to such a fact. Any really serious offenders might find themselves sent to the headmaster's study. Silence reigned in the classroom and along the corridors and staircases as we moved from one lesson to the next. No wonder that the eruption of noise on leaving the school at the close of the day was a volcano of sound. Every single aspect of life within that building was laid down as we responded to a small army of teachers dedicated to the virtues of self-improvement and the supreme value of learning, duty and obedience.

My first five years at Edmonton County School took me up to the Ordinary Level examination. We had classes in English, French, history, geography, biology, science, music, scripture, mathematics, art, PT (physical training) and woodwork. Sixty years on, these form

only a fragmented jigsaw within my mind. We were taught French
– badly – by a teacher who, most of the time, had his eyes fixed on the
girls in the class and one hand always in his pocket, for reasons which
only dawned upon me in retrospect. Music was taught by Mr Wilkinson,
one of the science teachers who had been landed with the topic. I had
little or no response to music at that age other than to know that I
never wanted to hear *The Sorcerer's Apprentice* nor sing 'Nymphs and
shepherds, come away' ever again. Mr Long taught geography, which I
enjoyed as I loved drawing and colouring maps. Miss Fothergill taught
mathematics. Again, I was good at geometry as it demanded graphic
skills, but hopeless at everything else. English was with Miss Haswell
and we worked our way through an anthology, bits of which stuck, such
as 'The Lady of Shalott' and 'My Last Duchess'. And then, of course, I
was a star at art and history all the way through. Each school year ended
with examinations and I could count on being first in art and history.

PT brought the dreaded Mr Bruneels into my life, who taunted and
baited anyone like me who couldn't leap over the vaulting horse or walk
across the bar. Then, one day, Mr Bruneels vanished without explanation. I vividly recall the ripple which went through morning assembly
when we were told. We were all aware that when someone vanished
overnight it could mean that something unsuitable for young ears had
occurred. I loathed all forms of sport and did anything to evade taking
part, prompting a remark in my annual report which read: 'I have seen
so little of him this year that it is difficult for me to write any comment.'
I remember that well, and regret that later I lent my school report to an
exhibition in aid of a charity, which never returned it. I do, however,
have a certificate which reads: 'This is to certify that Roy Strong Form
3A came first in the form at the yearly examination 1949.' In that year

I was fourteen and my father attempted to take me from school and put me to work. He had encountered a cartoonist on a newspaper who needed an artistically minded junior to assist him. Probably a combination of the form prize and pressure from the school ensured that that did not in fact happen, but it was a near miss and reflected the way he was thinking.

During the same period I remember being in hospital for an operation to remove a glandular lump on my neck. I was just old enough to be in the adult ward and was aware that someone in the bed opposite to mine had died, the curtains being drawn around it. I was seized with horror and a desire to get out of the place if I possibly could, so, much to everyone's surprise, I swung my feet out of bed and stood up. The operation had been on the previous day and the lump had gone, although a second one was still there, which was treated successfully by radiotherapy. I was never told what precisely the problem was, although I registered that my mother was ashen. For over twenty years I went annually to North Middlesex Hospital to be gone over by someone who became a friend, Dr Victor Levison, who felt me over for any new lumps. Life went on and I had forgotten all about it when one day my eldest brother happened to see a piece of mine in the *Evening Standard* in a series 'Me and My Health'. 'But you didn't mention Hodgkin's disease and we all thought you were a goner.' It is now called Hodgkin's lymphoma and is a form of cancer originating from the white blood cells. Suddenly it placed in perspective Dr Levison's comment, 'You'd be very unlucky if it recurred.' I now know that it would have been a death sentence. My current knowledge of it I owe to the Internet, from which I learnt that it occurs most frequently in two separate age groups, one of which being young adulthood between fifteen and thirty-five. A long and complex entry on the disease ended with a depressing list of those who had died from it or who were in remission. In my case the latter has gone on for sixty years. And in a way I wish that I had never been told that I had had it in the first place.

Some years later a teacher returned to me one of my history exercise books, from the school year 1947–8, when I was twelve. On its outside is a map of the Middle East and on the following page a heading in block capitals carefully filled in with red, 'THE SUMARIANS' and then, in joined-up writing, 'Archaeologists, by their excavations have discovered much about the cities', followed by drawings in coloured pencil of a spade, a trowel and a basket. And so it unfolds page by page, with short coherent sentences and drawings through the Babylonians, Egyptians and Greeks. Interspersed are short essays such as 'A day in the Life of an Athenian boy':

> The sun shines [*sic*] through the window of my bedroom as I awoke. I quickly put [on] my chiton and ate my breakfast of some figs and milk. I was told by my father that I would go the long way to school this morning past the Acropolis. I was very pleased at this because I loved to wathch [*sic*] the temples and statues.

Via the Roman Empire we arrive at 'Christianity in Britain', into which I had inserted a page from a picture book with 'Ecclesiastical Vestments' – cope, alb, stole and amice. Surprisingly, we learned about Islam and the book comes to an end with the Normans and a whole series of drawings of the various medieval architectural styles and the symbols of the Investiture contest – crozier, ring, mitre and cope – and a plan of Fountains Abbey.

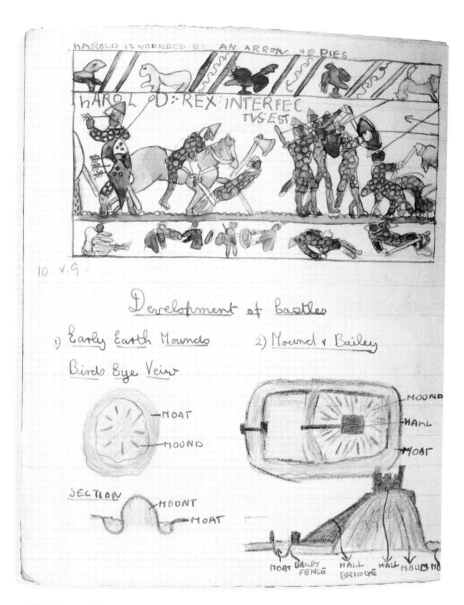

The lure of history: a page from my exercise book, 1947–8, on the Normans with the death of Harold in the Bayeux Tapestry and diagrams of a castle.

And what of life outside of school? That followed an unvarying rhythm in termtime, with little time for manoeuvre, for the burden of homework was considerable. Life seemed then to have a pattern set in stone. It was a period of fixed points in the compass which revolved around my maternal grandmother in Wood Green and, in the opposite direction, what had once been the market town of Enfield, which had been swallowed up by suburbia but still had fragments of its earlier incarnation left: an old church and a group of Georgian houses labelled Gentleman's Row. Going in the direction of the school but beyond it was the three-mile walk which took me to Edmonton, where there was a good public library to which I walked every Saturday morning. My debt to it remains incalculable, providing me with the books I lacked at home.

I shared my weekly walk to the public library with my particular school friend, the aforementioned James Platt: I think I must have sat next to Jim for four or five of the years which preceded the sixth form. Tall, thin and lanky, with bat ears, he lived within walking distance of Colne Road in a semi-detached house in Firs Lane. He was an only child, and what bound us was a shared alienation from our fathers. Jim's was a brusque north countryman from Accrington who perpetually taunted his son, telling him to get out on the football field – which, like me, he hated. Like me, too, he was a sensitive child born out context: his chief pleasures were his gramophone and listening to classical music.

On a Sunday afternoon Jim and I would often stroll together to Grovelands Park, designed by John Nash at the very end of the eighteenth century for a Quaker brewer. It had been purchased in 1913 by the local council, who turned the house into a Priory Clinic, so I never saw what, according to Lucinda Lambton, was 'one of the most delicate delights in all London', an octagonal dining room painted to resemble a bamboo birdcage through which one glimpsed a panorama of fields, woods and sky. All we did was walk there, do a turn around the lake and return home. This was my first exposure to an English country house.

My first experience of what I would categorize as a proper country house was Hatfield, accessible by Green Line bus. Hatfield had precious links with she who was to become my heroine, Elizabeth I, with the remains of the old royal palace in which she had passed her youth and where she had received the news of her sister's death. But it was the new great house, built by Sir Robert Cecil in the Jacobean period, which captured my imagination. It was crammed with treasures from the Elizabethan age, including the haunting 'Ermine' and 'Rainbow' portraits of the Virgin Queen, two images that were to recur in several of the books I would later write on the period. I certainly visited Hatfield in 1952, when I purchased a tiny booklet on the portraits by Frances A. Yates, in which I discovered what the various symbols in them meant. I was not to know then that four years later Frances Yates was to enter my life as my supervisor for a doctorate which included a study of the Queen's many likenesses. Hatfield was to inspire me with a lifelong love of country houses that would be reinforced during my National Portrait Gallery years, when I visited so many of them, and that, when the time came to spring to their defence, made me unhesitatingly stage *The Destruction of the Country House* as my first major exhibition as Director of the Victoria and Albert Museum in 1974.

Life was lightened by radio and programmes like *Grand Hotel*, *Songs of Praise*, *In Town Tonight* and serials based around the detective Paul Temple and the dramatization of great classics such as Dumas's *The Count of Monte Cristo*. All such programmes were listened to in ordered silence. *Children's Hour* retained its spell, with endless renditions of Enid Blyton's tales of 'The Famous Five', Richmal Crompton's 'Just William' stories or, more to my taste, Pamela Brown's *The Swish of the Curtain* and Noel Streatfeild's *Ballet Shoes*. At the time one was unaware that this was the finale of a certain period in the history of radio brought abruptly to an end when television entered the house in 1953.

There was no such thing as an annual holiday; we were too impoverished. The most that came my way was the result of a small financial windfall when I was taken for a deadening week on the South Coast with my mother and grandmother. But this privation fitted in to life in the early 1950s, when everyone guarded their privacy. Any social interchange happened on the doorstep; only relations penetrated beyond the front door. Neighbours were greeted and the time of day might be passed over the garden fence – but that was very rare. Thought would even be given as to what could or could not be put out on a line of washing for fear of comment. Internally our house began slowly to change as rooms rendered closed by the war came into use. I shared a bedroom with my brother Brian until 1954, when my eldest brother, Derek, married and I at last had a room of my own, albeit the minute box room above the front door.

In the summer of 1951 I took the Ordinary Level examination. It was taken for granted that I would leave school. One by one we had been interviewed by a group whose task was to guide us into the right arena of the world of paid employment. I was deemed artistic and so perhaps, it was suggested, I could have a future in textiles. I would begin, I was told, stacking bales of fabric onto shelves. But luck was on my side: by that year things were looking up just a little. My exam results were good, apart from failing in French, and the school was keen for me to continue. One thing was clear: as long as I never went near my father for money (he had never given me a penny of pocket money, ever), I could return.

———

And so I returned to Edmonton County Grammar School in the autumn of 1951 and the sixth form. Looking back, it was akin to being admitted to an elite club. This was another world. Alan Bennett's play *The History Boys* captures something of the hothouse atmosphere that pervaded these early days of the aftermath of the Education Act. Although Bennett's play was set in the 1980s, it depicted grammar school life of the kind Bennett himself had experienced, like me, in the 1950s. Here were gathered fewer than a dozen of us who, in the new dispensation of things, were to prepare ourselves for university entrance. There was no attempt to even consider applying for Oxford or Cambridge; it was a given that this was an empyrean beyond our wildest aspirations. Instead we hoped to be accepted by one of the top of the second eleven, London, Bristol or Manchester.

This return, like entry to the school at eleven, signalled another parting of the ways. The lanky Jim Platt, with whom I had shared a desk for so many years, left my life and went to work for Shell on the South Bank. I am devoid of even a snapshot by which to remember him. I was only to encounter him accidentally once more, in the interval of a performance of Ashton's ballet *Enigma Variations* at the Royal Opera House. Ascent in life inevitably produces casualties in friendship as the common ground once shared is eroded.

Once in the sixth form, my subject range suddenly contracted. Much to my joy, games and work in the gymnasium formed no part of the curriculum. This, I thought, was emancipation from servitude and ridicule. In the first year there were to be four subjects: English, history, art and Latin. In the second year one of these, in my case English, was dropped. I also continued for a time with French lessons: languages have never been my strong point and I had failed French at Ordinary Level so had to sit for it again. I was perceptive enough to realize that I needed to start at exercise one. And so Mr Elengorn took me under his wing and I worked on my own from an ancient textbook, doing one exercise every day and delivering it the next. And so I finally passed in 1952.

Latin was quite another thing. In order to read any arts subject at university one was required to have a qualification in Latin at both Ordinary and Advanced Level. There were just two of us in the class, Anne Berry and myself. And that is where the formidable deity of the sixth form, Doris Staples, entered my life. To her the sixth form was sacred and anything untoward that occurred was regarded as the betrayal of a trust bestowed. She was one of those women who had adopted a somewhat mannish appearance in the period between the two wars. In feature she veered towards the sharp, with piercing blue eyes, but she could equally, on occasions, burst into a radiant smile. She wore no make-up and her hair was cut in what was then called an Eton crop. She wore blouses and tweed jackets and skirts, the latter so long that she had a special device to lift them away from entangling with the mechanics of the bicycle she rode to and from school.

Miss Staples's dedication to the new dispensation was total. For two years, five evenings a week, Anne Berry and I stayed behind to have a Latin class with her. Every evening we had to do an exercise, returning to have it marked the following day. The set text was Book VI of Virgil's

Miss Staples, the benign ruler of the sixth form, with
Mr Long, the geography master, on a school outing.

Aeneid, which narrated Aeneas' flight from Troy and his voyage into
the Underworld. It is curious that it was never suggested that we read
the whole of the *Aeneid* in translation to place our set text in context.
The only way we coped with this in such a short period of time was to
learn by rote the translation written by Miss Staples and reel it off onto
the page for the exam. I recall how touched she was when I showed
her one of my major set pieces for submission for Advanced Level art
– a watercolour that I still have. It illustrates a moment from Book VI
when Charon, the Underworld boatman who ferries souls across the
river Styx, challenges Aeneas, whose companion, a sibyl, produces a

golden bough and thus dispels any opposition to his passage in search of his father.

Besides heading the sixth form, Miss Staples taught French to other classes in the school. It was during this period that there was a school production of Corneille's *Le Cid*, for which I designed the scenery and costumes. Miss Staples kept those designs and returned them to me decades later.

Quite an intense atmosphere pervaded this young band striving for passes that would secure them university entry and a county scholarship. This was the heroic period in the aftermath of the Butler Act. We were, I suppose, guinea pigs, some of the very first to enjoy the fruits of this opening up of advanced education to classes hitherto denied it. We were painfully aware of the privilege and seized with a desire to achieve. Competition was the name of the game and we felt no shame in aiming to win prizes. We were a motley lot; what we shared across the board was that we were the first in our families to aspire to a university education. Coming from a lower-middle-class background, I at least had a smattering of the social niceties. Some of my classmates, however, came from out-and-out working-class families, their speech and manner demanding adjustment to the world to which they aspired to enter.

At that stage my deepest desire was to read history of art at the Courtauld Institute, then in Portman Square. Later I was to discover that at that period entrants could generally be found only in Debrett. But I recall the courtesy of the then registrar in response to my application, registering his dismay that their admittance system worked in such a way that I could not gain entry until a year beyond my taking of Advanced Level. There was no way an interval of that length of time could be afforded, so it was decided that I should read history, if possible under Professor S.T. Bindoff at Queen Mary College. I would at least then be qualified to become a schoolteacher.

It is difficult for me to capture the ferment of those two years in the sixth form, the impact on a shy and in many ways repressed schoolboy suddenly having to shift from being the recipient of a lesson and leaving it at that to beginning to explore subjects on my own. Although Latin had to be learned almost mechanically, my other subjects opened my mind to new vistas. I regretted having to drop English, but it was not before my eyes and ears had been opened by the teaching of Mavis Emery. Nicknamed 'Emma', she was a large, short, jolly lady whose hair was a colour (as was written of Elizabeth I) unknown to nature. Empty gin bottles had been spied in her waste-paper basket and from time to time she asked the sixth form boys home. Her somewhat raddled rubicund features and roving eye told one everything.

I instinctively felt that Miss Staples did not approve of Emma, but she instilled in me a love of Shakespeare! Indeed, she was the author of my favourite comment in my School Report: 'Occasional flashes of rare insight into Shakespeare. These must be more frequent.' The play we studied was *The Winter's Tale* and in 1952 we were taken to the Phoenix Theatre to see a production by Peter Brook, which had begun its life at Stratford the previous year to mark the Festival of Britain. I have never seen it better performed, with John Gielgud as Polixenes, Diana Wynyard as Hermione and Flora Robson as Paulina. Looking down from the upper circle, I remember a moment when it was as though plugs had been removed from my ears and I sat entranced by the music of the language uttered by a great actor. With sets and costumes by Sophie Fedorovitch, it was beautiful to look at. So it was that I decided to design the sets and costumes for that play for my Advanced Level art submission. Soon after, I took myself to see the second Shakespeare play Gielgud had brought to London from Stratford, a celebrated production of *Much Ado About Nothing* with himself playing Benedict, Diana Wynyard as Beatrice, Dorothy Tutin as Hero, Robert Hardy as Claudio and Lewis Casson as Leonato. Once again, I was entranced.

This was the beginning of my lifelong love of Shakespeare and my fascination with Gielgud as an actor. Not long after this I went to the Lyric, Hammersmith, to see Gielgud as Millamant and Pamela Brown as Mirabelle with Margaret Rutherford as Lady Wishfort and the young Paul Scofield as Witwood in Congreve's *The Way of the World*. I recall Gielgud as Wolsey in a production of *Henry VIII*, a memorable Prospero at the Old Vic in a *Tempest* designed by Leslie Hurry, and a less memorable *Lear* in the Japanese manner at the Palace Theatre. What I could not foresee was that Gielgud was to enter my life much later via my wife, who worked with him on Jonathan Miller's celebrated television version of *Alice*, Tony Richardson's *The Charge of the Light Brigade* and Alan Bennett's *Forty Years On*, and was also to design the last play in which he appeared on the West End stage, *The Best of Friends*. By then his memory for his lines was failing and the set had to be designed in such a way that he was within reach of a prompt, the only dread being that he might dry up when he edged downstage centre to a table. In 1987 I asked him to open the ill-fated Theatre Museum in Covent Garden and we took him out to dinner afterwards. His impact on me is caught on what I wrote on my fifty-ninth birthday: 'Talked to Julia about people one admired who coped with age. Gielgud came tops for me, no *folie de grandeur*, prepared to do any job, major roles or a small character part and just plod on working, no power lust and no bitterness at not having this or that.'

But it was the melody and distinctive diction of Gielgud's voice that captured me. I had never really thought of the human voice as an instrument before and, for the first time, I began to listen to my own and consciously alter it. That transformation led to Miss Emery saying one day, as we did a Shakespeare reading, 'You have a good voice.' And so my North London vowels began to fade. Years later, in the middle of the 1990s, the remarkable Robert Elms interviewed me on Radio London about my Diaries. By then we had entered the period when any kind of received English was out; looking hard at me, he said, 'You changed your voice didn't you?' 'Yes,' I replied, 'if you came up in my period you had to.' What I said was greeted with a friendly smile of understanding.

For Advanced Level art I had to produce a portfolio of work plus the scenery and costume designs for *The Winter's Tale*. I have them still and they are full of debts to the prevailing designers of the day – Oliver Messel, James Bailey and Leslie Hurry. By then my knowledge of historic dress was so detailed that I could set the court of Polixenes in that of Philip II of Spain and that of Bohemia in late Valois France. In that I was apparently first in the country; but, alas, the aspiration to design for the theatre had to be laid aside. The Advanced Level art syllabus included art history, in this instance the Italian Renaissance painters, and poor Mr Woodward, the art master, seemed barely a chapter ahead of me as we ploughed through books like Berenson's *Italian Painters of the Renaissance*. These classes, with me as the solitary pupil, took place in the Art Room Store, a commodious cupboard full of plaster casts after the antique. Of course I had never seen most of what I wrote about, but my appetite had been fuelled by the reopening of the galleries after the war, the exhibitions and the revolution in art publishing. We are so sated with colour in art books now, not to mention all that can be seen on television or on the Internet, that it is difficult to recapture the huge impact of these post-war books with their tipped-in colour plates. Skira was one of the first publishers to produce such books. I still have the two which were given to me then, one on Fra Angelico and the other on Piero della Francesca. At that period of my life such books were so precious to me that I would take them to bed and place them under my pillow.

It was also during the sixth form years that, in response to my discovery of the Elizabethan age (to which I shall come shortly), I attempted to paint miniatures in the manner of Nicholas Hilliard. My fixation with them came too late for me to have seen the major exhibition on that artist and the French miniaturist Isaac Oliver at the Victoria and Albert Museum in 1949; the source of my inspiration was to be Carl Winter's *Elizabethan Miniatures*, one of the most beautiful of the King Penguins, published in 1943, in which they were reproduced in colour. This was the birth of a love affair that culminated in a book and an exhibition at the V&A in 1983.

One thing lacking from my art training was any drawing from the life, so it was arranged for me to attend the life class at Hornsey School of Art on Saturday mornings. I was desperately unhappy, crippled by shyness amidst a sea of extrovert art students, so I gave it up. I do not know what Mr Woodward made of me but one remark did stick in my mind. My obsession with portraits totally baffled him and once he said to me, as though it were a fate he would not wish on anyone, 'You'll end up working in the National Portrait Gallery.' He was right. I did.

My attempts at seventeen to be an Elizabethan miniaturist,
reproduced actual size.

Christmas card depicting a Macaroni sent to my history teacher,
Miss Henderson, when I was thirteen.

I enjoyed the sixth form. I was treated as an intelligent human being
and what creativity I had was put to good use. It was a period in my
young life that was an opening up and not a closing down, which to
some extent the undergraduate course that followed was. But I had
already set my sights on the portraiture of the Virgin Queen. This was
to become such a driving force that it calls for some explanation as to

how a schoolboy of seventeen opened a card index of her portraits. Its origin lay in a passion for the history of dress that went back to quite early in my teens. It was stimulated by colouring books of figures in historic costume but it can be pinpointed more precisely in a Christmas card I painted to send to my history teacher, Joan Henderson – to her I shall come shortly – which depicted an eighteenth-century 'macaroni' with a towering wig and a floral nosegay. I was in Form 3A and in my thirteenth year.

Through the local library I worked my way through the prolific works on dress by Iris Brooke and C. Willett Cunnington and thence on to those by Doris Langley Moore, whose collection of dress went on display in 1955 at Eridge Castle, to which I travelled. What set her apart was the seriousness of her approach in a period when the study of fashion was regarded as trivial. Her 1949 book *The Woman in Fashion* was a revelation. She used the photographer Felix Fonteyn, brother of Margot, to take the photographs of various friends, such as the Redgrave family, actually wearing items in her collection. Doris was to enter my life at the close of the 1960s, a huge character but not by any means easy. By then she was a formidable *grande dame* with quite an *hauteur* of manner. Doris had been born in Liverpool but was brought up in South Africa. She had a lifelong obsession with Lord Byron. Just after I became Director of the Victoria and Albert Museum in 1974 she gave a lecture on her passion for the poet, opening with a vignette of herself as a young girl at a ball coping with a young man who attempted to kiss her and was beaten into a retreat when she drew back from him and said 'Have you read *Childe Harold*?' Thereafter a tale unfolded, culminating with her writing an account of the notorious Byron marriage and its breakdown in a house in Portland Crescent just along, she thought, from the one in which she was writing. It transpired that the crescent had been renumbered and that she had been writing that account in the actual room where much of the event had taken place.

I once suggested to Jock Murray, who published Doris's work on Byron, that he should persuade her to write her autobiography but she never did. As a consequence she has become a forgotten figure. I treasure the various books she gave me, including one in which, she said, the reader was taken through the bedroom door for the first time. Her contribution to the serious scholarly history of dress cannot be underestimated. Her greatest legacy, however, is the Fashion Museum in the Assembly Rooms at Bath, to which I later gave the one suit which was to me the epitome of myself as an apostle of the Swinging Sixties. It was made for me by Blades of Savile Row, and was dark blue, very tight-chested, double-breasted and with side vents seemingly to the armpits. With it went a Turnbull & Asser shirt and tie in the same striped raspberry ripple fabric and a black fedora hat. Years later, the Fashion Museum took in stages virtually everything I had worn from about 1965 to 2005. 'That', their curator said, 'solves men's fashion for the late twentieth century' – and promptly put on an exhibition of my shirts.

So Doris Langley Moore was one thread in my dress life. Another was the stage designer Herbert Norris, and it was his work that led me to the portraiture of Elizabeth I. His books, published between the two wars in several large volumes starting in 1926, found their place in the reference section at Edmonton Public Library. This meant that they could not be borrowed, until one day a librarian relented and I was allowed to take home the two volumes on the Tudors, filled with drawings of costume and in particular with a large section on the Virgin Queen's wardrobe and dress. I worked like blazes, copying as many of

Gloriana enters my life: a costume drawing based on the famous
'Armada Portrait' of Elizabeth I made when was I was seventeen.

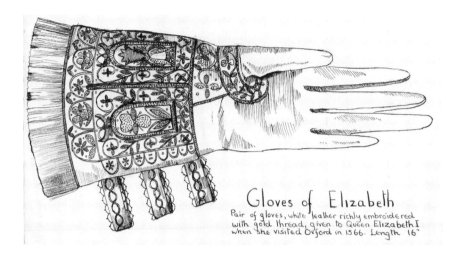

Gloves of Elizabeth

Pair of gloves, white leather richly embroidered
with gold thread, given to Queen Elizabeth I
when she visited Oxford in 1566. Length 16"

I draw Gloriana's glove.

these illustrations as I could in the time I was allowed, for this was an
era that knew nothing of the photocopier. Norris opened a door into a
part of the past which fascinated me. Decades later I did an interval
talk on Radio 3 which recalled that moment and how important it was
to me. E.H. Gombrich had heard the broadcast and told me how touched
he had been by it. More extraordinary still was the letter I received from
Norris's heirs and the gift of his personal set of his books, covered in
his own annotations.

I might have become a historian of dress but the subject became
crowded out of my life. However, I was the first chairman of the newly
founded Costume Society at the close of the 1960s, keeping the peace
around the table between the likes of Doris and the formidable antiquarian John Nevinson. The topic was rent with feuds. Stella Mary

Newton, who had been appointed to teach dress history at the Courtauld Institute, stood aloof from the new society. My most important contribution was to bring in Ann Saunders as the editor of *Costume*; she guided it over the decades to become a much respected scholarly journal. Today it has been largely forgotten what a struggle it was to gain academic recognition for the subject.

Herbert Norris's work belonged more to the romantic era of the Shakespeare productions of Beerbohm Tree and Sir Henry Irving than to modern scientific research. But Norris introduced me at an early age to the importance of original manuscripts, such as the inventory of the Virgin Queen's clothes of 1600 and the New Year's Gift Lists. Later in life they became the subject of an abandoned project, the editing of those lists and a book on the Queen's clothes making use of the warrants to the Great Wardrobe, which I began to study. I was to make occasional forays into this area with articles on Tudor and Stuart royal jewels and the dress of Charles I but I never took it any further. Janet Arnold later wrote the definitive book on Elizabeth's wardrobe and Aileen Ribeiro at the Courtauld brilliantly consolidated dress as an academic discipline.

Another person who fits into this excursus on dress and whose books were a great influence on me was James Laver. I was hypnotized by his book on Heideloff's *Gallery of Fashion* and came to know him a little in my National Portrait Gallery period, when we would occasionally lunch at the Beefsteak Club. His elegance and ease of manner and his wit set a standard for me. Although he came, in class terms within his period, from 'the wrong side of the tracks', he had an enviable sophistication and a polymathic knowledge of prints and drawings (he was Keeper of that department in the V&A from 1938 to 1959), as well as an ability to hold his own on *The Brains Trust* and *The Critics* and to write bestselling poetry and a novel, *Nymph Errant* (1932), later transformed into a hit musical by C.B. Cochran, starring Gertrude Lawrence. In a way he was the first media museum man, and of course stored up resentment and not a little envy among his less glamorous colleagues. In particular *Nymph Errant* stirred up a great deal of excitement and disapproval in the staid halls of the museum.

All of which brings me back to where I started as to why the portraiture of Elizabeth I became such a fixation. The answer to it lay in my interest in dress history but married to the effect on a young mind of studying Elizabethan political, religious and social history under Joan Henderson in the sixth form. This was to blossom into a friendship which was to last to her deathbed. Miss Henderson was someone who gave me what my own family never could: an introduction to another way of life, a cultured existence that followed art exhibitions and what was on at the theatre. Every Monday during term time she would rush off to attend Sir John Neale's seminar on the Elizabethan era at the Institute of Historical Research at Senate House. As far as I recall, Joan, as I eventually came to know her, was writing a thesis on the 1587 Parliament, which she never finished. At this early stage of my life there was an excitement about being at one remove from the epicentre of research on that era: in particular, Neale had written what still stands as perhaps the classic biography of the Queen.

As far I can remember, Joan Henderson remained virtually unchanged in appearance as long as I knew her, her dyed dark brown hair brushed back from her forehead, her cheerful animated features and receding chin. Her manner of speech was always very precise, with a tendency to end every sentence with the word 'altogether'. She dressed in sensible

Inspirational history teacher: Joan Henderson.

working clothes and flat shoes but to the end of her days believed that to be a lady meant having one good silk dress. Later I was to learn that she was totally undomesticated and lived in chaos, although during this early period of our friendship she lived with her mother in a rebuilt bombed-out house in Brondesbury Park. She was an inspirational teacher, who would tell me what exhibitions were on and where, and would often lend me the catalogue. To some of the more impoverished pupils I saw her slipping money. That gesture captures the intensity of this period in the history of post-war education.

During these two years I began to pass from mutely taking notes by the mile in class and learning every fact and date by rote to being introduced to the work of certain historians who have remained household gods to me ever since. It was Joan who enthused over the work of the future Dame Veronica Wedgwood, who inspired me with a love of history. Two of her works in particular were to become icons in my intellectual life: *The Thirty Years War* (1938) and *The King's Peace, 1637–1641* (1955), the first volume of a trilogy she never completed on 'The Great Rebellion'. Why was this? The answer, I think, lay in her deep sense of humanity, along with her acute observation of character, an approach which viewed the past as though it were some mighty canvas in which she used words as a great painter uses brushstrokes to give form, substance, depth and light and shade to a vanished era. The opening chapter of *The King's Peace* I hold as a masterpiece of historical writing, taking the reader by the hand on a journey through the England of 1637.

Alas, I had fallen in love with a form of history writing that was going into sharp eclipse. Veronica, as I came to know her, belonged to the great Victorian tradition of Carlyle and Macaulay. *The Thirty Years War*, written when she was only twenty-eight, sits within that tradition. But, as soon as I got to university, her work was generally referred to in a dismissive way as some kind of inferior form of life, although it did not impede her ascent to becoming a Dame in 1968 and the following year being appointed only the third female OM. It was at that period that I came to know her, for she was generous to the National Portrait Gallery. Perhaps she is best caught in part of what I wrote about her in my Diary on her death in March 1997:

> How can I describe her? Inclining to short with her hair tightly
> pulled back from the face into a bun at the back, a somewhat
> rubicund complexion and eyes that twinkled with intelligence and
> humour. In dress somewhat nondescript: shoes flat with no heel and

safe suits and skirts and blouses. But it was her voice which was so marvellous, alert yet endowed with an inner warmth. She always spoke about the past as though she was seeing it. ... She was a great historian, a great writer and a generous and gracious woman. I recall her writing in *The Author* an article saying how she had come to do what she did, how after her degree she had to choose between close-focus academe and 'the great tradition', history as narrative and literature. I was later to be faced with the same choice and decision. Veronica chose the latter. Jacqueline Hope-Wallace sweetly wrote to me that I had always been a 'true believer'. I always was. To me she was sacred and an ideal.

The second figure whose works came my way in this formative period of my life was a far more contentious character, A.L. Rowse. His early works were on sixteenth-century England and these were the ones I read: *Sir Richard Grenville of The Revenge* (1937), *Tudor Cornwall* (1941) and *The England of Elizabeth* (1950), the first volume of a trilogy called *The Elizabethan Age*. This is what I wrote on his death:

The papers are full of obits for Leslie Rowse ... I dedicated *The English Renaissance Miniature* (1983) to him and he dedicated his *Reflections on the Puritan Revolution* (1986) to me three years later. I still haven't read the latter. I've flicked through it, yes, but everywhere my eye fell there was that bias and diatribe which was his undoing. What an extraordinary man! He was as 'god' all those years ago when as a humble grammar school boy I read *The England of Elizabeth*. He fired me with a love of that age and for that I'm eternally grateful. But where did it in his case go off the rails? When did that ego explode to become 'infallible' and 'absolute'...? Rowse sat in that large rabbit warren of a house, Trenarren, with its ceilings falling in, the walls damp and books cascading in heaps everywhere. But the energy and intellect were always extraordinary. He was in many ways like a politician. He needed an audience in front of which to perform. No question of how are you or what are you up to? From the moment of encounter the floodgates were open, everyone, everything, every age, he knew it all. One didn't get a word in edgeways. And yet there was a twinkle there. Everyone was called 'dear' or 'sweetie', especially men ... I think that he was aware, as he bashed hither and thither, that it was all a bit of a lark really. That was what I liked about him. Otherwise he'd have been insufferable but in fact he wasn't. There was always a warmth that made up for the stupendous ego. He deserved to be honoured earlier than he was ... He was a great, maddening figure that caught the public imagination. There's no one else like that.

The third historian to whose work I was introduced in the sixth form was Muriel St Clare Byrne, whose books *Elizabethan Life in Town and Country* (1925) and *The Elizabethan Home Discovered in Two Dialogues* (1925) revealed to me the social life of the period. Both were delightful and betrayed a rare eye for detail. She was later to enter my life when I was an impoverished postgraduate student anxious to make a pound or two and applied to help with a Society for Theatre Research project. That never happened but thereafter our paths crossed from time to time. She was another of those between-the-wars mannish women in sensible, rectangular clothes and a hat close to a trilby. Most of her life, I later learned, was spent as an extension lecturer for nearly twenty years at Oxford and London, and also at RADA. The books of hers I studied as a sixth-former were hugely popular and went through numerous editions. But her life's work was editing the letters of Arthur Plantagenet, Lord Lisle, on which she started work three years before I was born and finally published in 1981. To my astonishment she presented me with a set. I recall her describing how through the war years she had clung on to what she had done, once sitting on the trunk containing her work as the bombs fell and the ceiling collapsed. The Lisle Letters are now recognized to be the equivalent of the fifteenth-century Paston Letters but for the reign of Henry VIII.

———

So windows began to be opened in my mind by a teacher who was to become a lifelong friend until she died at eighty-seven in December 2002. Joan Henderson was the one teacher with whom I stayed in contact, our friendship maintained almost wholly by correspondence. That it developed in that way I now realize in retrospect was because when I went up to university I felt lonely and at sea and Joan offered a much-needed sympathetic ear – inevitably the university world was completely incomprehensible to my family. What surprised me was that Joan kept virtually all my letters, stretching from 1953 to the year of her death. The ensuing chapters owe something to those letters, which her executors returned to me. I never forgot my debt to her. What other teacher would have sat in the British Library and copied in longhand the only published listing of the portraits of the Virgin Queen, F.M. O'Donoghue's *A Descriptive and Classified Catalogue of the Portraits of Queen Elizabeth* (1894)?

The life of the kind Joan Henderson had led when I was in sixth form went on for decades. Attendance at the Elizabethan seminar and friendships in the Institute of Historical Research were to be the bedrock of her existence, plus regular visits to Kew Gardens. On her death I recalled my last visit to her, in hospital, and attempted to sum up our friendship:

There seemed little of her left beneath the bedclothes. She had tubes stuck into her and a mask over her mouth. In spite of this she looked the same as I always remembered her. What can you do in such circumstances but just talk and I found myself on a stream of memory and chatter about the garden, the cats, the house, the weather and then suddenly I realized that she knew that it was me. Her eyes rolled and her head lifted itself and I found myself recalling the old days, how last weekend I had taken from the shelf *The English Icon* which I'd dedicated to her, how she had introduced me to the Elizabethan age, given me books by A.L. Rowse and C.V. Wedgwood to read, how I'd show her my costume drawings, how much I owed to her, to those years and that giving by a school teacher to a lower middle-class boy from nowhere at a grammar school but who was stage-struck and mad about the Virgin Queen and her many dresses and portraits. I couldn't sustain all of this for more, I think, than fifteen minutes or so. There was nothing I could do, no way that I could help. I could only offer her my love and thanks and say goodbye before my voice completely cracked with emotion.

Away from it all I did crack up. It was my childhood gone. I prayed that she would fade quickly and the prayer was answered, thanks be to God. I saw her at about one o'clock on the Monday and she peacefully passed away about four o'clock the following morning. It was as though she'd hung on knowing or hoping that I'd come and when I had it was somehow all right to let go. She was eighty-seven, so one mustn't mourn but give thanks that the end was quick and un-prolonged.

To one's schoolteacher one is always a child. I don't think that she ever grasped how much I had changed. She had been such a prop to me when, shy, awkward and retarded I went up to the university. Always a letter would come. I was so grateful for that amidst all the isolation. And yet the relationship worked on certain principles with parameters which were on no account to be crossed. Her letters after I married always opened 'Dear Roy and Julia' because I'm sure that she believed that a married man should not be receiving letters from an unmarried woman.

... Such teachers had a vision and social conscience to help those forward who never before had had a chance. But she would tell me about exhibitions on in London which I ought to see and lend me the catalogue. At that age those small things are so important, glimpses into worlds unknown to one's family, the worlds of art and history to which I was so strongly drawn.

There was a memorial service for her in the chapel of St Mary's College at Strawberry Hill. I went along and so did Norman Tebbit, who was also taught by her. It was a small but affectionate gathering at which I would so much have liked to have spoken, but I was never asked. I had after all been in contact with her for over half a century. What I publish now must compensate for that lost opportunity to pay tribute.

And so at the end of June 1953 these years came to an end, framed by two great public events: the Festival of Britain, which opened in the spring of 1951, and the Coronation in June 1953. I went to the Festival with my mother – not that I warmed to it that much, leaving a memory of the bright and garish and modern, already not to my taste. In the case of the Coronation, I was one of two pupils from our school chosen to join others from other schools to stand on the Victoria Embankment and watch the great procession pass by. That the choice should fall on me I feel was not accidental but reflected that they sensed I was made to view such a spectacle. And indeed I was. Although the day was wet, nothing dimmed the glory of the great cavalcade that on its surface reflected what seemed to be an Empire upon which the sun still never set. It was, of course, a mirage; but for those who lived through these early years of the new reign there was an optimism anticipatory of a new era. And I was to be part of it.

Dour sixth-former: myself in the year of the Coronation, 1953.

Eleven to eighteen is not an age when it would ever have occurred to me to form anything resembling an archive. But it is significant that I have treasured a handful of things from which I have never parted. There are the form prizes: Hugh Braun's *The English Castle* for 1948-9, Harry Batsford and Charles Fry's *The Cathedrals of England* for 1949-50, Berenson's *The Italian Painters of the Renaissance* for 1951-2 and Burckhardt's *The Civilization of the Renaissance in Italy* and H.A.L. Fisher's *A History of Europe* for the History Prize for 1952-3. All these vividly represent the preoccupations of my mind, with their seeds of a passion for Italy, which has lasted a lifetime, and an equal and even stronger passion for the heritage of England in the form of her ancient buildings and monuments, which is as strong now – perhaps even stronger – having spent a lifetime studying, exploring and expounding them.

And then there was that passion for theatre. I still have the two short one-act plays I wrote for Andrew House to present while I was in the sixth form, *Pavane for Dead Lovers* in 1952, about Mary Queen of Scots, and that for the following year, *The Abdication*, whose opening is so hilarious that I find it irresistible to quote:

ACT I

SCENE I. *The scene is a room in a royal palace somewhere in the Balkans just after World War II. The room is large and pleasant with a door at the back right and window to front stage right. A desk and chairs.*

The Queen Mother is writing at the desk.

Enter King Peter II.

Queen Mother   Hello Darling. What's wrong? (*continues writing*)

King   The peasants are in revolt.

Queen Mother   Again! Don't they ever work? I suppose you have sent the Imperial Guard to suppress them?

King   We have no Imperial Guard. Mutiny broke out last night.

Queen Mother   Well, you should pay them more often...

It is as well that the public has been spared my career as a playwright.

But I do leave these years haunted by a sense of loss. I have always held on to a huge folio crammed with my artwork. The earliest item in it that bears a date is a copy of a Velázquez portrait of an Infanta inscribed in the bottom right-hand corner: 'R C Strong 19 June Age 12 ½ 1948'.

Then follow other sketches and watercolours, above all for the scenery and costumes for *The Winter's Tale* that were part of my Advanced Level submission. I still stare at them with a sense of mourning for a career for which I had yearned but which was doomed never to happen. In the years that followed I gradually relinquished pencil, paint and brush forever and put all my energies into what could be achieved by the pen. All of this was only to reach a resolution on 10 September 1971, when I married the designer Julia Trevelyan Oman.

The final judgement on me from the headmaster, H.B. Champion, reads as follows:

> He is a lad of real character, quiet and unassuming, but full of ideas and ready to work really hard to carry them through. He has three times been awarded the Form Prize for all round effort. He is quite outstanding in his attitude to his studies, and few boys of his age are capable of his devotion to the task in hand.
>
> He is outstanding at Art. He has studied the history of costume on his own account and illustrated Vergil's Aeneid for the sheer joy of doing it. He has many times designed and painted scenery and costumes for school plays, both French and English.
>
> He leaves us with our complete respect as a lad of single-hearted purpose and unswerving integrity.

So far, so good; but there was a long way to go. What I learnt early on was an ability to work ferociously hard on my own. It was only when I reached university that I was to realize the yawning gap between those who had been born into an educated family and those who had not, and it took me a long time to make up for that. Most arrived with a familiarity with the work of some of the great novelists such as Jane Austen and Charles Dickens, which would have been on the family bookshelves, and it would have been taken for granted that by sixteen you would be able to hold your own, however modestly, in a conversation at table. All this I had yet to learn. Public schools endowed pupils with a social assurance which ensured that those who went, even if only to a minor one, assumed the nature of an unassailable caste. One of my earliest encounters on reaching the university was with a girl who cross-examined me as to which public school I had attended and to which London club my father belonged. My negative replies meant that I was immediately cut. When I reflect on this phase of life I call to mind the post-war film *The Guinea Pig* (1948), in which the young Richard Attenborough played a tobacconist's son who won a scholarship to a public school. This caught pretty accurately the travails of what was an emergent meritocracy in the country's still rigid class structure.

THREE

MARKING TIME

1953 to 1956

M Y EARLY ICONOGRAPHY is meagre, more than made up for later in life when I discovered that I was photogenic and a whole litany of celebrated photographers were to record me in various guises: Beaton, Brandt, Snowdon, Bailey, Donovan, Lategan and Swannell among them. But here an emaciated face peers out, a mugshot taken for some identification purpose during my first visit to Italy in 1955. By the time it was taken I was a virtually penniless wanderer, travelling as cheaply as I could through North Italy. What it does demonstrate is that times continued to be hard well into the 1950s. These were the years when I was living at home, eking out an existence on a county grant, if I remember rightly, of £150 per annum.

———

By the mid-1950s I was growing up. Having passed my Advanced Levels in the summer of 1953, I was ready to take up my place to read history at

Queen Mary College at the University of London. The History School at Queen Mary had been created under the aegis of Professor S.T. Bindoff and, like the History School at University College (for which I was not considered bright enough), was a centre of Tudor studies appropriate to my obsessions. The College itself had its origins in late Victorian philanthropy to the impoverished citizens of the East End of London. It was reconfigured in 1934, when the original Queen's Building was given over to the arts – which included history – and this was where I was to be based for the next three years. To get there from the suburbs of N21 involved a lengthy journey by public transport, either wholly by bus or by bus combined with Underground, alighting at Mile End station and walking the rest of the way along the Mile End Road. The advantage of my epic daily commute was the huge amount of reading accomplished during the journey: I vividly remember that this was when I first read Milton's *Paradise Lost*.

That drear commute to and from the Mile End Road was to dominate these three years. All I ever seemed to do was travel to and from North London to the East End or to Senate House at Russell Square, for either lectures or the university library. And then, once home, to work in what was the dining room but in effect became my study, where I would sit with my face glued to a book. Accounts of gap years, today regarded as some kind of rite and right, leave me astonished, let alone the notion that undergraduate life should be one long party. I was there on a county scholarship and I knew that any failure would bring to an abrupt end what I aimed to achieve. These were years of unremitting slog. The little appointment diaries from that period, which I still retain, are largely empty. At the front of two of them I listed off my week, which I here synthesize:

Monday	11 am	European History (Senate House)
	2.45 pm	Florentine Special Subject (Bedford College)
Tuesday	11.30 am	Political Theory (QMC)
	2.30 pm	Essay class (QMC)
Wednesday	10.30 am	Modern English History (QMC)
Thursday	10.30 am	Medieval English History (QMC)
	2.15 pm	Renaissance Optional Subject (The Warburg Institute)

At the end of each year there was an examination, and everything led up to Finals, in my case in the summer of 1956.

What is striking, and again parallel to my grammar school years, is that my arrival at Queen Mary coincided with the government's belief that the extension of higher education was the key to the economic prosperity of the country. In 1945 only 2 per cent of the population went up to a university; by 2003 the target was 50 per cent. The period to which I belonged was one when the grammar schools had taken the bright and motivated members of the lower middle and middle classes and catapulted them into the ancient or, at least, relatively old universities. It was a short-lived period, cut short when Labour's Secretary of State for Education and Science, Anthony Crosland, followed, incredibly, by Conservative prime ministers Edward Heath and Margaret Thatcher, embarked on their destruction of the grammar schools, thereby hacking down the ladder of social mobility that had served the country so well for so many centuries. When I think of many of those I came to know, such as A.S. Byatt, Peter Hall or Alan Bennett, we all belonged to this brief swathe of time that produced a short-lived meritocracy. Virtually all of my friends who came up and through the system at the same time and who were successful, married and had families, were to send their children to private schools as the state system by the 1970s had gone so far downhill. Even worse was the fact that those who went on to teach in the universities spent the first year teaching undergraduates what in our day they already knew on arrival.

A group photograph of the History School of Queen Mary College is, I think, a sharp mirror of the times. Few if any young faces captured here would have dreamed of being able to go to university as little as five years before. At school one was thrown together with children who at least shared a locality in common. At university suddenly the mix of social background and area of the country was on a national scale. I think of people like Clare Toms, a fresh-faced country girl who missed the cows on her father's farm. Most, like me, were products of the aspiring suburban classes, sons and daughters of middle-range families

whose fathers worked in business of one sort or another. Gathered here is all three years' intake of the History School. Two particular friends I spy, Michael Bridson, who married almost as soon as he left college and worked for Thorn Electric, and Cedric Holland, who went on to become an archivist. I quickly lost touch with the former but not the latter. Tragically, he was afflicted by diabetes and in the end went blind and died young. And then, in the front row, sit the staff of the Department of Queen Mary College with the benign avuncular figure of Professor S.T. Bindoff presiding in the centre with his hands on his knees.

Queen Mary College, or QMC as it was known, only re-established itself in the aftermath of the war. The masonry of the main building bore the scars of bomb damage and, along with most other London buildings at this period, it was virtually soot-black. Its distinguishing feature was

The History School of Queen Mary College in 1956, all three years. I am in the back row, second from the left, between Cedric Holland and Clare Toms. In the front row Professor Bindoff sits in the centre, flanked to his right by Dr Chew and his left by Dr Leslie.

the clock tower in the forecourt; otherwise it was architecturally totally forgettable. The History School, when I arrived in the autumn of 1953, was only in the third year of its existence. Professor Bindoff I recall with huge affection. He was a big-built man, benign of aspect and gruff of voice. There was a certain shyness about him, which, as often happens in the case of the shy, made those dealing with him tremulous. Patrick Collinson, the distinguished ecclesiastical historian, wrote of Bindoff: 'The pipe, the gruff and slow-moving voice: these were what laboriously animated the most important experience of their lives for many of these pupils.' His memorable Penguin History entitled *Tudor England* appeared in 1950 and the following year he became the first holder of the History Chair at QMC. This was a golden era for Tudor historians, with Bindoff at QMC and John Neale and Joel Hurstfield at University College. The seminars over which they presided (to which I will come in the ensuing chapter) were alive with excitement and vitality. But what I most liked about Bindoff was his avuncular kindness and the fact that he took on board that what interested me were the aesthetic and cultural aspects of the period, and he never stood in my way of pursuing them.

To the new History School Bindoff was able to attract a number of extremely talented academics. Years later, at the annual al fresco lunch held for the staff and close friends of Westminster Abbey, I was tapped on the shoulder and a friendly voice said, 'Hello, Roy.' I turned round to come face to face with the person who had taught me medieval history, Barbara Harvey. That had been her first post as an assistant lecturer but her brilliance was perceived almost immediately, for she became a tutor at Somerville College, Oxford, in 1955 and was succeeded at QMC by Dr Dione Clementi, whose interests centred on medieval Italy. Thus Barbara stepped back into my life in the year 2000 after a gap of forty-five years, as her great work on life and death in medieval England was the result of the first serious examination of the unique records of the Abbey preserved in the Muniment Room: in that same year I had taken on one of the Abbey's honorary posts of High Bailiff and Searcher of the Sanctuary.

Barbara's other medieval colleague had been Dr Helena Chew, whose masterwork had been on ecclesiastical tenants-in-chief. She it was who taught us early political theory, starting with Plato and Aristotle and moving on via St Augustine to Aquinas and Marsiglio of Padua. But she also lectured on early English history and certainly inspired in me a love of the Anglo-Saxons, so much so that Joan Henderson sent me Sir Frank Stenton's magisterial Oxford history on the period. I was stimulated by movements until that point unknown to me, such as the twelfth-century Renaissance; as my cultural bent was well known, Barbara Harvey asked me to present at one of her essay classes in 1954 something to do with the arts. What I wrote to Joan Henderson catches very well my extreme hesitancy and shyness at this phase in my life:

> I appeared armed with drawings of medieval costume. I was afraid for a moment that I would dry up as usual but once I had started I chatted on quite merrily for half-an-hour. Afterwards everybody, including Miss Harvey, said how interesting it had been. It is quite all right when I am talking about something I know about but when questions turn up like 'What was the significance of the coronation of Otto III' I just feel like crawling under the carpet.

Only in retrospect have I been able to realize that I arrived at the university at a particular moment in the teaching of history which conditioned what one was taught and the slant put upon it. Social history was beyond the pale; sad when I recall how much delight I had

had at school from the Quennells' *A History of Everyday Things in England* (1918-34) and G.M. Trevelyan's *English Social History* (1944). Anything connected with culture or art was not exactly dismissed but viewed as periphery and a soft option. Instead the focus was almost wholly on economic and constitutional history. The preoccupation with the latter was reinforced by a recent phenomenon, *The History of Parliament*. That owed its origins to Josiah Wedgwood, who believed that the nation's history could be mirrored by writing the biographies of some 75,000 MPs. The project was state-funded five years before I arrived at QMC and was based at the Institute of Historical Research. The historians involved in this project, Neale, Bindoff and Sir Lewis Namier, virtually set the history agenda.

The other dominant tide was a left-wing to Marxist one obsessed with class. Its approach was epitomized by a new journal, *Past and Present*, set up by the Historians Group of the Communist Party of Great Britain, including Eric Hobsbawn and Christopher Hill. Oswald Spengler's *The Decline of the West* (1918-23) was much talked about but not, I believe, widely read. In the QMC History Department all of this was embodied in the volatile Dr R.F. Leslie. Historians who went along with the Marxian analysis of the past inevitably focused their interest on the Civil War period and a keen preoccupation with what was billed as 'the rise of the gentry' and 'the world upside down'; they were also obsessed with the peasantry. Years later I remember shocking a journalist by saying that I had absolutely no interest in them at all.

Sir John Drummond read history at Cambridge; his autobiography *Tainted by Experience* (2000) exactly mirrors my own. In those days at Cambridge biography was regarded as a lower form of life, social history was not even to be referred to – and as for literature, music, architecture and the arts in general, they never warranted more than a few paragraphs or a chapter at the close of any book on a particular period. John was to come into my life later (he had entered the BBC simultaneously with my wife), when I was asked to do one of the programmes in a major television series entitled *Spirit of the Age* (1975).

In addition to the run of British and European history that we were required to study, we could choose an optional and a special subject. For my optional I chose the Renaissance and for my special Florence in the Renaissance. The former course took place at the Warburg Institute, then housed in part of the old Imperial Institute in South Kensington before its demolition. I will reserve a description of this remarkable place for the chapter that follows. The latter was taught at Bedford College in Regent's Park.

The Renaissance course was the Warburg's only concession to providing any instruction to undergraduates. In January 1962 I recalled the importance to me of this course in a letter to my Dutch friend, Jan van Dorsten: 'one term cosmology, another neoplatonism, another humanism, another art history and Vasari. It has stood me in good stead many times.' In effect it introduced me for the first time to a multidisciplinary approach to the past and opened my mind and eyes to things I had never even thought about before. Needless to say, I was the only male member of this little band. Classes were conducted seminar style, with whoever was teaching seated at the head of the table. The opening ones were taken by the already celebrated E.H. Gombrich, benign and brilliant, who had only four years previously published his landmark *The Story of Art*. The first term was devoted to art and Vasari's *Lives*. I scored an immediate hit. As the first slide was projected he asked whether anyone knew what it was. 'It's the Margaritone in

Mind opener: Charles Mitchell of the Warburg Institute.

the National Gallery', I piped up to a somewhat surprised Gombrich. But these classes were not the trot through the evolution of style I had expected from reading Berenson, oh no, for we were asked to think about why Vasari wrote what he did, a story of art as an evolutionary tale with its first hero in Giotto and its culmination in the work of Raphael, Leonardo and Michaelangelo.

The whole of this course was revelatory. Virtually all of the rest of it was taken by the fiery, argumentative Charles Mitchell, one of those untidy, sprawling academics who looked as though he had just fallen out of bed. Before the war he had worked at the National Maritime Museum, Greenwich, but after it became a lecturer at the Warburg; in 1960 he migrated to the United States, where I was to encounter him again in 1965. Mitchell, like Gombrich, had a polymathic cast of mind. He loved winding us up and I lived in mortal dread of him. Often a class would begin with a page of Latin text being distributed and one by one we were called upon to translate a section of it. Part of his technique was to make one feel ignorant. When a girl in the class was unable to name four cardinal virtues, he roared: 'How dare you come to this class? Where ever were you brought up?' while the rest of us all looked at the surface of the table.

In a curious way Mitchell's approach spurred one on, ashamed of one's utter ignorance. But then there were lovely surprises, as when we were taken to the V&A where he had arranged that a medal by Pisanello should be produced from its case for us to look at, demonstrating that these were designed as tactile objects. There was also the startling gulf between what we studied and that taught to others doing more prosaic subjects. We were asked little by little to enter the thought context of another age which took a belief in astrology as a given, or to share in its exploration of classical antiquity by means of a new activity: archaeology. It was a hugely exciting course in which we traced the survival of the pagan gods of antiquity, in the main through the astrological tradition, to their reawakening in the Renaissance. We studied humanist texts and scripts, topics such as Ciceronianism and Neoplatonism. Castiglione's *Book of the Courtier* introduced us to a refashioning of courtly ideals in terms of dress, manners, deportment and the art of love. Charles Mitchell sprang to life even more when he spoke about his own researches. There was a wonderful class on Sigismondo Malatesta's *Tempio* in Rimini, taking us through stage by stage how Mitchell had worked out his thesis as to its true meaning as a building celebrating its only begetter.

Side by side with this was the special course under the aegis of Marion J. Tooley. Bespectacled and with her hair scraped back, she looked the part of the academic lady but possessed a sensitivity that endeared her to us. For our final class with her we clubbed together to buy her a potted plant, a gesture that brought tears to her eyes, which she failed to conceal. That course was at Bedford College, another part of the University of London that had begun its life in the Victorian age as a place for the education of young ladies. This was still writ large in the mid-1950s, when two of our class were being presented at court that year. On one occasion a girl arrived with her presentation dress in a large bag; when she pulled it out, her overexcited friends screamed with dismay: 'Oh no, not pale kipper!' A girl called Anne Longley and I were the only 'outsiders', which we frequently felt keenly in what at times resembled a finishing school rather than a college in a major university.

I started the course buoyed up with the notion that I would be floating along on a cloud of Botticelli and Fra Angelico, only to find that it was concerned with the power struggles of the great mercantile families of Florence like the Strozzi and the Medici to gain control of the city. For that we had to read works by Machiavelli, Savonarola and Guicciardini, so I enrolled in a course of Italian evening classes at Birkbeck College. Each class lasted some two hours, with a short break during which many who were on it, having worked for a living all day, laid their heads on the desk before them and went to sleep.

———

I do not recall this period of my life with a sense of anything other than that it had to be got through. I was not only cripplingly shy but aware that sexually I was ambiguous. These were years in the aftermath of the two homosexual spies Guy Burgess and Donald Maclean fleeing to Russia. Prosecution of homosexuals as criminals reached a peak with the famous cases of Sir John Gielgud in 1953 and Lord Montagu of Beaulieu the following year. For someone who is now in his late seventies it is difficult to communicate to a generation where everything can be – and is – said and done what it was like to come to sexual maturity in the middle of the 1950s. If I had been born in 1945 and not in 1935 I should probably have lived the life of a gay man in a society which by 1980 accepted such orientation. There will be readers of this book who will identify what I record here either in themselves or in family members or friends at this period. If I had gone to boarding school or done National Service I would have found out much that I was only gradually to piece together. An old friend of mine, Brian Sewell (of whom more later), captures this period very well in describing how he abandoned his volition to become a Catholic priest and took a very different path in life from the one I chose. For that I respect him, for he too could, he admits, have married. The other path was to know that that volition was there, tucked away at the back of part of one's mind, an isolating experience which can now, in the vastly changed ethos of the early twenty-first century, be admitted.

I was struck forcefully by this in an interview I gave to a courteous journalist from the *Evening Standard* in 2011, who went for the jugular with me on the gay or straight issue. I saw what he meant; but for we who lived in the 1950s it was all so much more complicated. Any mention of such a tendency was then unthinkable and even if I had faced up to it I would not have known what to do about it. At twenty I was totally bottled up and inhibited. There was a homosexual side to myself, that much I knew; but whenever, later, I got glimpses into that world I knew equally that I did not wish to enter it. There was another side to me:

emotionally and intellectually I was also hugely attracted to women and I knew that, if I found the right person, I would like the stability of an old-fashioned Christian marriage.

But the 1950s were still the age of innocence and reticence. Sex as a subject of conversation was simply taboo in any form. Decades later, when I was filming a pilot for a television series (which never happened) on the changes in society during the present Queen's reign I recall making use of a scrapbook which included a picture of myself and others from my year at what was the one great annual social event, the Charter Week Ball at the Royal Festival Hall. The year was 1955. There we sit at a table of eight: me wearing a dinner jacket for the very first time, with my date, Jackie Smith, in a strapless dress, Anne Nash in a halter neck, and Colin Bowden and three others. When I opened this page and showed it to two girls already high on cocktails and busy making themselves up to go clubbing, they just shrieked with laughter at what they saw: 'Look at them, a load of twenty-year-old virgins!' They were right. But that is how it was before the sixties changed everything.

For me this was an awkward period when I was looking for some framework to my life. The fate of my generation of 1950s meritocrats was that access to education separated us progressively from our own families as bit by bit there was less and less common ground. In effect I was living two separate lives, emphasized by the fact that I still lived at home, where life continued virtually unchanged. I maintained my interest in the theatre and in all the great exhibitions at the Royal Academy. But almost daily contact with highly educated teaching staff and intelligent fellow students opened my mind to other worlds. My friend Cedric Holland, who had left the Courtauld to read history at QMC, introduced me to music. Together we would go, for example,

Fifties innocence: the Charter Week Ball at the Royal Festival Hall,
1955, the first time I wore black tie.

to hear Purcell's music for the funeral of Queen Mary at Westminster
Abbey. There were visits to concerts and I went to see some of the early
revivals of Handel operas at Sadler's Wells. I also took myself off to a
modest hotel in Stratford-upon-Avon to see plays at the Royal Shakespeare Theatre, including *King Lear* with Michael Redgrave. At the
Old Vic there was more Shakespeare, including a memorable *Tempest*
directed by Robert Helpmann and designed by Leslie Hurry.

These were the years when certain threads which were to run through
my life began to come together. Some, as I have written, were already

there by 1953 – the theatre, the ballet, fashion, history and what we now designate as 'heritage'. Each of these was to find expression during the coming decades in a torrent of books and articles, lectures and exhibitions, radio and television programmes, and in formulation of policy for two of our national institutions. Some of these threads were to go underground during these undergraduate years, to resurface later, while others took on sharper definition.

One event during these years was to have long-term significance. Cedric had become involved in the Anglican Chaplaincy to the University of London, established in 1948 by the then Bishop of London; by 1955 it was based in 13 Woburn Square, in proximity to Christ Church. The chaplain, Father Gardiner, was going to Walsingham and there was room in his car for one more; I was offered the place. Church was not then part of my life. For a time I had gone to a Methodist church and Sunday school but that had long lapsed. What I experienced in Norfolk late in September was something very different: Anglo-Catholicism at its most fervent.

Looking back, is there any construction that I can put upon this sudden event? I recall at the time that this unexpected visit triggered within me a realization that there was a huge void at the centre of my life. My other great friend during this period, Michael Bridson, was a devout Catholic and indeed the College's Catholic Society was the most socially active at QMC. In retrospect this was a hangover from the between-the-wars Monsignor Knox period when conversion to Rome became fashionable and the universities in particular were targeted. I was later to catch the tail end of this when, as the young National Portrait Gallery Director, I was placed next to the legendary Monsignor d'Arcy (his many converts included Evelyn Waugh), whose eyes lit up at the sight of me. My response to the Christian faith was an immediate and I suppose emotional one, not one reached through either argument or analysis. It was at the time an overwhelming impulse. There was no discussion with the family, not that there ever was about anything anyway. No comment was made as suddenly off I went to church and a framed postcard of Perugino's *Crucifixion* in the National Gallery was pinned to my bedroom wall as a kind of manifesto. There was, of course, an aesthetic appeal and I became enamoured of the Oxford Movement, which was part of the history course. The childhood visits to the crib at Catholic St Monica's lingered in my mind and I loved the sense of mystery, the almost balletic movement of the clergy, the music, the visual panoply of vestments, incense and images attendant on Catholic practice. Later I came to realize that they were the icing on a cake (in Anglican terms they are 'things indifferent') of incredible and profound richness which would see me through all the ups and downs of my life.

The Shrine of Our Lady of Walsingham, one of the greatest sites of pilgrimage in medieval England, had been destroyed in 1538. But in 1922 the vicar of Little Walsingham, Father Hope Patten, re-created the image of Our Lady from the seal of the medieval priory and a revival began that goes on to this day. The Anglican shrine church arose in the 1930s and the effect on those who come to it has grown over the years. In the autumn of 1955 it made an overwhelming impact on me, as someone who had never been in contact with people whose faith was so transparent and so powerful in its commitment. The holy face of the mother superior of the community at which we stayed haunts me still, as does the darkness of the shrine with its guttering candles and devotion of the kneeling pilgrims. I suppose that I went through what is crudely categorized as a conversion experience. It is one I have never regretted.

On my return to London I asked to be instructed in the faith, only once wavering as to whether or not I should become a Roman Catholic. But Father Gardiner lent me Father Kenneth Ross's *Why I Am Not a Roman Catholic* (1953) and loyal Anglican, albeit of a High variety, I have remained to this day. I love the Church of England for many things, among them its bravery in keeping doors open and also admitting that some things we do not know – or, perhaps, are meant not to know. My diary for 1956 is the usual sea of blank pages but there are two entries for February. On 4th: 'Afternoon of devotion – Went to my first confession. Fr Hester (Clerkenwell)'; and the next day: 'Confirmation by the Bishop of Stepney. Went to High Mass at All Saints, Margaret Street.' The Bishop of Stepney who confirmed me was that fearless man Joost de Blank, who the following year became Archbishop of Cape Town and, even more importantly, took on the role of being the scourge of apartheid.

All Saints, Margaret Street, has remained part of my life, on and off, ever since. It still reigns as the cathedral of Catholic Anglicanism, in spite of the loss of those who could not accept the ordination of women (which I wholeheartedly support). David Hutt, the priest who was destined to be my best man when I eloped and married in 1971, and later a confessor, was vicar of All Saints for some eleven years in the 1980s. It is one of the rare churches left in London where Mass is still said as often as three times a day. I know of few other churches which have such a powerful atmosphere, charged with the attributes that deep prayerfulness and the intensity of acts of penitence bestow. Years later I recalled in an introduction I wrote to a guide to the church:

> I was aware that I was standing not only in one of the monuments of Victorian church art, arguably William Butterfield's masterpiece, but also in one of the penultimate expressions of its revived faith

within a tradition that stretched back to the Caroline divines in the seventeenth century, down through the Oxford Movement in the nineteenth to our own day.

From 1956 I attended the Sunday High Mass at my local church, Holy Trinity, Winchmore Hill, a brick building dating from 1907, where the priest was Father Frank Hadkinson. I remained there for several years, embalmed in an Anglo-Catholicism of a kind that was later to change so radically after Vatican II, when the Church of Rome embraced liturgy in the vernacular. This was the era of the non-communicating High Anglican Mass when only the priest communicated. There was a prie-dieu at which one knelt to make one's confession and an image of Our Lady before which to light candles. On the great festivals there were processions with crucifer and acolytes and two censers swinging clouds of incense in every direction. The rituals of the Veneration of the Cross on Good Friday and the new fire on Easter Eve were observed, leading in to the first Mass of Easter; there was a Midnight Mass at Christmas, when the Christ Child in the form of a doll was carried by Father Hadkinson in procession and laid in the crib. In retrospect, so much of this was an Anglo-Catholicism that had run out of steam. Today Holy Trinity is one of those churches that has refused to come to terms with women's ordination and is served by what are known as 'flying bishops'.

I was yet to be exposed to priests who were extraordinary in themselves; this did not happen until 1968, when I moved to a flat in Morpeth Terrace in Westminster, overlooking the Roman Catholic Cathedral. It was then that St Matthew's, within easy walking distance, entered my life in the form of the unforgettable figure of Father Gerard Irvine. This was a church in which so many of the best architects and designers of the Victorian age were involved, Sir George Gilbert Scott, George

Frederick Bodley, Sir Ninian Comper and Martin Travers. It had arisen in what was then virtually a slum area of London and had, from the outset, been closely associated with the Catholic heritage of the Church of England. Sadly, the church I knew was destroyed by fire in 1977, although it was rebuilt and reopened seven years later.

There was no one quite like Gerard. The image of him I most remember was as a young man in a many-buttoned cassock standing by a Bentley. He was an Anglo-Catholic priest in the late Victorian mould with a bit of Ronald Firbank thrown in. Cherubic of countenance, he was endowed with a quick-fire, darting intelligence and a huge sense that life was fun. There was an attractive dottiness about him. At early Mass, I recall, it was not unusual for one of his beloved Siamese cats to jump up and walk across the altar. The Clergy House during Gerard's incumbency was an amiable, disorganized clutter of furniture and pictures and religious bits and pieces. You never knew quite what would happen next or who would suddenly blow in: his connections in the world of letters was prodigious and included Iris Murdoch, Barbara Pym, John Betjeman and Anthony and Violet Powell. At Christmas it looked as though a paper storm had hit the place, the rooms garlanded with cards and paper chains. He loved being given presents and also loved staging milestone celebrations of his priesthood. But he knew the people in the Peabody Buildings and the stallholders in Strutton Ground, and there was always room for a down-and-out. Prayer and the ministry of the sacraments were as natural to him as breathing. And he was endowed with a timeless optimism.

For almost twenty years Gerard was my confessor and I owe him much, above all for arranging in 1971 my elopement with Julia Trevelyan Oman. By then she had soared to stardom as the designer of Jonathan Miller's

Eccentric and beloved priest: Father Gerard Irvine.

famous television production of *Alice*, which won her the Designer of the Year Award, and she had gone on from there to work with Tony Richardson, Alan Bennett and Patrick Garland. Her father, Charles Oman, Keeper of Metalwork at the V&A, had passed on to her a rare engraving of Elizabeth I and told her to go and see young Strong at the NPG if she wished to know about it. I recall that visit. Ages after we were married she described how she had watched me retreat, thinking 'He needs looking after.' The attraction between us was instant but totally divorced from what one thinks of as London in the sixties, the world of David Bailey and *Blow-Up*. Both of us, beneath it all, were shy people born out of context and there followed a gentle, old-fashioned courtship until at last I plucked up courage and proposed to her in St James's Park. But all of that takes us far beyond the confines of this book. Gerard never batted an eyelid. He knew all about special licences and, being on the High Church circuit, was able to arrange that he would marry us at the tiny church in Mary Arden's village of Wilmcote on 10 September 1971, the day after the first night of Julia's *Othello* for the Royal Shakespeare Company. By then David Hutt was Gerard's long-suffering curate, bringing careful planning to what could have dissolved all too easily into the chaos familiar from the Westminster Clergy House.

Gerard died having reached ninety in 2010. His funeral was unforgettable. He had left very detailed instructions. It was at the church in which he had served during his final years, St Michael's in Brighton, living close by in Montpelier Road with his sister, Rosemary. Here is part of what I wrote at the time:

> St Michael's is my sort of church, a vast Victorian Gothic Anglo-Catholic pile filled with mystery, images and the whiff of incense. As I entered half an hour before the Mass I was confronted by a huge congregation jammed into the chairs. Rosemary Irvine was at the front, large, encased in fur and looking lively and shattered. She had never known what it was like not to have Gerard, who was two years ahead of her. In the centre aisle lay the coffin upon which rested a crucifix, a stole and a biretta with a red pompom on the top. This was the overture to a two-hour service presided over by a bishop assisted by twenty clergy all in white and gold chasubles. Gerard had specified everything as he wanted it, so it was a kind of joyful High Mass of requiem using the new Common Worship rite but with bits added ... There were three addresses, one too many, by a priest, by A.N. Wilson and by Imogen Lycett-Green, Betjeman's granddaughter. I sat next to Donald Buttress who had re-done St Matthew's after the fire, and on the other side I had the Betjeman Society delegation. Andrew's eulogy spoke directly to Gerard as though he was there. He is very good at these addresses. I loved the story of the bishop who asked Gerard which church he'd most like to work in. 'St Cuthbert's, Philbeach Gardens', he replied. 'That', the bishop replied, 'is the Church of England at its most effete. Why on earth would you want to go there?' 'That's *why* I want to go there', was the reply ... Once he had helped a

down and out who stole from him and everyone else. He dossed in St Matthew's. The man was sent to jail on the Isle of Wight. Down Gerard went to see him and, when he was released, Gerard took him in again. I don't think that priests like that exist any more. He loved the Church of England and never left for Rome ... This was the living world of Barbara Pym and Rose Macaulay. Dearest Gerard. God rest you.

In October there was a final requiem presided over by the Archbishop of Canterbury and Gerard's ashes were laid to rest and a memorial plaque unveiled. The last time I saw Gerard was when A.N. Wilson and I took him out to lunch to celebrate his eighty-ninth birthday. Realizing that this would almost certainly be the last time that I would see him, I broke down and wept in the taxi back to the station.

When, from 1973 onwards, we settled in Herefordshire, life took a different turn and churchgoing met in the middle: Julia was inclined to Low and I to High. And so it was a succession of country churches where dwindling congregations caterwauled and well-meaning clergy did their best to maintain what was so often a sinking ship. But I held in there, remembering always Father Gardiner's valedictory and wise message on the occasion of my confirmation: 'Stay with it. At this moment your faith is intense but it will fade or ebb and flow but hold on to it through the dull periods. In the end it will all come right.' I know this to be profoundly true.

The only period when I lapsed from seeking the absolution of a priest was at the close of all those years at the Victoria and Albert Museum. David Hutt, by then vicar of All Saints, Margaret Street, took me on in what was a return to the faith. To mark this new phase in my life as a Christian he bestowed on me a special blessing which meant much and moved me greatly. Later he was to see me through the loss of

Julia and bestow on me, at my request, a second special blessing for the final phase of my life as I placed her ashes in the memorial urn which stands in her orchard at The Laskett. I knelt on the grass and he laid his hands on my head. I need not nor can write more...

A new phase in my spiritual life opened up when I began going to Hereford Cathedral after my wife's death in 2003. Decades before, Frances Yates, who will dominate the next chapter of this book, said that she saw me as an old canon in a cathedral close, writing a vast tome on the mythology of the Church of England. In a funny sort of way she was right as my old age is lightened by a close association with two great churches, Hereford Cathedral, where I am an altar server, and Westminster Abbey. The Abbey may be grand but at its heart it never forgets that it began its life as a Benedictine house. I once had the privilege of living in the Abbey for quite a time (David Hutt was by then a subdean) and recall the powerful prayerfulness of that building, empty and silent in the early morning, when the few gather for the first Communion of the day in one of the side chapels or at the Shrine of St Edward. Hereford Cathedral has given me something resembling a family in my old age. Like most of our cathedrals it has undergone a renaissance, attracting a large and lively congregation in response to a warm ministry of welcome, a dignified and inclusive liturgy and fine music. The Anglican tradition of 'the beauty of holiness' is everywhere in evidence and suits my temperament, which remains firmly rooted in the poetry and prose of George Herbert, Henry Vaughan, Thomas Traherne and William Law.

So the thread has remained constant, since 1955, through both my outer and inner life's journey. In 1977, sensing the urgency of the times, I felt compelled to stage an exhibition at the V&A entitled *Change and*

Decay: The Future of Our Churches. This was the second of the great heritage exhibitions of the 1970s but, unlike the ones on country houses and gardens, it never triggered the impact that it deserved. Haunted by a sense of failure and aware of the ever greater urgency, thirty years later I wrote *A Little History of the English Country Church* (2007) and went on the road – or rather into the pulpits – for two years, preaching (for want of a better word) on the importance of church adaptation. All of this was the consequence of that chance visit to Walsingham in 1955. I still find it incomprehensible how anyone can go through life unsustained by some kind of framework of belief.

Belief of virtually whatever kind brings and imposes points of reference and a discipline that frames human life. Catholic Christianity calls for the exercise of self-examination and therefore a coming to terms with an admittance of failure, although that action goes hand in hand with the bestowal of forgiveness. It also provides words and ritual with which to clothe life's most joyous as well as its most tragic moments. Those who were present either at my wife's funeral in the country or the service of thanksgiving at St Paul's, Covent Garden, will know what I mean as they saw me bear in my arms behind the coffin or lay on the altar a great sheaf of rosemary from The Laskett garden, an outward and visible symbol of something that words could never articulate.

———

The arrival of faith is inevitably a huge event, changing one's view of life and its purpose. In a different sense one other experience from these years was also to be life-changing: my first visit abroad. It was deemed necessary as part of the course on Florence and the Renaissance that I should go to Italy. That was made possible by a loan of £50 from the benign and better-heeled Aunt Elsie. The trip was more than a month

in all, during which I attended a course in Florence and stayed at the
Pensione Bianchi on the Lungarno Amerigo Vespucci. It was a lonely
month: tense and introverted, I sat at table silent and alone, and walked
the streets of the city as a solitary figure visiting every historic church,
monument and gallery described in my guidebook. The emancipation that would come later was missing, but this was nonetheless the
beginning of another lifelong passion: Italy.

A postcard to Joan Henderson dated 6 August, written at the end
of the fourth week, captures something of my reaction to this 'very
beautiful city':

> Still cannot believe I have actually seen the originals of some of
> the world's greatest paintings. At the end of this week I travel on to
> Ravenna – mosaics, Ferrara – the Este, Padua – Giotto and Donatello.
> Then, I hope, three days in Venice.

Eleven days later I wrote her a second card:

> Ravenna was a really wonderful discovery both as a city and for
> its contents – a whole new horizon opened up when I saw just how
> beautiful mosaics can be. There was not a lot at Ferrara – also
> difficult because all the museums were shut for a national holiday
> – still walked all over the town. Padua was wonderful – with its
> cathedral, its great centre of pilgrimage – St Anthony – and, above
> all, as you would expect, the great thrill of seeing Giotto's Scrovegni
> Chapel. Lastly Venice – surely the most beautiful city I have ever
> seen. Built for pleasure – a combination of dazzling white and blue,
> and of the unique and beautiful.

I still have the 1899 Baedecker I took with me, with all its underlinings
on the pages on Florence. Perhaps what I wrote to Joan Henderson a
year later captures its impact on me more vividly. She had sent me a
card from Florence; in response, I wrote:

as you can imagine for a moment I was there with you drinking in that view of cluttered rooftops, the indescribable green of the foliage and that blue blue sky. The view over Florence is one of those unforgettable things whether seen from the roof of the cathedral dome, the Palazzo Vecchio or from one of the hillside towns near Florence. There are so many things that I hope you have managed to see – the dusty Boboli gardens, the manuscripts in the Laurenziana, those two superb Brunelleschi churches – S. Lorenzo and, on the other side, S. Spirito with their innumerable side chapels, the Michaelangelo tombs in the sacristy at S. Lorenzo ... S. Miniato al Monte – that grey-green marble, the Strozzi Chapel in S. Maria Novella – the hierarchically ordered heaven and the gruesome torments of hell, the view of the city at night from the Piazzale Michaelangelo, S. Marco and Fra Angelico which even commercialization cannot kill, the English cemetery – an island of greenery amidst a sea of traffic where Elizabeth Barrett Browning was buried, the Botticelli St Augustine in Ognissanti – so different from the way one imagines it from reproductions in books, the little Franciscan monastery at Fiesole where the monks made one welcome – and their little cloister full of flowers and birds, or the rigours of the Carthusian house set rugged on top of a hill – and its little Farmacia which sold the most superb liqueurs, those wonderful frescoes in the Capella Spagnuoli next to S. Maria Novella which placed before one the whole medieval world – and so on, and so on, ad infinitum!!

Thus a lifetime's fascination with and love of Italy was kindled. In fact it began the moment the train crossed from France and entered the Lombard Plain. I peered out of the window at what has always been for me a golden land, as indeed it has been for generations of English people. It is a love affair whose course should perhaps be charted a little at this moment of its birth.

I was not to return to Italy again until six years later, in 1961, when I travelled with John Rowlands, then my editor at the Clarendon Press,

Oxford, but who subsequently joined the Department of Prints and Drawings at the British Museum. Even in the early 1960s there was still an element of adventure about travel within the Peninsula, which I think is caught in a letter I wrote to my Dutch friend Jan van Dorsten, in the October of that year:

Italy was so intoxicatingly beautiful that I can't find words to describe it. The clear blue sky and the shades of green that one sees nowhere else. As you know I went with John Rowlands and we had these touring tickets – just over £14 for a month all over Italy ... I have seen enough art to last me a lifetime. We started off in Turin which is not terribly nice but one gets some idea of that curious Savoy court. The churches are architecturally very odd and have a Spanish Catholic quality about them. From thence we moved on to Brescia where no one goes much except the Germans, a charming town with a delightful twelfth century baptistery cum church next to the cathedral and a good art gallery. Then on to Verona's fair city – that wonderful Roman amphitheatre – and then to Vicenza with the Palladio architecture and the Teatro Olimpico where they still do things like Monteverdi operas. It is the strangest thing ever, absolutely intact and I sat mesmerized, drinking it in ...

After that we stayed three days in a little town twenty miles from Venice called Castelfranco where, in the church, there is a chapel with the famous altarpiece by Giorgione. No one stays at Castelfranco much and we stayed at the only hotel, the Stella d'Italia, which was unbelievably cheap and where all the locals came to eat and gossip and so the food was correspondingly good. All the walls still stood around the town which was only a few hundred yards wide and still with its moat around it. In the golden evening light one could understand Giorgione's paintings in the same way that last year, as we ate in Middelburg and looked out at the sunset on the red brick houses, it dawned on me what Vermeer was about.

... Onwards we went to Padua and it was good to see Giotto's Arena Chapel once more and this time I managed to see the famous fourteenth-century Salone, a huge room covered with astrological frescoes dear to the Warburg's heart. Thence onto Ferrara for the Schifanoia palace and more astrological frescoes. Ferrara is a horrid place now and it is impossible to imagine how it could ever have been the Italian home of northern chivalrous pursuits in the manner of the court of Burgundy. At Mantua we saw the Mantegna exhibition which was stunning and set the old brain-box working on the importance of renaissance epigraphy, archaeology, etc. It was held in the ducal palace in a series of beautiful renaissance rooms each decorated with Gonzaga *imprese* which gave a wonderful idea of the civilized life of that court.

By then we were dead beat at the end of our first week or – as John says – we were on our 'benders'. John is more susceptible to art than I am and it was touch and go whether he would pass out before I managed to get him back to the station. In a state of utter exhaustion we zoomed straight through Florence down to Arezzo which we thought would be a sweet, charming, little old hill town. Arrival by night can be wildly deceptive. It was in this case. The street leading from the station was lit up like Piccadilly Circus and the hotels cost the earth so that, disillusioned, we ended up sharing a bed in the matrimonial room (camera matrimoniale – life is full of new experiences) in a dreadful pensione. Came the dawn and Arezzo turned out to be everything I had hoped that it would be and we found a good hotel right next to the church where the famous Piero della Francesca frescoes are. Fortune smiled and we hit on the best local restaurant where the proprietor was dedicated to food and where, after two meals, we were having drinks on the house. Arezzo is beautiful set amongst the Umbrian hills and from it we visited Assisi, glistening white on a hill top, touristy (St Francis on toast racks and what have you) but still wonderful.

... From the very moment that I knew that our tickets included a crossing to Sicily I had been bent on going ... The crossing to Sicily is indescribably beautiful. I would never have believed that the Mediterranean was really as blue as that and as clear. Sicily was wild,

mountainous, full of orange and lemon groves and palm trees ... We
saw the Hohenstaufen tombs and went up to Monreale where the
church is covered with famous mosaics and next to which there is a
set of cloisters which have to be seen to be believed. Sicily seemed
to me to be a nodal point of civilization. The churches had, many of
them, been mosques and Christianized with mosaics. There were
the Normans, the Angevins, the Hohenstaufen, all mingled, and, of
course, finally the Spaniards...

... And so we ended up in Rome, everything grand and yet not overwhelming. I still see that St Paul's in London wins hands down over St
Peter's. The Bernini things are wonderful and I realized for the first
time that one really ought to know about baroque Italian art...

Italy became almost an annual fixture in my life but it is interesting to
compare these initial responses to what became a lifetime's romance with
a diary entry from January 2000. From 1993 onwards Julia and I went to
Florence every year in January or February. This is how I reflected in my
diary on the city forty years on from these initial encounters:

What is striking after so many decades of coming to Florence is
how one's preoccupations have changed. All those years back in
1955 I came starry-eyed about the quattrocento, brain-washed by
Berenson. And now one's pleasures are fixed and different. I stand
in amazement at the Medici funerary chapel, not the Michaelangelo
tombs. The whole concept of the place, the staggering richness of the
materials, the craftsmanship, the overwhelming arrogance of it, all
those multicoloured marbles and stones in claret, coral, puce, ochre,
crimson, white, aubergine, grey, black – mottled and marbled and
flecked – the vast golden statues of the dukes. The thought of this
arising in the 1590s must have astonished all Europe.

... In the Uffizi I gravitate to Piero della Francesca's portraits of
Federigo da Montefeltre and his wife, a bit like the Gozzolis really
with that backcloth of landscape in which my eyes love to wander ...
No sign of the return of the Valois Tapestries to the great encircling

corridor. I miss them dreadfully ... But no matter, I love that corridor with its windows, its ceiling arabesques, antique sculpture and friezes of portraits, good, bad and indifferent, and for the stunning panorama across the city downwards to the Ponte Vecchio, one of the world's great views. Now when I come I don't *have* to see anything and bless the release from that world of academic compulsion. I just want to visit old friends that lift the spirits and give me joy.

How many thousands of others must have made this journey of the mind and the eye! Over the years Italy was to bring me so much, both in terms of art and gardens and also – even more – of friendships. Here I met those great editors and art historians Hugh Honour and John Fleming in their villa near Lucca, then that master of innuendo Sir Harold Acton at La Pietra, with the formidable Susana Walton at La Mortella, nursing the legacy of her husband Sir William and the great garden she had created with the aid of Russell Page. There were the annual visits to that lovable man and genius of a couturier Gianni Versace, both in his flat in Milan and at his villa on Como. And finally, and still punctuating each August, there were days with the brilliant publisher Franco Maria Ricci and Laura Casalis near Parma. All of these have enriched my life and taught me so much about the art of living, *la vita*, to delight in things visual and tactile, not only those from the past but those in the present. Life, I began to learn from them, is for living.

Some of these people I have already written about but others call for placing in the pattern of my life. My only account of Hugh Honour and John Fleming was in March 1995, but these words from my diary could as easily have been written twenty years earlier:

Hugh Honour and John Fleming are people whom you would have to invent if they did not exist. Expats of forty years standing, they're

still in the Villa Marchio at Tofori outside Lucca. It was an awful
day, rain non-stop, so we couldn't walk around Lucca as planned
but hid in a café guzzling coffee and ice cream until Hugh picked us
up. They both looked better than I last remembered them, still very
1950s Austin Reed. Hugh, however, had abandoned his slicked-down
hairstyle in favour of it being short and wispy, a great improvement.
But he was in the usual corduroys and checked sports jacket. John is
now quite rotund and in cords too but with a pullover of no taste. Both
were deaf-ish, John more so.

But the villa retains its magic, such a superb space for living and
working, with gracious high-ceilinged rooms with smaller ones off
... they were hungry for British gossip and we were hungry for theirs.
Their circle is now sadly diminished, with Harold Acton and John
Pope-Hennessy gone ... For them the world is that of art history with
its rippling circles of mainly gay friends. How wonderful to be free of
that. But the villa is beautiful with its pond and lilies, box topiary and
persimmon tree.

Hugh and John entered my life as editors of a book on the celebrated
Van Dyck portrait of Charles I on horseback in the National Gallery,
which was published in 1972. This appeared as one of the first in a series
called *Art in Context*, one of three, the others being *Style and Civilization* and *The Architect and Society*, which are now recognized as among
the most important short-subject art histories of the late twentieth
century. John met Hugh when up at Cambridge and together they
moved to Italy in the middle of the 1950s, rapidly joining the expatriate
community; from 1961, when they moved to the Villa Marchio at Tofori
outside Lucca, anyone who was part of the art-historical world had to
make their way there if only for the gossip about everyone and everything connected with that closed world. As editors they were superb:
when working on Van Dyck, for example, they opened my eyes to sources

that I had missed. For decades Hugh and John were a phenomenon known collectively as 'the Flemour', whose annual visits to London caused those who inhabited the art-historical dovecot to flutter.

That circle belonged to a certain period which to a great extent ceased after I left the V&A at the end of 1987. By then Franco Maria Ricci had entered my life in the form of his magazine *FMR* and through his astounding art books, having a style and taste hitherto unknown. Franco's passion is for his homeland of Parma and every year I go to stay with him at his villa near Fontanellato. Not far from the house there is arising as I write a huge complex: a chapel, a museum for his art works and books, a restaurant, an educational centre and performance arena, all set within a gigantic maze of bamboo. All the people I have admired most have been originals and he is on that list.

So, too, is perhaps my greatest Italian friend, whose memory I continue to cherish, Gianni Versace. There is a bookcase in my library reserved for books by or about people who have most influenced me. Inevitably the works of the great polymathic Renaissance scholar who taught me, Dame Frances Yates, are there. So too are the diaries and many other books by or about Sir Cecil Beaton, who transformed my life as the young Director of the National Portrait Gallery and whose impeccable personal style had a profound effect on me. That was an enduring friendship, which ended when I was an usher at his memorial service at St Martin-in-the-Fields in 1980. Another shelf is reserved for the great Italian couturier Gianni Versace. These books are lush essays in what might be described as bibliophilic bling, many of them lavish trips into the visual imagination of this extraordinary man. Twenty years on they unfold like scrapbooks, evoking a period of brash glamour that some might label vulgarity. The pages are filled with such electrifying juxtapositions as a Jacobean portrait of a lady in a ruff and an embroidered gown opposite a muscular hunk reclining erotically on a sofa in Gianni's Milan apartment. They establish at once that this was a complex human being, a man of contradictions who adored neoclassicism as much as what he called *il mondo del pop*. Both his Milan apartment and his villa on Lake Como were crammed with neoclassical paintings, sculpture and artefacts. Equally, *il mondo del pop* cast its spell and he was drawn to the likes of Elton John, who became a friend, and Madonna. Unlike my friendships with Frances Yates or Cecil Beaton, my connection with Gianni Versace is less easy to place in my life. We were drawn to each other by a mutual sympathy, quiet and unspoken. The Gianni I knew bore no relation to his public image. When he was murdered by a gay serial killer outside his Miami mansion on 15 July 1997, I lost a precious and private friend.

On my first visit to his villa on Lake Como he took me to his shop on the Via Spiga, deciding that I had to be dressed. Various items were tried on and then my eye fell on a crumpled brown silk suit, the acme of style. I tried it on and, for a moment, hesitated before asking Gianni whether or not I could carry it off. In that beguiling Italian English, he said: 'You can wear anything. In this you look like an old colonial planter.' I wore that suit for some years, although it nearly came to grief in the residence of our ambassador to Spain, Lord Nicholas Gordon-Lennox: one's suitcase was seized on arrival and unpacked, and the crumpled silk was ironed flat by the maid. It is now in the V&A dress collection.

Not long after that I appeared in a film on the great Victorian photographer Henry Fox Talbot, made by Harlech Television and shot at Lacock Abbey. To appear in it I needed that iconic 007 garment, a white suit. Gianni promptly obliged and it was flown in from Italy overnight. The V&A dress collection pursued that item for several years and in the end I handed it over.

The following passage is from the obituary I wrote soon after Gianni's death:

> This was a man of quite exceptional energy and drive with an untold ability to assimilate visual information ... His public image totally belied the man as I knew him. Publicly it was hype, glitz, extremes, the stars, over the top. My memory is of a quiet, shy, gentle, generous and thoughtful man enshrined in his monochrome neoclassical palaces. There was never a raving 'scene' at Como ... We met at meals and talked or sat in happy silence. He felt secure with us knowing that we didn't need impressing, didn't need a 'scene', just the pleasure of being with him.
>
> He always seemed so lonely to me. Antonio d'Amico [his partner for eleven years] was usually around, lovable, laid back and funny. Gianni had a prince-like quality; or perhaps he resembled more than anyone I have known what it must have been like to be in the orbit of a renaissance prince: the splendour of the interior decoration, the elegance of his table, the art collections which spread everywhere – the utter madness of some of it. There was also a restlessness which accelerated as he got into his forties and as New York and Miami were added and then an adumbrated house in London. He worked in theatre and moved on to home furnishings, including ceramics, and then there were his Instante and Versus collections. The empire never ceased to expand.
>
> He described me once to his Milanese butler as *'un uomo molto fino'*. And he would ask my opinions about things. One felt a joy in his presence. He was one of those people who lifted everyone and everything around him. I shall miss him. A light has gone out.

I wrote two descriptions in my diary of those weekends at the Villa Fontanelle, one from May 1993 and the second two years later. The earlier weekend was doubly memorable for the presence of the great American photographer Richard Avedon, whose genius was bestowed on Versace fashions shoots. In 1993 the visit occurred only a few days after the first night of a new ballet at Sadler's Wells by Gianni's friend the choreographer Maurice Béjart. The Empress Elisabeth, known as Sissi, was the subject of Béjart's ballet, memorable only for its opening tableau in which prima ballerina Sylvie Guillem stood in Gianni's version of a dress by the first great couturier, Charles Worth. It was a Winterhalter painting brought to life. Gianni had just purchased his Miami house:

> Dick Avedon arrived at the Villa Fontanelle, a small Jewish New Yorker with tiny hands ... After lunch he showed us the proofs of his huge autobiographical volume. It is his greatest and falls into three parts. Over all it is a huge statement on beauty and its loss, on life and death, on bloom and decay, said so often through photographs of his family capturing his father from middle age to death and his sister, who went mad. This is a man with an extraordinary eye, brilliant at the observation of surfaces and any line which is the essence of fashion, at penetrating the veil or rather lifting it, recording how laughter can turn so quickly to a scream. I found it very moving.
>
> In the afternoon we went into Como to pick up Gianni's friend Nene Bellotti and walked happily in the rain. There was dinner for seven with everyone relaxed and happy with the conversation flowing from the nineties depression to the royals. Avedon recalled how at long last Nancy Reagan came through. Her opening words had been 'Hello Richard. Do you retouch?' And he gave a wonderful account of photographing the army's gays.

We never got to the Miami house but I sent Gianni mount-ups and a plan for his courtyard garden with a spectacular grotto, all of which were realized.

Three years later the mood had changed. This time the visit was for the first few days of June:

This time we were strolling in the grounds when Gianni appeared. We waved and he came down to us and we walked together. He is an extraordinary man but I always see him as vulnerable and alone, like Atlas bearing the world, in his case the world of his own commercial empire. As the weekend progressed much emerged, for at dinner that evening I noticed that he had visibly aged (he will be forty-nine this year), his face pale and transparent. But then he told us that he had had a cancerous small growth in proximity to a nerve near his left ear. He opined that that was traumatic enough without friends like Elton John ringing up in floods of tears. The cortisone treatment had been unpleasant but he said he's OK but it all took a toll and I could see that ... He was so tired that we were all glad to enjoy each others' company, to laugh, to catch up and to go to bed early and sleep in the afternoons, and to stroll. To be quiet with someone is a real index of friendship. Nothing need be said. There is no scene. It is the private side of the man and one feels very close to him, to someone caught in the web of his own success and creation in a way which makes me glad that I escaped such a fate.

Every Christmas a gift would arrive. One year it was a scarf, which I still wear, with the message 'It's going to be a baroque Christmas'. Another year it was a dinner service for twelve. And there would also be some item of clothing waiting for me on visits to Italy. He always saw me in purple, for some reason, his last present being a floor-length dressing gown in thick purple silk, a clone of one he had made for himself which he wore occasionally in the evenings. Often when I am on my own I have my bath and descend wearing it for the evening, remembering him.

The Miami phase of Gianni's life always puzzled me. More than once he castigated Americans as ignorant, uneducated peasants, but then he suddenly fell in love with Miami. By then Elton John had entered his life: 'I am trying to educate him', Gianni would say. I could not bring myself to go either to the funeral or to the requiem Mass in Milan Cathedral, which had all the pizzazz of Princess Diana, Elton and Sting. That was the side of Gianni with which I didn't particularly empathize. I had known the private man, the man who had once told me that he hated being touched but who put his arm through mine as we once strolled by Lake Como.

By 1995 I had travelled a long way from the hesitant, awkward twenty-year-old student of four decades before, now able to move with confidence on a far wider scene than the narrow world of academe and museums.

———

I had gone up to read history at QMC with one end in view, to write a book on the portraits of Queen Elizabeth I, and my letters to Joan Henderson continued to record my unremitting pursuit of that goal. An undergraduate course had to be endured in order for that aim to be achieved. Early in 1954 I recounted that I had told Dr Chew that I aspired to 'write and illustrate books on costume. She was very interested [and] hoped that I would one day get a post at the V&A for instance.' She then went on to say that I ought to do postgraduate research at the Warburg Institute, 'which is supposed to be much better than the Courtauld'. Two years later, in February 1956, I was still anxious to do research and still hankering after the Courtauld, which Bindoff, when I went to see him in January, dismissed as 'a waste of time'. Like Helena Chew, he had a respect for the Warburg and arranged for me to be interviewed by Gertrude Bing, its formidable Director, and E.H. Gombrich. Afterwards I wrote to Joan:

They seemed a bit sceptical and were especially keen that I should have Courtauld training. However, the mention of Elizabethan portraits seemed to clear a lot of ground. They liked the idea because no one seems to be doing much on them and also portraiture is so specialized that Courtauld training could be dispensed with.

At that stage it was proposed that I should do a Master's degree jointly supervised by Frances Yates of the Warburg and David Piper, Assistant Keeper at the National Portrait Gallery: 'It is what I always longed for, and an incentive to work hard.' But everything depended on getting a studentship, of which there were few, and of course on the results of Finals. Then, suddenly at the end of July, everything was resolved when I got a First. 'Apparently', I wrote to Joan, 'my First was second in order of quality out of the whole university History School.' I was showered with congratulations but, even more to the point, it brought with it a scholarship worth what to me was the large sum of £300. On 23 July I went to see the future Dame Frances Yates for the first time and a new chapter in my life began.

But I end this chapter with a letter I wrote to Miss Staples on 26 July 1954, at the close of my first year at QMC. She sent this back to me years later, along with my designs for the school production of *Le Cid*. The main part of it reads as follows:

> I would also like to take this opportunity of telling you how I am faring so far in my scholastic career. In my first year I deliberately dropped the pace of my studies in comparison with the exhausting 2nd year 6th [form]. I have tried to a certain extent to conserve energy for the last two years which will really count.
>
> The sessional examinations turned out much more favourably than I had imagined. It is surprising that the majority of students are not so brilliant as you imagine them to be – and the results proved that I was

not so way down below as I thought. I got a B+ for the European paper and B (I was told I would have got B+ if I had finished the paper) for the English history [one] down to 1215. I came fifth in the general knowledge paper thanks to my essay on art and economics. So you can see I have not done too badly. I suppose next year will be spent eliminating the question mark elements in my papers ...

QMC is not exactly one's ideal of a college (what a dreadful building! What awful surroundings!) and I must admit the journey through the not very salubrious parts of the East End is extremely dreary, tiring, expensive and time wasting. I also have periodical yearnings for the Courtauld Institute ever since I was told by a friend of mine about the contents of the course. I do hope to be able to go on to the Warburg – that is if the grant continues or I can get a scholarship. I realize that one degree is not really of much use – interesting jobs are so difficult to get. All I want to be is something like the Director of the National Portrait Gallery or the Head of a Department in the Victoria and Albert Museum! And then the whole time I have to keep in mind the question of National Service – dreaded thought.

So you can see that life gets more not less complicated. I hope the coming years will see either my artistic or my historical interests get the better of me or perhaps I might reach a compromise. I am still madly interested in designing for the theatre and in the History of Costume – neither of which seem to fit in anywhere at present. So you will gather that my varied interests are leading to complications.

When this letter was returned to me I had no idea that the Warburg as a destination was already so firmly in mind when I was still only eighteen, let alone the aspirations in respect of both the National Portrait Gallery and the Victoria and Albert Museum. It was an extraordinary premonition of all that was to happen – but what I could never have guessed was that both aspirations were to be fulfilled by the time I was thirty-eight.

I get a B+? for the European paper and B (I was too I would have got B+ if I had finished the paper) for the English history to 1815. I came fifth in the general knowledge paper thanks to my essay on art and economics. So you can see I have not done too badly. I suppose next year will be spent in eliminating the question marks elements in my fu...

QUEEN MARY COLLEGE

(UNIVERSITY OF LONDON).

to be is something like the Director of the National Portrait Gallery or the Head of a Department in the Victoria and Albert Museum! And then the whole time I have to keep in mind the question of National Service — dreaded thought.

So you can see that life gets more not less complicated. I hope the coming the years will see either my artistic or my historical interests get the better of me or perhaps I might reach a compromise. I am still madly interested in designing for the theatre and in the History of Costume — neither of which seem to fit in anywhere at the present. So you will gather that my varied interests are leading to complications.

I do hope the present 6th Form is living up to the old standards and would wish them luck in their examination results. Hoping that you too are in the best of health and enjoying a pleasant holiday.

Yours Sincerely

R. Storey

My aspirations revealed in a letter to Miss Staples dated 26 July 1954, when I was still only eighteen. Note the somewhat Elizabethan signature.

FOUR

A CLOSED WORLD

1956 to 1959

I OPEN with the only visual record of me during these three years. One of my brothers must have had a camera which caught my somewhat prissy presence. Smooth-faced, my lips quite tight, my eyes concealed behind thick glasses and hair slicked back. My look is cast down on to papers spread before me and I look withdrawn into other worlds – as indeed I was and had been since a childhood playing with toy theatres. I look purposeful, which I was, but not much fun, which was probably also true. I had yet to discover and respond to the present. Everything I had done so far had buried me in the security of the past. Three years' postgraduate research was to reinforce that.

———

In my interview with Gertrude Bing and E.H. Gombrich I had been warned that pursuing the past in the way advocated by the Warburg Institute generally rendered a person unemployable, citing the problems faced by more than one of their students in finding a job because the topics on which they worked fell outside the conventional subject boundaries. What, the reader might well ask, was this Institute which swelled the ranks of the educated unemployed? And yet, more than any other place I had experienced, it was to widen my horizons dramatically and change forever the way in which I approached the past.

The Warburg Institute was founded by Aby Warburg (1866–1929), an avid and highly erudite student of the art and culture of the Renaissance. Realizing that this called for an approach which was not fragmented but interdisciplinary, he began to assemble the extraordinary library that bears his name and still today lies at the heart of this institution. It was and still is to me revelatory, being arranged in its founder's division of human history into categories: Action, Orientation, Word and Image. To the average reader this might sound somewhat off-putting and abstract but it works on the premise of thought progression, one subject leading on to another. Founding texts are followed by books and articles on the topic, one thought sequence effortlessly flowing on to another. There was also the advantage of actually being able to work in the library stacks and explore where such sequences led. It was so very different from any library in which I had ever worked before. Parallel with the book collection there was an equally extraordinary photographic library arranged in a very similar manner. All of this encouraged the student to plunge into subjects for which he was totally unqualified, hoping for the best. Frances Yates used to say: 'Jump in, splash around a bit. You'll probably make some mistakes but, on the other hand, it may be hugely rewarding.' And, of course, it was.

The Institute had arrived in England in 1933 from Hamburg before Nazi anti-Semitism sealed its fate. In 1944 it became part of the

University of London and, in the aftermath of the war, was relocated to Imperial Institute, where its staff seemed to occupy a series of plywood boxes as offices and the library meandered in every direction. It is the only library I can recall which had ashtrays nailed to the baluster rails. The atmosphere was unique, intense I might say, headed by a band of scholars led by Fritz Saxl. I have always regretted not meeting that remarkable man, knowing how he combined scholarship and practicality, the latter not being a shining attribute in the main amongst the Institute's staff. Frances Yates once described to me how Saxl would be seated typing an article on Mithras and the next minute go into another room and save the Institute. That description stuck in my mind, my own aspirations being to do both.

The roll call of those at the Warburg Institute who changed the face of scholarship in their chosen fields included already, when I arrived in 1956, such towering giants as Erwin Panofsky, Ernst Cassirer, Rudolf Wittkower, Edgar Wind and Ernst Gombrich. Frances Yates had yet to join that pantheon with her revolutionary books on the hermetic tradition, Giordano Bruno and the art of memory published in the 1960s and 1970s. That lay in the future for her when I arrived in the summer of 1956. I was lucky enough to catch the tail end of the Institute's great days.

———

Dame Frances Yates was to occupy such a seminal place in my intellectual development that it is difficult to know where to begin or how explain why this female academic was to have such a hold over me for so very long. But then this was the age of the academic empire builders, kingmakers who revelled in their intellectual satellites whose careers

PANTHEON OF SCHOLARS

Mastermind: E.H. Gombrich, 1975 (*top*).
Dominant Dame and academic deity: Frances Yates, 1968 (*left*).
Prickly, precise but benign: Francis Wormald (*right*)

they advanced in return for eternal pinches of incense being offered
to the Great One. A number of other people at this period of my life
and into my early years at the National Portrait Gallery fell into this
bracket. Professor Sir John Neale was one, Francis Wormald another
and Sir John (Jack) Plumb a third. It was a role I swore that I would
never occupy in my own career.

Frances Yates does not wholly fit into this category but it was clear
from quite early on that Warburg students were seen as standard-bearers
of the ideals of the Institute into other areas of the cultural arena of the
nation. The Institute was linked with the Courtauld Institute of Art,
then in Portman Square, but I do not think that there was much love lost
between the two. I remember Frances Yates sighing and fingering the
script of an article by a Courtauld person for the *Journal* the institutions
shared, saying, her voice verging towards the withering, 'It's one of
those Courtauld articles. I suppose we'll have to print it.'

As I have already written, I had first stumbled upon the work of
Frances Yates in 1952, in a little booklet she had written on the alle-
gorical portraits of Elizabeth I at Hatfield. Told that she was to be
my supervisor, I wrote a postscript in a letter to Joan Henderson in
June 1956: 'Read Yates's article on Queen Elizabeth as Virgo-Astraea
– most odd.' What that introduced me to was a wholly different way of
thinking about sixteenth-century monarchy, studying its presentation
to its public by way of art, poetry and pageantry as valid reflections of
its political, spiritual and cultural ideals. Back in 1956 this was a wholly
new way of thinking and looking at the past, which now, half a century
on, has entered the mainstream. In fact the article 'Queen Elizabeth as
Astraea', first published in 1947 in the *Journal*, had begun its life even
further back, in 1945, as a lecture in manuscript form read by the great

Saxl. That in itself is interesting, in that Saxl himself, Yates once told me, would never pursue an analysis of the elements which made up what we now recognize as the machinery of 'ruler-cult'. The reason was, of course, the rise of Hitler. The article crossed the subject boundaries in what was to me a total revelation. There was no hesitancy in moving from political and religious history to the history of ideas and on to that of literature and symbolism. And all of it was placed firmly within the Western classical and Christian tradition. In the long run it was to result in my book *The Cult of Elizabeth* (1977). In 1956 such an approach was way out of kilter with what was going on in normal postgraduate research.

What that baffling article told me was that my whole approach to the past was to become unlike anything that I had experienced up until then. It was to be polymathic. It was also to move between word, image and ideas. It was to treat seriously material dismissed by the majority of historians as frivolous, irrelevant froth such as court entertainments, poetry and portraits. It was also postulated on the premise that you must somehow attempt to enter into the minds and thoughts of people at the time. It explains why, for instance, Yates always valued histories written closer to the time of a particular event just because they were nearer to it than we were. She was to define the Warburgian approach as the 'history of culture as a whole – the history of thought, science, religion, art, including the history of imagery and symbolism'.

The fact that she could take what was in retrospect such an extraordinary line was owed to her unique background. Yates had never been brainwashed by the existing English academic system. Born in 1899, she was the youngest of three daughters of a naval architect. The family background was an upright and sober middle-class one where hard work and intellectual pursuits were a given. Her first degree was in French, for which she was awarded a First, as an external student in the University of London. She then proceeded to an M.A. Very little of her education was formal and structured in the way mine had been on the escalator of a system; in addition she had another great advantage, thanks to modest family financial resources, of being able to follow her own star. None of the preconceptions and barriers which ring-fenced academic disciplines impeded her and she could let her mind wander in any direction in which her research led her. Yates was introduced to the Warburg Institute in 1936 and joined its staff five years later in 1941. Saxl must have realized the importance of recruiting a member of the country of his adoption but one whose free intellectual background would be attuned to the Institute's unique orbit.

When I became one of her postgraduate students in 1956 I was, she once told me, only her twelfth student – which is some indication of how rarefied the place was and how far removed from the degree factory of the modern university. Somehow one always felt that we students were a burden that had to be borne, taking one's supervisor away from the exercise of their higher spheres of the intellect. That what I was about to embark upon would be unlike anything that I had experienced until then was reflected in the huge list of books I had to read during the summer holidays of that year. It included the whole of John Foxe's *Actes and Monuments* (1563 and later editions) as well as John Nichols's monumental three-volume *Progresses and Public Processions of Queen Elizabeth* (1823). The former I never got beyond dipping into but the latter I read from cover to cover, making copious notes page by page. It was taken for granted that one could read Latin, French, Italian and German, with all of which, never having been a natural linguist, I struggled.

Many times Frances would dwell upon the virtues of toiling away in the dark, seeking the truth of other ages and never needing any form of recognition for it. Later I was to interpret this obsession with the virtues of obscurity as meaning a desire for exactly the opposite. In a sense Frances never was nor could be material for a biography, although an American scholar has attempted one. What I discovered from that was that she was 'a depressive, moody, frequently unhappy woman whose salvation ... was incessant work and an intense spiritual life'. I am not sure what form the latter took, for although her upbringing was stoutly Anglican I recall Joe Trapp, the Director of the Warburg after Gombrich, being quite upset that, at her cremation, the officiating cleric had edged towards claiming her for his own. Reading that attempt at a biography leaves a mass of unanswered questions, and the material gathered there suggests that something happened in her life in the 1920s, of which she left no record. An acquaintance of hers once observed that she 'tended to fall in love with people'.

Margaret Drabble in her biography of the novelist Angus Wilson speculates that Frances Yates was in love with a colleague at the Warburg, Perkin Walker. Walker led a double life, one side the silent, melancholic scholar toiling away on the remoter paths of Renaissance hermeticism and magic, the other an alcoholic homosexual with a taste for flagellation. Walker was to buy a house in Suffolk not far from Angus Wilson and his partner, Tony Garrett, and was a regular at their annual drag ball. Frances from time to time was Walker's guest.

It was through this connection that Frances Yates found herself on the periphery of the gay circle that centred on the benign novelist. In that context Frances has remained in the running as the prototype for a character that appeared in *Anglo-Saxon Attitudes*, the Wilson novel published in the year I began working under her. The character in question was Dr Rose Lorimer, a senior lecturer in medieval history, an eccentric and bizarre bundle resembling Margaret Rutherford as the dotty medievalist in the post-war Ealing comedy *Passport to Pimlico* (1949). Four academic women in all are in the running as Wilson's prototype, better regarded, perhaps, as an amalgam of elements from all of them. Frances had a direct connection with Wilson through Walker and in common with Rose Lorimer had a slightly wild side to her, as she sank her mind deeper and deeper into the past. She was also large and untidy and in her madder moments, lubricated by whisky, she could resemble another memorable character played by Margaret Rutherford, that of the medium Madame Arcati in Noël Coward's *Blithe Spirit* (1945).

I wrote at length about Frances in my diary in the year of her death, and although that has been published it also belongs here:

> One's encounters with Frances Yates left a deep impression. I was quite overawed by this extraordinary woman ... She must have been in her mid to late fifties when I first knew her, large of build, wearing flat sensible shoes, always a straight skirt and jacket with a blouse or jumper on to which she usually pinned a little gold brooch of two birds. Her hair was already almost white, worn rather long, and she was always aware of its untidiness, from time to time hairpins falling out of it on to the floor. The structure of her head was leonine, no beauty, her features could move from those of a hooded intensity with the gaze of a seer into the beyond, to ones invested with a kind of mad gaiety. Her eyes, which were pale blue-grey, were her best feature. At that period she chain-smoked Craven-A cigarettes in a holder which struck an unexpectedly sophisticated note. In attitude and appearance she belonged to that first generation of middle-class English women who had been allowed to have

a university education (however odd hers was). She fits neatly into a gallery which includes Dorothy L. Sayers and Muriel St Clare Byrne. To be intellectual was equated with the affectation of a certain mannishness.

Frances's journals for 1956 find her 'down and worried' and 'frightfully worried'; her biographer records that much 'appeared to revolve around the concerns she and Bing had about Roy Strong's M.A. thesis'. There was much coming and going between Frances and Bindoff as she edged me off the portraits beyond them being, as I wrote to Joan Henderson, 'one aspect of the build-up of Elizabeth into a propaganda figure clothed in suitable imagery and also an aspect of the Elizabethan revival of chivalry as a buttress to the new monarchy'. That was where we had got to by June. In August I wrote to Joan that

> the Warburg people thought I might do Lord Mayor's Shows but now Bindoff has agreed to the portraits I am not budging. One snag, an American woman, Miss Sherley, is working on the portraits, has been for 2 or 3 years, so I have got to settle that first. According to [David] Piper she is hopeless.

In the end the die was in fact cast: I was to do a thesis on Elizabethan court pageantry with the portraits somehow on the side. In this I was in at the beginning of what has since become a minor academic industry, the study of court festivals. Up until the middle of the 1950s such topics impinged only on literary students in the form of the Stuart court masques. Frances's interest in festivals stemmed back to the chapter she wrote on Valois ones in her *The French Academies of the Sixteenth Century* (1947). That was followed by a paper on 'The Magnificences for the Marriage of the Duc de Joyeuse, Paris, 1581' at a colloquium staged in Paris and organized by Jean Jacquot under the aegis of the Centre de la Recherche Scientifique, and a second in 1955 on 'The Entry of Charles IX and Elizabeth of Austria into Paris, 1571' at another such conference. The latter was incorporated into the first volume of what was to be a pioneering series on this wholly new subject, *Les Fêtes de la Renaissance* (1956).

Thus the opening up of court spectacle and entertainment as subjects worthy of serious research was, in 1956, completely new. A year ahead of me Frances had a second postgraduate student, Sydney Anglo, who was busy on the early Tudor period and there was logic to the arrangement that I should take on the second half of the century. Sydney had one enormous advantage: he was not working in an area colonized by Frances Yates herself. She never took kindly to any form of correction or criticism, as I was very soon to find out. Soon I was set on my way studying Lord Mayors' Pageants in the sixteenth century, eventually presenting my researches in neat, typed-up form in December that year, thanks to the purchase of an Olivetti Lettera 22. What I do recall is her sigh of relief as she handed it back to me telling me that I could write.

On New Year's Eve I wrote to Joan Henderson:

I think you will agree that the change from the undergraduate to the research approach is quite a wrench. I am only just beginning to feel on the postgraduate level, the difference from accepting other people's views to accepting nothing unless there is adequate evidence and feeling that your own theory is just as good as theirs.

By then the topics I was to tackle had fallen into place: the popular celebration of the Queen's Accession Day, the Accession Day Tilts, the

Order of the Garter and, but added later, the Queen's entry into London in 1559.

Already work on the tilts had led me to my earliest discovery. In the *British Portraits* exhibition at the Royal Academy that winter there was a full-length miniature by Nicholas Hilliard tentatively identified as Elizabeth's last favourite, Robert Devereux, 2nd Earl of Essex. This depicted a knight in costly fancy dress with a favour, a glove, tied to his right arm and skirts worn over his armour, which included a device with the motto *Dum formas minuis*. I spotted in the antiquary William Camden's *Remaines* (1605) that this motto was borne by the 'late Earl of Essex'. And so David Piper publicly acknowledged my contribution to the new identity of the sitter in a footnote to his article in the *Burlington Magazine* in 1957.

By then life with Frances Yates had settled into a pattern that was to remain unaltered until the middle of 1959. I quote from my 1982 diary account of what this was like:

> Our encounters in term-time were every Monday at 3 p.m. Punctuality was not her virtue and she had no compunction about leaving one standing outside her door for up to forty-five minutes. Once in the room one sat in a low chair and she swung on her desk chair, the smoke from her cigarette arising like incense around her. Early on she got the file of portraits of Elizabeth out of the photographic collection and we sat down to look at them together. Her flights of fancy would at times know no bounds. She would stroke ermine in a picture and mutter 'Purity', or, if the Queen were holding a jewelled chain, wonder whether it was an allegory of Aristotelian justice as number and measure. She would suddenly embark on long expositions of sixteenth-century interpretations of the Apocalypse, once narrowing her eyes and bending down towards me saying, 'You know, we've got to the get to the bottom of this Whore of Babylon

business.'... But her attitudes stuck. When confronted with a thesis on Elizabethan Pageantry as Propaganda I said 'I can't do that, it's English literature', to which the reply came: 'A trained mind can do anything. You take the book from the shelf and read it.' That was what was extraordinary.

While one's contemporaries at the Institute of Historical Research seminars were slogging away at recusants in Cheshire, MPs in the Parliament of 1581 or who did or did not pay Ship Money in Buckinghamshire in 1636, I was in full flight on triumphal arches, chariots, masques and ballets and, even more, leaping through them into music, theatre, poetry, the history of images and ideas, political and religious history, any tack to which the evidence led. The boundaries of knowledge widened dramatically. I was taught to think horizontally.

Research took me, of course, to original manuscripts in what was to become the British Library, the Public Record Office, the Bodleian Library, Lambeth Palace Library and the College of Arms, to name but a few. 'All the manuscripts I have had to deal with so far have been in the most foul condition!' I opined to Joan Henderson. 'The Public Record Office is a really dreadful place as though time had stood still in the year of the Great Exhibition.' The octagonal reading room there was presided over, if I remember rightly, by the likes of Roger Ellis and Noel Blakiston, tight-faced, old-fashioned English gentlemen who would peer over their spectacles with disapproval at those slaving below. Unbelievably, in winter a fire burned in the Victorian grate behind their seats. Such repositories were arcana into which, it seemed, we were admitted with some reluctance. A lot depended on whether they liked the look of you or whether you came with the right credentials.

The Department of Prints and Drawings in the British Museum was notorious, and it was a very long time before I eventually managed to study all the engravings it held of Elizabeth I. The College of Arms was another mysterious place and not easily accessible, but the benign Garter King of Arms, Sir Anthony Wagner, took to this intense, be-spectacled young man and the College's unique material on Tudor tournaments was transferred to the British Museum so that I could read it at ease. In a way these were halcyon days spent consuming and examining mounds of material, with a freedom which was never to return once I assumed the practicalities of the workplace. As nearly all the books I needed to consult were sixteenth-century ones, I soon had a permanent seat in the North Library where I recall toiling, for example, through the British Museum's vast collection of emblem books. This had been the habitat of novelist Angus Wilson, who had resigned the year before I arrived.

———

Into this emerging circle of those who were to preside over my future came another scholar, Francis Wormald, who then held the chair in palaeography at King's College, London, and later, in 1960, became Director of the Institute of Historical Research. Francis, as I was eventually allowed to call him (what a contrast to Frances Yates to whom I still wrote as 'Dear Miss Yates' as late as 1975!) came from a family of Yorkshire blanket manufacturers. He was an eminent and punctilious art historian and liturgist, and a friend of Frances Yates. I have concluded in retrospect that he was disposed towards me as we were both Anglo-Catholic; he never hesitated when I asked him to be a referee to support me, whereas others I knew were turned down. Perhaps that link of a common faith is caught in his charge to me on being appointed Director of the National Portrait Gallery in 1967 (for

Friend for life: the future Keeper of Manuscripts at the British Library,
Michael Borrie, about 1970.

which he was one of my referees) that I read the Rule for the abbot in
the Rule of St Benedict. Only later did I learn that there was a theatrical
side to Francis, although I never saw his turn wearing a tutu, and obits
refer to his brilliance as Cariola in *The Duchess of Malfi* when he was
at Cambridge. That submerged or suppressed theatricality was also
there in Frances Yates, who prided herself on being descended from the
famous Mrs Yates. Her lecturing style had a strongly thespian streak,
with arms uplifted and the occasional ecstatic upward gaze.

Francis Wormald taught the new postgraduate students palaeography.
Michael Borrie, a fellow student at the time and eventually Keeper of
Manuscripts at the British Library, describes these classes well in his
entry on Francis for the *Oxford Dictionary of National Biography*:

> His palaeography classes at the IHR could be an alarming experi-
> ence. He would distribute photographs of apparently indecipherable
> scripts to the class, and require each victim in turn to read his text

aloud. Any prompting by others would infuriate him; he had a sharp tongue when provoked, but his essential kindness ensured no lasting hurt to those who felt it.

I can see the formidable dome of Wormald's bald head in my mind's eye now and, beneath it, the glint of his steel-rimmed spectacles peering mercilessly downwards. He had a particular penchant for fifteenth-century banquet menus, documents that were to re-enter my life over forty years later when I wrote *Feast: A History of Grand Eating* (2003).

This was a period in which such people were held in awe and Francis Wormald exerted an immense influence thanks to the numerous committees on which he sat. I almost certainly owe to him the support I needed for my third year of research when I became a Fellow of the Institute of Historical Research. To those on the inner circle – of whom at that period I was not one – he was known as Puff or Puffy or Wormie. In 1935 he had married an heiress, Honoria Yeo, and this somewhat eccentric couple gathered around themselves a motley crew of artists, aesthetes, priests and scholars whom, from to time, they helped out.

Francis was precise, neat, exact and waspish. Outside our weekly encounters, we came together early on in an incident that affected a book by Frances Yates which was already in the press, *The Valois Tapestries* (1959). These wonderful creations, now in the Uffizi in Florence, depict French court festivals of the late sixteenth century. Frances was never at her best handling visual material, for which she always lacked the eye, but she had decided that these were designed by the Flemish painter Lucas de Heere, and sent as a 'politique' plea for religious toleration to Henri III and his mother, Catherine de' Medici. Brilliant, stimulating and extraordinary though she was, if Frances had made up her mind on something, every bit of evidence was bent to fit her conviction. I had cottoned on to this early on, writing to my Dutch friend, Jan: 'Although this is strictly between ourselves, this book is a bit hard to swallow I think.' It fell to me to tell her that one vital piece of her evidence was wrong. A book of costume drawings by de Heere was in the British Museum. It contained a portrait of Elizabeth I which I had examined and saw immediately was copied from a 1592 engraving and inserted years after the manuscript was compiled. The document came up quite by chance at one of my tutorials with Frances, and I pointed out that I was certain that she was aware that it had been inserted into the manuscript at a later date. The effect on her was electric: within forty-eight hours I was subjected to a very long letter from her listing off every reason why she was right. A meeting was then arranged between her, Francis Wormald and me in the Manuscripts Department of the British Museum. Francis took one look at the portrait and said 'Of course, Strong's right.' Unfortunately it radically affected her argument, for this image in her words 'proves conclusively that Lucas de Heere could have done the business of placing the portrait heads of royal personages onto the costume figures to form the foreground portraits of the Valois Tapestries'. The book was already in production, so a slip was pasted at the bottom of the page, not mentioning that both it and the map which followed it were later additions but merely saying that they did not 'have the same water-mark'; it continued: 'This may, but need not, affect the argument in the last paragraph of this page.' In fact it demolished it.

This was not the only incident of this kind that I experienced but it captures well enough Frances in one of her moments of frenzy, when every circle had to be squared to accord with her conclusions. She could, on the other hand, be both helpful and generous to her students and protect them from other more predatory academics.

Another of my weekly chores was to attend every Monday evening in term time the seminar of Sir John Neale, that hallowed shrine to which Joan Henderson went. This took place in another building that dominated these research years, the Institute of Historical Research. This had been founded in 1921 by the Tudor historian A.F. Pollard and in 1947 moved into its present premises in the north block of the University of London's Senate House in Malet Street. Its library contained on the open shelves a vast repertory of printed calendars and other papers, which were hugely useful to me. It emerged rapidly that Sir John's seminar was not for me. I had already reached that conclusion by December 1956, when I wrote to Joan: 'from my point of view [the seminar] is a bit of a bore – I am afraid that my sphere is just dead to him.' Or it was until a certain subject raised its head.

I wish that I could say that I warmed to Neale. I did not. Patrick Collinson neatly categorizes him as 'one of the last of the old-style power brokers'. I began to attend his seminar a year after his knighthood, a year before the appearance of the second volume of his *Elizabeth I and Her Parliaments* and the year of his retirement from the post of Astor Professor of English History at University College. His aim had been to make the Department there 'a nursery of professors', to the end that he might place them as satellites in the universities of Britain and the United States. Most of those gathered around that seminar table he put on to this or that aspect of parliamentary history about which he wanted to know. It was difficult to reconcile this ruddy-faced, balding, rotund little man with the author, thirty years earlier, of what arguably remains the best life of the Virgin Queen. The seminar was billed as on the

Elizabethan age but it rarely if ever left its one track of constitutional history with its never-ending biographies of this or that member of parliament.

What Frances had set me to work on meant nothing to Neale and I was ignored until one meeting in 1957, when he announced that he was going to the United States to deliver a grand lecture on the occasion of the four-hundredth anniversary of Elizabeth's accession. He said that he would be dealing with topics such as the celebration of her Accession Day and also her state entry into London before her coronation. Inevitably I piped up and said that I had been working in detail on those topics. 'Oh, you will let me have it won't you?' he requested, his eyes ablaze, taking a sudden interest in me for the first time. Shattered, I rang up Frances, who immediately said 'Don't go there again', rescuing me from what I later referred to as Neale's 'predatory activities'. The result was my first article in the *Journal* for 1958 on the popular celebration of Accession Day.

The second seminar at the Institute of Historical Research to which I was bidden was presided over by the avuncular Bindoff, puffing away at a pipe, with the assistance of Joel Hurstfield. These meetings were ponderous affairs and usually one or other of us was expected to give a paper on our latest discoveries. I recall one on the Dutch Sea Beggars, little more than pirates in the Channel, which went on for an hour and half of mind-blowing tedium, at the close of which Bindoff puffed and said: 'Is it all as exciting as this?' Anything I produced was greeted with amused astonishment. One paper led into Elizabethan apocalyptic theory with the dramas of the Last Days and the beasts of the Book of Revelation making their entry. 'So, Strong, that's what you think it was all about', to which I replied with clenched teeth, 'Yes, that is what I think it was all about.' The other comment of Bindoff's which I recall vividly was: 'I suppose that when we open your thesis a triumphal arch will pop up.'

What was read and garnered in these years was to cast both a ray of light and a long shadow over the decades to come. I had, for example, gathered a mass of material on James I's eldest son, Prince Henry, which was only to take book form in the 1980s. Such a period of wide-eyed freedom was never again to be experienced once I had embarked on a museum and gallery career. The Warburg and Frances Yates had opened a whole new world to me. I was to exchange that for one that was inevitably both intellectually and physically constricted in a manner which Frances was never to experience. She came into the Institute Mondays and Thursdays, otherwise spending her time researching at home or in various libraries. She never administered anything or dealt with any practicality. Her sister Ruby acted as cook and house-keeper in their comfortable 1920s house at Claygate in Surrey. In a way I worshipped her but the seeds which were later to divide us were in fact there from the outset, if I had thought about it. She never understood what it was like to be tied to an office or to deal with officialdom or the public. Worse, she had a barely concealed condescension towards anything that smacked of antiquarianism. As I moved forward in time she made me feel that I had betrayed the principles that both she and the Institute stood for, until in the end I was forced to break free and cut the apron strings that had tied me to her.

All of this can be traced in the substantial correspondence I had with a new friend, Jan Adrianus van Dorsten. As we engaged in a

Ladykiller: my Dutch friend and confidant Jan van Dorsten,
around the time I met him in 1959.

correspondence that ran on through three decades, it seems right to
etch him into my life at the point when he entered it: the summer of
1959. Jan was an Anglo-Dutch scholar and a member of the post-war
Sir Thomas Browne Institute in the University of Leiden, founded to
encourage research and publish material on the cultural relationship
between the Low Countries and Great Britain. It was presided over by
Professor A.G.H. Bachrach, generally known as Fred, whose surname
was so difficult for some English people to get their tongue round that
I recall once at the National Portrait Gallery a door being flung open
and the arrival of a 'Professor Switchback' announced. Bachrach was
a remarkable man, not that I realized it at that period. He had had the
most terrible war, interned in a Japanese prisoner-of-war camp where he
was starved and tortured; but he could never bring himself ever to talk
about that. Instead, to me he seemed a rather upright, old-fashioned
Dutch professor of English whose major research project was a life of

the Dutch humanist and ambassador Constantine Huygens. Fred was forever tut-tutting about the amours of Jan but himself ran through three wives. Immediately upon retirement he dumped his Dutch wife, moved to England to marry his mistress and settled in Twickenham.

Jan was one of the few compulsive womanizers I have known. We first met at Cumberland Lodge in Windsor Great Park, which in 1947 had been made over to be a meeting place where students and those who taught or were in public life could meet and discuss the issues of the day. Once a year a group from the English Department at the University of Leiden came for a week dedicated to this or that period of English cultural history. In 1956 it was the Elizabethan period, which accounted for my presence. It was there that Jan entered my life, and we decided we would write a book together on the festivals staged to welcome Robert Dudley, Earl of Leicester, as Governor of the Netherlands in 1585–6. This slim volume, entitled *Leicester's Triumph*, eventually appeared in 1964.

We must have formed an odd pair for Jan was a tall and good-looking Nordic specimen with wavy blonde hair and blue eyes, keenly aware of his attractiveness to women. His attitude to them was, however, condescending, and I could always tell when he was on the phone to one of them by the change in the tone of his voice. At this time he was married to his first wife, a somewhat characterless but sweet woman whom he had wed on the rebound. Jan's mother was a widow living in Utrecht and his upbringing during the war and after was there, his father having been killed, if I remember rightly, just before or early in the war in what was then the Dutch East Indies. Jan's knowledge of edible mushrooms was prodigious. It had had to be, for in the aftermath of the war the population edged towards starvation. He was very Dutch, loved anything to do with the water and had a boat which he sailed on the Zuiderzee. When the canals were frozen over in winter he donned his skates, once even emulating the seventeenth-century challenge of skating from Leiden to The Hague without smashing the clay pipe which was perched in his hat.

He was to have two more wives and I omit the various women, including a Siamese princess, in between. His love life was expensive in terms of divorce settlements and I once wrote to him saying: 'Live with them but don't marry them or you'll be ruined.' He was extraordinarily ordered in terms of paperwork: above his desk there was a shelf with all the letters to him from his various correspondents, including those I had written. His widow photocopied the whole sequence for me, providing a unique window into this period of my life because they were written before the age of the mobile phone and the invention of email. Hence the letters I wrote to him are akin to retrospective diary entries. Jan's great aim was to obtain a chair in English literature at a Dutch university, something he never achieved. But he had a joyous, somewhat gypsy attitude to life of a kind I was yet to discover, equally an ease of social manner and good humour absent in me at this period of my life. In sharp contrast, I was awkward, cripplingly shy and lacking social graces.

Two themes run through my letters to Jan during this period. One was the loneliness of my early years at the National Portrait Gallery (to which I shall come in the next chapter) and the other, which I shall follow here, was how Frances Yates pecked away at me, insinuating that I had opted for a lower form of intellectual life. What I can see now is that her disapproval rose in inverse proportion to my emerging success. That must be set in the context of her judgement on me, as recounted to me years later, in the early 1980s, by her good friend Jean Robertson, Professor of English at the University of Southampton. Jean had once asked Frances as to the prospects for 'the boys'. 'Anglo, straight to the top', was the reply. 'Strong you'll never hear of again.' Unfortunately her predictions turned out to be wildly wrong.

But I must polish off the saga of the thesis. As in the case of several colleagues, there was no way that it could be written and presented by the time I started work at the National Portrait Gallery in September 1959. Individual chapters had been written and I thought that putting these together would be sufficient, so it was something of a shock when Frances said: 'Now we have the block of stone we can set about sculpting it into shape.' By March 1961 I wrote: 'It occurred to me yesterday that I would be running into a sixth year by the time it went in; a feeling of guilt and remorse seized me.' My thesis was finally presented at the end of the year, typed by myself as I was too impoverished to afford a profes-sional typist. The viva was fixed for 28 February, which proved not to be my lucky day: the thesis was referred. The examiners were Frances, Joel Hurstfield and Professor D.J. Gordon of the University of Reading, a great crony of Frances. Gordon was a chronic alcoholic homosexual who in the end, thanks to a scandal, had to be quietly removed from post; but in his time had been a brilliantly innovative professor of English, opening literary studies in a way heavily influenced by the Warburg. Joe Trapp, Gombrich's successor, had begun his career under him, as indeed had Frank Kermode. Gordon apparently was the one who would not budge on referral: the others wished to pass it but for me to re-edit the appendices, transcribing original documents.

The effect on me at the time was devastating. Frances, too, realized that she had given me no guidance whatsoever as to the correct editing of texts. Generous, but also seized with a sense of guilt, she advised me to read Kafka and handed me a cheque for the professional retyping of the work. What was so awful was the fact that I travelled down to see Donald Gordon to seek his advice on editing those texts. He said that he never edited any texts himself but paid someone else to do it. At any rate it was resubmitted in June and passed. The same month I chanced to bump into Francis Wormald, now Director of the Institute of Historical Research, and reported to Jan: 'Before I had time to say anything I was told theses weren't for people like me but for nitwits ... I was told I was above such things.'

Theses are not books. That the University of Chicago turned it down hardly surprised me, nor that Frances showed little enthusiasm for reading any of my revised versions. Bits appeared as academic articles but did not solve what to do with the material until a decade on when I drew it together, adding new pieces I had written in my early years at the National Portrait Gallery on the celebrated procession picture of the Virgin Queen, Nicholas Hilliard's most famous miniature known as *The Young Man among Roses* and the memorial portrait of Sir Henry Unton. A book eventually appeared in 1977, entitled *The Cult of Elizabeth*, to appreciative reviews by A.L. Rowse, John Barton and Christopher Hill. It was to go through more than one edition and finally, in 1999, into paperback. Years later I happened to come across a book which dealt with advances in English literary scholarly method, finding, to my surprise, that my book was cited as responsible for the new historicist approach to English Renaissance literature. In the preface I had paid tribute to the fact that it owed 'much to many enlightening conversations with Frances A. Yates, whose work and teaching remain a constant source of inspiration'.

The thesis episode reveals Frances at her best, as did her belief that one of her tasks was to get her students jobs. 'I've just been down to the

National Portrait Gallery', she would say. 'There may be a vacancy.' At the same time she cultivated Oliver Millar, Surveyor of the Queen's Pictures, with the same end in view. And, of course, that led to my appointment as an Assistant Keeper at the National Portrait Gallery. But having sought me such a position she could never come to terms with the fact that what it entailed did not square with her view of how one's time should be spent. This is vividly caught in a letter I wrote to Jan van Dorsten in February 1963:

> I had a long and somewhat disillusioning session with the Lady
> Frances who more or less implied that I was wasting my mind work-
> ing on this sort of thing [i.e. Elizabethan portraiture and painting]
> and why wasn't I working on something big to do with the history of
> thought and not English. She was sweet [looking back, I wonder...]
> but one did see what she meant – on the other hand I've worked like
> a slave and produced stacks and the National Portrait Gallery is not
> exactly the place to work on Pico, Ficino, della Porta and the rest of
> them.

In March I wrote: 'I shall steer clear of her for a time. She's a dear but really she has no contact with reality. To tell me I wasn't getting anywhere when all the doors are as it were beginning to open wide seems lunacy to me.' This is a sore which runs through my letters to Jan, culminating in one in which, at last, I crossed the bridge. This was written in March 1966, a year before my appointment as Director of the National Portrait Gallery:

> I saw Yates last Monday. It was an annihilating experience. After
> two hours I left wanting to put my head in the gas-oven and have
> felt mentally depressed ever since. Her main theme seems to be an
> implication that nothing I had produced was any good and it was a
> 'lower form' of work and really useless anyway. I was painted in lurid

colours as a glossy, successful young man who had sold himself down the river to a life of glamour and ostentation. I have thought a good bit about what she said and feel that it was, on mature thought, a bit much when I think how genuinely hard I work and of the things I have produced. In spite of doing all the normal administrative work in the National Portrait Gallery it is nothing short of a miracle. I could have sat back, like certain nameless colleagues, and done nothing and escalated upwards not lifting a finger.

I believe *passionately* in the Gallery and its future and in my work and its use. The older one gets the more one realizes that it is the facts one finds which last and the conclusions which are ephemeral. She obviously hates the art world and its glitter, sees exhibitions and display work as a waste of time, cataloguing as fit only for mental drudges. There is obviously a parting of the ways here. It is difficult to see things in perspective but somehow now her world and its ambience seem so very narrow and inward-looking. I feel that I have benefited from other contacts with circles beyond the academic. I don't see why I should axe them off and live in a cloistered cell reading Bruno for an eternity. Ever since I went to the Gallery there has always been this effort by her to belittle the type of work one does there. I think and know it is valuable.

Forgive this screed on F.A. Yates, but this kind of lurch makes one need to sort oneself out mentally. She remains always someone for whom I have a deep affection. She was super to me all those years ago, bless her heart. But, oh dear, she is not of this world. I can't understand her. She got me the Gallery job and all she does when I see her is to make me feel miserable and unhappy about it and small when I have done all I can to make it something positive and exciting.

Not long after, I was to write to him again:

in retrospect the encounter with Yates was cruel and unnecessary and unjustified. Perhaps one senses a tinge of jealousy in the old bird when she sees her fledgling begin to spread his wings and fly on his own. The 'old' Strong (to whom she mystically referred) depended on her – the new can stand on his own. Women's minds are difficult to fathom and however much Yates believes she has mastered logic she remains, like all women, bound to muddle in her emotions. However I have made a vow (a) to avoid seeing her *pro tem* (b) if I do see her I would not allow her to cross examine me in such a way again.

This was to all intents and purposes the end of something. Although I dedicated *Holbein and Henry VIII* to her the following year, it was accepted grudgingly with insinuations that she knew really what the painting was about. I have learned since that such ruptures often happen, a kind of moment when a student no longer wishes to be yet another star in the Great One's coronet but someone in their own right, with their own view of things and their own path to tread.

But I never forgot her or how much I owed to her. When, on the only occasion I was taken out to lunch by the man who dealt with Honours, I was asked if I knew of anyone who deserved one, I, of course, nominated her and it followed. She did congratulate me on becoming Director of the National Portrait Gallery but I was mortified that she did not even scribble a postcard when, at thirty-eight, I became Director of the Victoria and Albert Museum. In a way I sense a streak of envy there. I was loyal to her to the end, wrote a fulsome review of her book *Astraea: The Imperial Theme in the Sixteenth Century* (1975) in the *Times Literary Supplement* and letters of congratulation on her OBE and then DBE, but something had snapped. She died in the autumn of 1981, only a few months before I was knighted. By then she had been taken up as a cult figure by Hugh Trevor-Roper and Jonathan Miller, while her books became wilder and wilder as she grew older. I wrote an account of her depressing cremation in Leatherhead and reflected on that relationship which had done so much to open my mind and also, at times, to destroy it:

> Looking back on it from a personal point of view the prodigal son had been received back! This was happy, because I knew that I was looked upon as a kind of write-off for years. Now I know that she would ask after me and in fact was really full of affection for me and saw that one had achieved something by a different path. To me she was always 'Miss Yates' and it was only last year that she signed her letters 'Frances' – so I think that meant something and was a signal.

Not long after I was knighted, Joe Trapp sent me a little book of poems by Edmund Spenser inscribed in childish handwriting within: 'Frances Amelia Yates her book'. Later followed a 1581 edition of Petrarch's poems which had been hers. I treasure both still and they rest on a shelf along with all her other works. On shelves below extend those of two other people who were central to my creative life, Sir Cecil Beaton and Gianni Versace, of both of whom she would have strongly disapproved. But then she never did really understand me.

To Frances Yates, knowledge of the kind she cultivated was not to be communicated to the uninitiated. 'They don't *know*' was a phrase she often used, with a heavy accent on 'know'. By this she meant that special access to an understanding of the minds and actions of people in other ages that she believed only a Warburgian could hope to 'know'. She despised journalism or any form of populism as tainting knowledge by communicating it to the uninitiated public. I had heavy warnings from her when I joined the National Portrait Gallery that David Piper wrote journalism, a warning which only made the possibility attractive. My first attempt at doing that kind of more popular writing, *Splendour at Court: Renaissance Spectacle and Illusion* (1973), was damned by her as 'entirely derivative'. In that judgement she missed the point, which was to synthesize what scholars had discovered in that field since the early 1950s and open up the subject to a wider audience. That was the divide. All of my life was to be concerned with communicating to the public, opening up the gate of knowledge, keeping the drawbridge down and not, as she did, pulling it up and retreating into her tower. A phrase from Sir Philip Sidney's prose romance the *Arcadia* was to be the guiding principle of my life, to purvey 'the riches of knowledge upon the stream of delight'. There let it rest.

———

But what of the Virgin's Queen's portraits, that mad adolescent passion that had led me along this path in the first place? Devoid of any training or guidance, I had slogged on, cataloguing her images under media, paintings, miniatures, wood engravings, medals and so on. In April 1960 the result, along with its introduction, went to Oxford University Press with recommendations from Gertrude Bing and Ernst Gombrich. 'I certainly think that it is the best thing that I have done', I wrote. The usual slow passage through the press followed. Eventually, in 1963, *Portraits of Queen Elizabeth I* appeared. At the end of the previous December I had written to Jan, on receipt of an advance copy, saying: 'It looks strangely tiny ... One looks through and realizes that now one could do better, still it is an advance on 1894.' Two thousand copies were printed and the reviews were favourable – very, in fact. The review in *Punch* hailed it as 'a work of immense beauty and precision', while that in *The Times* closed with the comment: 'The scholarship Mr Strong has put into this work is rewarding.' The book was taken up by television, as I wrote to Jan:

I did it on television with lute music twanging in the background and the face of Eliza gradually getting older on the screen ... It was fun in every way and this time I just relaxed into it. As I left the studio they said 'See you again', so that I felt a line had been established. Actually I was terribly pleased that that had happened as it means that the book was held up and appeared on the screens of millions of homes, far more effective than any of the old reviews.

This was one of my earliest appearances in that medium whose use of me over the decades to come was to ebb and flow with the occasional series, a programme or two and, as I get older, endless interviews about this or that person I have known. But I was never to be taken up as one of the immovable gang who present everything. In the case of the subject, Elizabeth I, I revisited it for the last time in the late 1980s in *Gloriana: The Portraits of Queen Elizabeth I* (1987), which was to appear in paperback in 2003.

———

Those who are obsessed with social mobility, to which I am a minor monument, forget that there is a downside as well as an upside to it. Education permits you to ascend but at the same time it progressively creates an ever-widening gulf between yourself and your family. Educated conversation gradually becomes a norm, along with the manners and social behaviour of what would in the 1950s have been designated as 'a better class of person'. Life in our suburban terrace house in N21 continued on exactly the lines I described in my opening chapter, although tempered by an increasing prosperity as the decade drew to a close. One by one the rooms returned to their pre-war use. The dilapidated settee and armchairs from the late 1920s gave way to a three-piece suite in uncut moquette in an unutterable shade of red.

The 1956 Clean Air Act banished the fire around which we had gathered for so long, to be replaced by one of electric bars. DIY arrived and rooms in the house were progressively painted and papered. Outside, the chickens vanished along with the vegetables, to be replaced by lawn and flower beds. Visits to the cinema declined as the television set became the focus of domestic life – and to it I owed much in an era when the mandate of Lord Reith still prevailed, one in which, for example, George Bernard Shaw's *Back to Methuselah* was staged in its entirety over several evenings, something inconceivable by the close of the 1960s.

But living at home became progressively more and more constricting for someone who was within reach of his twenty-fourth year. There never had been an open-house policy of welcoming anyone to the house. It remained a citadel. But I was living on a few hundred pounds a year, just about able to afford a modest meal out or a visit to the theatre and a quiet few days in a guesthouse in Stratford upon Avon to see the plays, but that was the sum total. In a sense I created small private worlds of my own within the tiny compass of its walls. The dining room, used only for lunch on Sundays, was colonized and a desk given to me by my parents, to mark my twenty-first birthday and the award of a first-class degree, was sited in the bay to the right of the chimneypiece. On that and on the dining table in the centre of the room I worked unremittingly all through those years. I had some bookcases made, which were progressively filled with the books so signally lacking in any form in the rest of the house. I also had a record player and began to explore the joys of classical music. Home was exactly as it had always been: an impregnable fortress in which I led my own solitary existence.

And what of life outside and beyond this voyage of the mind? Looking back, these years were dominated by two circles, both created by the throwing together of people of roughly the same ages in the same educational institutions. One of them was inevitably the Warburg, which was certainly not teeming with young blood – far from it. The prevailing view of things seemed to be summed up by Frances Yates's dark reference to a student who had let the side down and, on inquiry as to how, the word 'marriage' slipped from her lips. There was a touch of the virginal and monastic about the place.

Conversation always centred on this or that aspect of the past and where a particular person had got to in their research. The group I came up with all became dyed-in-the-wool academics, distinguished in their fields of endeavour. Amongst them figured Michael Kauffmann, a prolific and polymathic art historian who combined his knowledge of the likes of Constable with his status as an authority on Romanesque manuscripts. He was later to enter my life as Keeper of Prints and Drawings at the Victoria and Albert Museum and then, for a decade, Director of the Courtauld Institute of Art. Jennifer Montagu was to carve out a career for herself as an authority on Charles Le Brun and Italian baroque sculpture, while Mary Webster, who worked in the Institute's Photographic Collection, made Johan Zoffany her life's work. I took quite a shine to her but she was to marry Ronald Lightbown, who became the V&A's Librarian. That alliance of people all delving into this or that aspect of the past fed a virtually closed world. My 'twin' under Frances Yates, Sydney Anglo, was to become a professor at the University of Wales and marry Margaret McGowan, who also worked on court festivals and became a major pioneer of early dance history. In a sense these marriages were alliances of minds as much as passions.

A second, livelier circle existed in the Institute of Historical Research, where the great event of the day was tea in the Common Room. Here were gathered those who were to fill the posts of lecturer, reader and, hopefully, professor in the expanding or new universities which sprang up in response to government policy on higher education. They formed a desultory group, among them William Lamont, whose life's work was to be the polemicist William Prynne and the Muggletonians and who became Professor of History at the University of Sussex; Bernard Hamilton, who ended up Emeritus Professor of Crusading History at the University of Nottingham; Valerie Cromwell (later Lady Kingman), who was also a Professor at Sussex; and another medievalist, Teresa Hankey. To them I can add Michael Borrie, who became Keeper of Manuscripts in the British Library (of whom more in Chapter 6). Somehow after these hothouse years we became geographically dispersed and my career was to be so radically different from theirs that contact gradually ceased. Bernard Hamilton was a particular friend during these years (we shared our Anglo-Catholicism) but towards the end of the research period he converted to Rome, married, and left London for a provincial university.

However constrained I was by living at home some social life began to burgeon. Valerie Cromwell and Teresa Hankey were great party-givers at Bedford College. Teresa, a striking and incisive woman, was daughter of the Dean of Ely and her mother in turn was daughter of Frank Harris, the author of the notorious *My Life and Loves* (1922). I recall the latter asking me one day whether I was a member of the Bloomsbury Group. Both Teresa and Valerie went on to be Fellows of Newnham College, Cambridge, where from time to time, they gave rather smart lunch parties. I lost contact with Teresa but not with Valerie, who went on to marry the future Sir John Kingman, Vice-Chancellor of the University of Bristol. Their friendship with the Anglos also ensured that they, too, never quite vanished from my life. But my career in the museum world and then my marriage into that of theatre effectively cut me adrift from academe. I was also, in the long run, to find academia constraining and dull, and in that respect I could never have achieved what I did without breaking away.

This was university life at the opposite end of the spectrum from the world of *Brideshead Revisited* – but not so far from that of Kingsley Amis's *Lucky Jim*. Every subsequent visit to a university only reinforced my belief that this was not for me. This was a world devoid of any panache or style or glamour, all of which I had glimpsed from afar. But the late 1950s remained a world of deference, respectability, conformity and restraint. Although 'teddy boys' had arrived like a sartorial bombshell, the most I achieved was a yellow waistcoat.

One cloud hung on my horizon: National Service. It had been introduced in 1947, and all eighteen-year-old men were liable to spend at first eighteen months and then two years in one of the armed services. I dreaded it and it had been progressively put off as I pursued my postgraduate education until, in the spring of 1959, to my horror it raised its head again. I wrote a remarkably full account of this to Joan Henderson:

> I have been through the most ghastly four months of my life but now everything has turned out all right. The National Service business has been frightful, four months of heart-rending traipsing to and from medicals and hospitals. I moved heaven and earth to get out on the grounds of what I had wrong with my neck [Hodgkin's disease] but they didn't go for that. But the Army did arrange for me to go and see a specialist – I did not know for what. After three visits to a hospital ending in three doctors looking at my inside through

an X-ray machine they marched across the room and told me they thought I had a hole in my heart. Up until then I did not even know I had been seeing heart specialists, let alone that this horror was to be launched at me plus the fact that, in my case, they would be unable to operate. I am afraid when I got home for the first time in my life I really broke down. Thank goodness the day after I went away for a fortnight of peace and calm in the Cotswolds which I much needed and enjoyed. As you can imagine all sorts of wild thoughts about my health went through my mind but when I came back to London there was at least a letter from the Army rejecting me on medical grounds. Further, mother had arranged for me, on advice from an aunt of mine [the ever-blessed Aunt Elsie] to go and see ... *the* heart specialist in Devonshire Place. With fear and trembling I went, but the doctor was delightful and within an hour showed me a tracing of my heart and exactly where the Army specialists had gone wrong – *laus Deo*! So I know now that I have a perfectly normal heart, which is such a relief as you can imagine.

Not long ago a friend returned to me a letter I had written to David Piper at the National Portrait Gallery on 8 January 1959, in which I sent him a copy of my early article on Nicholas Hilliard. In it I wrote: 'This also gives me an opportunity to say how very interested I would be if there should be any possible post at the NPG. It would, of course, be ideal and I am flattered that my name should have been mooted.' So the Gallery must have had its eye on me.

In June the National Portrait Gallery post was advertised and I applied. In those days you had to put down on the form your father's occupation. Frances Yates, seeing that I had written 'commercial traveller', made me change it to 'businessman'. The old hierarchies were still in place. They were there when I was appointed Director in 1967, when Sir Geoffrey Agnew, doyen grandee of the art trade, remarked about me to the future Sir Hugh Leggatt of Leggatt Brothers: 'No one of that class should ever have been appointed.' But that's how things were back in the 1950s and '60s, when scaling the mountain of the old establishment was no easy task.

The interviews were in July. I do not remember much about the board, except that there was the usual Civil Service chairman, Kingsley Adams, the Gallery's Director and the distinguished art historian E.K. Waterhouse, by then Director of the Barber Institute of Fine Arts in the University of Birmingham, and, I think David Piper. The Gallery was anxious to recruit someone who would undertake cataloguing its sixteenth-century collection and in that sense I fitted the bill. After three years at the Warburg, however, I was living in an academic dream-world of Yatesian fantasy and I recall that, as I went on at them in just such a way, Waterhouse leaned forward and said: 'What would you do if the window cord broke?' That has always stuck in my mind. It was a much-needed wake-up call from the world of reality and practicality. But I got the job, much to my mother's delight. For her a post in the Civil Service, with job security and a pension attached to it, was all that anyone could ever aspire to. Her father had had a lifetime of self-denial so that when he died there would be some small accumulation of capital producing a modest income for his widow. My father's job brought with it no pension and the idea of providing for my mother barely crossed his mind: 'You don't have to worry, your boys will look after you.' And that is what happened.

———

What am I to conclude from these years? Bindoff always said that the research years were a voyage of the mind and that they were in a sense unreal ones. He was right: they were. But they did equip me to work on my own, with a keen sense of purpose, with the ability to research and write – since then I have never been without a book in the making – and instilled in me the importance of that simple fact that has seen me through some of the darkest periods of my professional career. I developed the ability to go into my workroom and open a book and enter another world, which no one could violate. The interdisciplinary approach of the Warburg taught me to move across several fields of study and hope for the best. Later that was applied in a very different way, when I bravely turned my hand to writing on garden design. What it did not prepare me for was the practicalities of the workplace. In retrospect that was perhaps the greatest indictment of post-war university expansion. It had little if any connection with the world of work, which seemed to defeat the object of this vast explosion of academe. In a sense all it did was produce more academics and a multiplication of ivory towers. There was little if any attempt to cultivate bridgeheads to the real world, so that when the tap of government money was eventually turned off there was little sympathy or support from the community without. In my case I would have benefited from a placement for a few months in a museum or gallery in order to gain hands-on experience. Instead, one was encouraged to inhabit and glorify living permanently in an intellectual fairyland. Worse still, any form of life other than theirs was cast by those who inhabited the ivory towers as some lower form of existence.

Soon all of that was to change. My progress so far had coincided at every stage with some evolution in post-war society, which in effect put in place and facilitated the ladder of ascent for a new, short-lived breed: the meritocrats. We all worked ferociously hard, were obsessively competitive and knew precisely where we wanted to go. Most of the other thrusting meritocrats seemed to be left-wing ideologists, thrilled by John Osborne's *Look Back in Anger* and the arrival of Joan Littlewood's Theatre Workshop, fans of the novels of Kingsley Amis and Angus Wilson, marching in favour of nuclear disarmament. In sharp contrast, I was entranced by the past: a committed royalist; an Oxford Movement Christian; a lover of Old England, its great houses, churches and landscape; in short, at this stage of my life, a prototype of the later Young Fogeys, conservative by instinct and not at all an Angry Young Man of the Colin Wilson/John Osborne variety. And so, with this contradiction of character, I was to join that most conservative and old-fashioned of all the national collections, the National Portrait Gallery, in September 1959, on a salary of just over £700 per annum. It all seemed curiously apposite. But then the following year was 1960 and with that I entered a very different decade.

FIVE

SHADOWLANDS

1959 to 1963

THIS IS A DETAIL from a rare photograph of the entire staff of the National Portrait Gallery in the early 1960s, arranged in hierarchical order from the seated figures of the Director, curatorial and secretarial staff through the standing ranks of the warding staff. The Director, Charles Kingsley Adams, sits centre stage, flanked by his Assistant Keepers, John Kerslake, David Piper and myself, and librarian Caroline Brown. The setting is what might be described as the High Victorian Gallery at the very end of what was then called the Duveen Wing. Behind the assembled company we glimpse Sir George Hayter's portrait of Queen Victoria in her coronation robes. On either side of her hung portraits of worthies such as Gladstone and Disraeli, as acolytes. The Gallery vanished in this form almost half a century ago. Looking at this drear line-up it is hard to imagine that the photographic world of David Bailey was about to explode on the scene. It is staid, stately and dull, everyone knowing their place in a world which seemed immutable.

There I sit. It was employment but I was not particularly happy as I found myself seemingly trapped and frustrated in an institution from which there seemed to be no escape.

———

The National Portrait Gallery when I arrived there in 1959 bore little resemblance to the vibrant institution we see today. Apart from the Victoria and Albert Museum, which under the aegis of Sir Leigh Ashton had become the most exciting museum in London, this was in many ways a dead period in the history of many of the national collections. Recovery from the war was slow and nowhere slower than in the NPG, reigned over by the formidable Sir Henry Hake. His next-but-one successor, Sir David Piper, in his unpublished, fragmentary but revealing account of the Gallery in Hake's period (now held in the National Portrait Gallery Archives), described him as 'a militant romantic, and a man of violent passion'. The portrait of Hake in the Gallery's collection records him as opinionated, fish-eyed and querulous.

There was no middle ground with Hake. There was a clear grouping of the loved and the loathed, the latter being by far the larger group. He loathed all journalists, dealers, auctioneers, millionaires and social climbers. That eliminated a small army of people in his world for a start. The hit list of specific people was a long one and included all those involved in any way in the creation of the Courtauld Institute of Art: the distinguished art historian W.G. Constable, its first Director, whom I met once in Boston where he was Curator of Paintings at the Museum of Fine Arts, the art patron Lord Lee of Fareham and the financier Sir Robert Witt, who together drove through the creation of the Institute. To them could be added one of Hake's predecessors,

Sir Lionel Cust (I was told that every time a bluebottle buzzed in the NPG boardroom Hake would scream, 'Swot it! It's Cust come back to haunt us!'); Sir Karl Parker, an outstanding Director of the Ashmolean Museum, Oxford; and Carl Winter, an equally outstanding director of the Fitzwilliam Museum, Cambridge, and author of the King Penguin on Elizabethan miniatures that had inspired me as a schoolboy. And then there was the future Lord Clark, the nearest thing in Hake's book to a living Antichrist. Members of the short approved list include the NPG's first Director, the great Sir George Scharf, and Fritz Saxl of the Warburg Institute. Hake wrote very little except a British Academy lecture entitled 'The Historic Portrait: Document and Myth'. Charles Mitchell, sorting out those he regarded as the men from the boys, snapped this at me once, asking what I thought of it. I snapped back 'Very good', to which came the reply: 'You're in.'

Hake exercised a deadly hold on the NPG, of which he was Director for almost twenty-five years, dying in fact in harness. He had been dead for eight years when I arrived in September 1959 but it didn't feel like it. In a sense he was somehow still there. When I became Director in 1967 I was determined to exorcize him, for I was the first total break with Hake since I did not even remember him. On finding to my horror an envelope in the directorial desk labelled 'Pieces of paper found on Sir Henry Hake's death the day he died', I shot it on sight into the nearest wastepaper basket.

This was an era of dead men's shoes and on Hake's death in 1951 they all moved up one; so it was that Charles Kingsley Adams became Director. Hake had treated him in a manner akin to the proverbial squashed cabbage leaf, forever taunting him about his lack of Oxbridge education. Piper was generous in his description of Kingsley, as we

Identikit establishment: C.K. Adams in composed greyness, 1964.

called him, writing of his 'humility and goodness' and of his 'self-effacement'. 'Only later', he wrote, 'did I realize that he was some kind of lay saint, entirely uninterested in self-promotion, a dedicated acolyte in the service of scholarship and of the public, and of the NPG.' I would thoroughly concur. His manner was dignified, slow and courteous. To me, however, coming in from the outside, the place seemed stuck in a deferential time warp.

And what was this 'place'? The National Portrait Gallery still stands at St Martin's Place, its entrance opposite the monument to Edith Cavell and its main façade facing up Charing Cross Road, over a garden surrounding a statue to Henry Irving. The site was an awkward one, wrapped like a skin around the National Gallery, but Ewan Christian gave the main façade all the appearance of a Florentine Renaissance palazzo. The Portrait Gallery's existence is owed to the three men whose busts preside over the entrance: Philip Henry Stanhope, 5th Earl Stanhope, and the two great Victorian historians Thomas Babington Macaulay and Thomas Carlyle. The Gallery was created in 1856 as a tangible response to the Victorian exultation of the role of the great in the nation's history, told in a manner we now categorize as Whig. It had the good luck to have Scharf as its first Director, who guided it through its early decades and died only shortly before the present building opened in 1896.

From my schooldays onwards I had visited the Gallery in the post-war years. The lighting fittings, which resembled divers' helmets, had been installed before the war but as no one had bothered to record which went where when they were dismantled in 1939, no one knew what to do on their return in 1945. The result was gloom and the top-lit galleries on the upper floor had to be visited during daylight hours since otherwise it was virtually impossible to see anything. This was not helped by the fact that all the pictures were glazed and few were cleaned. Indeed, cleaning was regarded on principle with the deepest suspicion and the only person allowed to do it was a Mr Vallence of Holders. The sole change in the public galleries after they were reinstalled by Hake after 1945 was a multiplication in the number of the portraits on display, Kingsley, on his appointment, apparently telling the warding staff to 'fill up any gaps'. The NPG was not fully restored to its pre-war state until 1956, just three years before my arrival.

I cannot begin to describe the utter loneliness I felt in my early years at the NPG. Until then I had always been one of a group, at school, at college and as a postgraduate. But now it was just me and three other members of senior staff. There was no question of fraternizing with the secretaries, who still drank warm milk at eleven every morning as Hake had thought that they looked peaky. Sometimes whole days would pass with barely a word exchanged. Isolation was intensified by the fact that the Gallery's offices had been converted from what had once been public galleries. A long, echoing corridor acted as its spine off which opened spacious rooms for the Director's office and boardroom, the typing pool and so on. By means of a narrow iron spiral staircase I descended to the basement, in which I sat at a partner's desk looking out onto a well, lined with white ceramic tiles, leading on to – if I looked up – the iron railings behind Irving.

Upstairs, in what was called the boardroom, Kingsley sat at a desk sited at the end of the meeting table. There he quietly presided, white-haired and pale, his face somewhat sad and browbeaten. He was long-suffering – and you would need to be to be married to Christine Adams. Kingsley had his own secretary, Maureen Sloan. My only daily contact with him was at teatime, when a tray was placed at the opposite end of the room and by a process of osmosis we were to assemble, grab a copy of *The Times*, *The Burlington Magazine* or *Country Life* and sit at the table with a few hesitant exchanges of conversation like 'Has anyone got into Drayton?' or 'How many Duchesses of Bedford are there?' If I wrote a letter to anyone with a title it had to be looked at by the Director to see that the correct form of address had been used. It was Hake who had coached David Piper in how to behave towards the upper classes, with reserved friendship, politeness but not subservience. I always feel torn in my judgement of Kingsley. On the one hand I have a deep sense of gratitude for his kindness to me but, on the other, it is difficult not to feel that he was gutless and stick-in-the-mud. In a way Hake had neutered him. I always felt that what I did when I became Director must have come as a terrible shock to him, the changes were so quick and abrupt and so successful. Cancer took him but by then – and typically – he had put me up for membership of the Athenæum, a true gesture of reconciliation.

I suppose that judgement 'gutless' springs from one incident which took place during my years in the Gallery's basement. The NPG had on loan from the Duke of Leeds Goya's famous portrait of the Duke of Wellington, not that much was made of the fact. In 1961 the loan was withdrawn and the portrait was put into the saleroom, where it was purchased for £140,000 by the American collector Charles Wrightsman. The National Gallery had wanted the picture and when the government decided to step forward and purchase it for the nation it was to the National Gallery that it went, to be stolen shortly afterwards. What I could never understand was Kingsley's resignation to this sequence of events that was, I felt, deeply humiliating to the NPG. It was the attitude that this sort of picture was not for us and beyond our means. I could not understand why he did not fight for it but just passively watched it slip away. It left an indelible impression on me and I swore that if ever I became Director and a similar situation arose I would fight tooth and nail for the object. Almost within weeks of my appointment a lender was going to put Thomas Hudson's portrait of the composer Handel with the score of *Messiah* before him into the saleroom. My response was to launch the Gallery's first-ever public appeal and Joan Sutherland sang *Messiah* in the Albert Hall in aid of it. As a consequence the portrait hangs still in the NPG today.

Herald of sixties change: Pete, alias David Piper, relaxed and alert, 1965.

Now David Piper, or Pete as he was always called, was a very different character. His background, like that of so many other people in museum service at the time, bore no relation to what comes now from the Courtauld Institute of Art 'production line'. He had left Cambridge in 1940 with a First in medieval and modern languages. Joining the Indian Army, he had the misfortune to be captured by the Japanese in Malaya and spent over three years in a prisoner-of-war camp. The effect on him was inevitably traumatic and I recall that he could not even go into a room if he knew a Japanese person was there. The American man-of-letters and impresario Lincoln Kirstein reckoned that Piper's novel *Trial by Battle* (1959) was one of great books of the Second World War.

Immediately after the war Pete had married and wanted initially to take up where he had left off in academe, until Professor Vivian Galbraith pointed out that there was a vacancy at the NPG. Hake, in Pete's words, wanted 'some reliable young man, a blue-eyed boy, to cheer his declining years'. Pete was fortunate enough to fulfil Hake's three criteria: he had to have an Oxbridge degree, to have had 'a difficult or nasty war of it', and he must have no connection with the hated Courtauld Institute of Art.

Pete was a multi-talented man and I have often wondered whether Hake ever appreciated how remarkable he was. I think not. R.J.B. Walker described him well in the *Oxford Dictionary of National Biography*:

> Striking in appearance, slim and elegant, Piper was tall and elegant as a young man, with large brown eyes. Latterly a scholarly stoop disguised his height. At all times his rather lugubrious face could suddenly be lit up by an enormous and friendly smile.

He was devoted to the National Portrait Gallery, wrote the seventeenth-century catalogue and one apposite book, *The English Face* (1957), an elegant and delightful introduction to English portraiture. Essentially, however, I see him as a man of letters and I often felt that his mind was elsewhere. He wrote novels under the name Peter Towry and his house on Hammersmith Mall was a haven for the avant-garde of the Royal Court. His *Companion Guide to London* (1964), for which Pete would walk the streets of the capital in the early hours before arriving at the NPG, ran through several editions. He was, in addition, an accomplished broadcaster and journalist. In retrospect I wish that Frances Yates had not attached a health warning to him – although that in fact tended to incite in me a wish to follow in what she regarded as the same tainted footsteps. Pete, like Frances Yates, was kept going by cigarettes. Once an hour or so he left the building to walk round the block smoking a cigarette and then come back in again to resume the task in hand.

His role as Director of the NPG, and subsequently of both the Fitzwilliam and the Ashmolean museums, lay in the future in 1959. That year finds him as number two. In 1946 he had described his role as administering the rostering of the warding staff to cover a six-and-a-half-day week and dealing with all the complexities of their pay. It also included liaising with the Ministry of Works, which maintained the building and the boiler and provided the nightwatchmen. In addition, he dealt with Her Majesty's Stationery Office (which Hake hated and with which he refused to deal) and coped with the library and the ordering of books. What was to happen in the coming decades was that gradually new staff arrived and took on one or other aspect of his multifaceted job.

Looking back from the second decade of the twenty-first century, it is incredible that such a great institution was not far off a one-man band. By the time I arrived things had moved on. John Kerslake had been appointed as an extra Assistant Keeper, and onto his shoulders fell the library and the ordering of books, together with the putative eighteenth-century catalogue. My advent, to another new post, meant that the library and books now came my way, while Works were passed to John.

I had been warned that my first two years would be spent in penury. They were. In 1946 David Piper was paid £517 per annum as an Assistant Keeper II. In 1959 I received a little over £700, supplemented a little by an allowance recognizing the expense of living in London and fees gained from inspecting works of art to decide whether or not they should be exempt from tax by the Estate Duty Office. But real change only came in August 1963, when I was made an Assistant Keeper I and my salary suddenly doubled to £1,400.

So I sat in the basement in an area that had been cleared for me. On the partner's desk I found a blotter, a container filled with blue-black ink and a pen. Behind me was a bookcase filled with *carte de visite* photographs by Camille Silvy. No one ever looked at them; photography at that stage was no part of the scenario. In fact, photographs were regarded with a sniffy condescension: the only photograph hanging on the Gallery's walls was one of Mrs Beaton, the cook. Over tea we would be regaled with terrible stories of how an academician had once been unmasked painting over a photograph and how we had to keep our eyes open to guard against such deceptions. The NPG had something called the National Photographic Record, a ghastly mechanism whereby once a person had risen to a certain status he sat for a photographic portrait. Also before my arrival, the Gernsheim Collection was offered to the NPG but it would have involved having to take on Helmut and Alison Gernsheim, regarded as people who were more than difficult. The fact that this did not happen was viewed therefore with some relief. In 1963 their collection went to the University of Texas.

In front of me stretched serried ranks of thousands of old saleroom catalogues and it was my task, with the assistance of another new member of staff, Caroline Brown, to sort through them and dump the superfluous. I was also put on to filing photographs of portraits. Not long after, I began to be let loose on the public, members of which could arrive any afternoon clutching a portrait and ask for it to be verified. Primitive though all this may seem, it is in fact a marvellous way to learn. A person arrives and unwraps a picture which has to be placed in terms of costume, style and identity. In addition, one had to acquire finesse in terms of courtesy and the choice of words when delivering the verdict to the owner.

Every Monday afternoon, when the auction houses were active, there would be a visit to Christie's and Sotheby's and, occasionally, Bonhams. One always took the catalogue and was expected to annotate it as to what this or that object was. Then, over tea, it would be decided what should be photographed. From time to time there would be the bonus of expeditions to country houses or to the Royal Collection, all of which were filled from floor to ceiling with portraits good, bad and indifferent. Until then I had never learnt how to examine a picture as a physical object. The result of all this baptism by fire was that you learnt an awful lot. Even now, half a century on, I can still go round any country house and get virtually all of the attributions of the portraits right. I can still examine a canvas or a panel in terms of its physical condition and whether the surface has been extended or reduced, as well as being aware of over-paint and later additions.

To me also fell that drudgery *The Annual Report*, a slim volume which followed a set format, listing off the Trustees, a few succinct paragraphs on this or that followed by a catalogue of what had been acquired during the year. In the report for 1958–9 there were forty-two portraits acquired, the Purchase Grant rose from £1,200 to £4,000, there was a series of six public lectures attended by an average of sixty-nine people and there were two modest exhibitions, one of portraits of Oliver Cromwell and the other of Elizabeth I, it being the four-hundredth anniversary of her accession. Not much had changed by 1962–3, when thirty-seven portraits entered the collection, the Purchase Grant stood at £4,756, the seventeenth-century catalogue was published and the average attendance at lectures was seventy-one.

That annual chore went hand in hand with another, the annual display of the principal acquisitions, which always opened on Boxing Day, working on the theory that the critics would have nothing else to write about. The presentation was drear, the framing done under the aegis of Barbara Isherwood Kay, the widow of an Assistant Keeper at the National Gallery whom Kingsley Adams had rescued from penury. From the moment I arrived I knew she had taken against me, reducing me at times to a stutter. Her task was to keep the Gallery register. Otherwise she spent her time cutting out awful brown-paper mounts and checking on her stock-market shares in *The Times*.

The hub of the Gallery was the Guthrie Room, so named because it had once housed Sir James Guthrie's group portrait of the leading statesmen of the victorious allies in the First World War. If you were interested in British art, as I was, which was rare, the Guthrie Room was a gold mine, crammed with unpublished material. There were ranks of solander boxes filled with photos of portraits under kings and queens, filed alphabetically by sitter, artist and painter. That was complemented by a massive paper index, filing drawers stuffed full of references. Stretching around the walls and out through other rooms were shelves laden with peerages, copies of *Who's Who*, catalogues of private and public collections and others on portrait painters.

The days hardly changed in their routine, year in and year out. The working hours were 9.30 a.m. to 5.30 p.m., Monday to Friday. A Saturday roster was formed and if you did Saturday you got Monday off. That suited me very well, as the only single member of staff. On Saturday I had the freedom of the place to work on what I fancied. There was another bonus: the Gallery paid for one's membership of the London Library in St James's Square. All I had to do was fill in a slip of paper with the printed heading 'Mr Roy Strong presents his compliments to the Librarian and requests the loan of the following books' and a warder would go off to fetch them.

Relationships were extremely formal, although slightly less so than under Hake, for the senior staff now called each other by their first names. But the secretaries were always referred to as Miss This or Miss That. They were recruited via *The Lady* and the thickness of the notepaper and the address were studied to establish whether the applicant was well enough provided for to work for the poor pay we offered. There was no ladies' lavatory, so anyone wishing to use one had to walk past me, key in hand, and proceed through a door at the end of the room to the public facilities. There had in fact been no public lavatories of any form until David Piper presided over their installation after the war.

Members of the warding staff were referred to by their surnames in the tradition of officers and men. Friday was payday, when they lined up and were handed it in cash in a brown paper envelope by the Head Warder. There were no female warders. Warders operated the switchboard and served behind the counter in what passed as some kind of shop, selling only photographs of every single portrait in the collection (a point of pride) and a selection of postcards printed in sepia on card which curled. There were a few coloured cards but they were regarded with suspicion as bearing little resemblance to the originals. The guide to the Gallery was unillustrated, yet if a portrait was removed or introduced to the display it was a cause for major consternation. Mrs Isherwood Kay would survey the existing text and work out how an adjustment could be made without disturbing any other page. My favourite memory is of her inventing the phrase: 'Now we take a backcast up the stairs' to match exactly the number of letters being replaced on the page.

Yet again I found myself enmeshed in another timeless, closed world. As the Guthrie Room contained photographs of portraits in private collections, it was not easy of access: there was a strong feeling against communication to the wider world. It was as it were an arcana for the few. I recall saying to David Piper what a disgrace it was that the Gallery had been in existence for over a century and yet was devoid of any proper catalogues. I was swiftly put down, being told that it was a very vulgar thing to communicate information, which, coming from him, was somewhat surprising. But such an attitude was then fairly prevalent in the national collections. It lingered on in the Victoria and Albert Museum when I was appointed Director and discovered, for example, in the case of the Keeper of Sculpture, John Beckwith, that as long as he was head of department no scholar was ever allowed to examine a single object under his care.

I was, as I said, lonely and isolated, so much so that in my second year I really wanted to get out of the place. Frances Yates, who had found me the job, was far from pleased when I told her: 'as she rightly said, the successive volte-face in subject matter on my part makes me not very attractive to an interviewing board.' She was peeved but I was terrified that if I left it for another three years I might never be able to escape. The problem was that those who had come up with me were now scattered to the various provincial universities, where at least there was a more lively social interplay. I had yet to make friends and put down roots in what was a new field: the museum profession.

Everything in the Gallery centred on the Trustees' meetings. These happened four times a year: in February, June, October and December. On those occasions the place was swept, dusted and polished – above all the corridor floor, which always reeked of disinfectant on meeting days. After the event we all gathered for tea to discover what had been accepted or purchased, or any other decision they had made. The Trustees were appointed for a term of seven years by the Prime Minister; as far as I was concerned in those early NPG years, they might just as well have been beings from outer space. I sat and cowered in the basement until they had gone. There was no informal mingling with the curatorial staff. The Trustees were as gods.

Shortly after I arrived I was exhumed from the basement to be presented to them like some exotic specimen. I only have memories of the reaction of two of them. One was the chairman, Sir Geoffrey Keynes, brother of John Maynard, surgeon, bibliophile, friend of Rupert Brooke, Blake scholar and balletomane. His was a welcoming and benign presence. He was to remain Chairman until 1966, the year before my appointment as Director. That, as far as I remember, was my only encounter with him for, as far as the Board was concerned, we were 'below decks'. I do, however, remember a happy encounter later, years after I had married, at the Royal Opera House when there was a revival of the ballet for which he wrote the scenario, Ninette de Valois's *Job*, with its Vaughan Williams music and sets by John Piper, based on the drawings of William Blake. By then I had arrived and was married to a descendant of the Oxford Victorian intellectual aristocracy.

Keynes was one memory; the other was Sir Harold Nicolson, diplomat, politician and writer, as well as husband of Vita Sackville-West of Sissinghurst fame. I remember this very distinctly, as it was though a stave had been driven through me. As I was steered towards him he just looked at me and said 'We never appointed you', and turned his back on me. That incident still rattles around in my mind all these years later: a sense of social rejection by a man who, with his wife, dismissed anyone they considered 'bedint'.

During those early years the Trustees were just names on a piece of paper to me, and were to remain so until I became Director. They included the likes of Lord Ilchester, Sir Thomas Merton, Viscount De L'Isle, Field Marshal Sir Gerald Templer and Robert Wyndham Ketton-Cremer. They came and they went, as to their ranks were added Lord Euston, soon to be Duke of Grafton, the novelist Anthony Powell and the painter Lawrence Gowing. Their term of office was, as I said, seven years, and what set our arrangement apart from other institutions was that at the NPG that term of office could be multiplied *sine die*. The Trustees were chosen to represent and pronounce upon different fields of national endeavour, such as the Army, the Navy, the world of letters and the arts, scholarship, and so on. The Board was virtually without exception the old Establishment: male, white, public school and Oxbridge, only partly aristocratic and belonging to what was still at that time more or less an interrelated caste. My wife's aunt, Carola Oman, Lady Lenanton, the first-ever woman trustee of a national collection, was the only woman – which at least reflected a degree of enterprise. But the NPG Board did stand apart from those of similar institutions, as Andrea Geddes Poole's recent study has demonstrated, by the fact that there was no bloodbath between trustees and the executive as happened so often elsewhere. This was due more than anything to the skill and tact of the directors, including, surprisingly, the querulous Hake, but also to the fact that the Gallery's focus was not aesthetic but historical, with the consequence that the Board was not stuffed with opinionated aristocrats and each member was chosen for a particular expertise they could bring to the table. It was also aided by the fact that there were no dramatic changes or innovations proposed to fuel division and dissent.

At that period no one but no one was appointed whose prime role would be that of laying their hands on money. That lay two decades off. Nothing as squalid as finance ever raised its head, but rather nods of assent or dissent as to whether the portrait of this or that person was worthy to be admitted to the national pantheon. Access was circumscribed by something called the Ten Year Rule: that no likeness of anyone who had been dead for less than a decade was to be brought before the Trustees. It was later to be my task to begin the process of sweeping that away.

There was something stifling, feudal and sterile about this. It was a means whereby the old Establishment maintained its hold on affairs in the new democratic age. Lloyd, Lord Kenyon, already a Trustee when I arrived, was to be Chairman of the Board from 1966 to 1986. He was educated at Eton and Magdalen College, Oxford, and a monument to a litany of boards, hospitals, libraries, the University of North Wales and the National Museum of Wales among them. He spent his life moving from one board meeting to the next as, he once told me, part of his aristocratic duty of service. He had arrived at the NPG thanks to a conversation over lunch at the Beefsteak Club with one whom he knew as Stavvy Ilchester. But over the next few years things began to shift. I always associate this with the arrival of the future Sir 'Jack' Plumb, whose background was grammar school and University College, Leicester, before he found a foothold at Christ's College, Cambridge. Plumb was a herald of a new establishment group, the academic powermongers. As Kenyon once dismissively said to me with distaste, 'He's the sort of man who buys other people's silver.' The Trustees were never seen between meetings, they never appeared at any private view of an exhibition and I never recall encountering one of them, ever, in the public galleries – although there was an annual inspection of the galleries, which most of them generally skipped. They were, however, absolute, and even chose the ghastly wallpapers.

And yet these were the years when the NPG was crying out for a fighter, for the National Gallery was at its most aggressive, planning to swallow up the NPG and for us to be accommodated in a new building on what was referred to as the Hampton Site, now occupied by the new wing of the National Gallery. This came to the surface in 1963; my lowly role was to measure up the linear footage required to hang all the existing portraits on display in a single line at a 44-inch centre. I had no idea what was going on and was never told. Virtually everything was reactive rather than proactive. There was a sense of drift and the endless repetition of an immutable fixed cycle of how things should be done. The idea of an exhibition programme, a publication and education policy did not exist, and this, as time went by, rendered the NPG increasingly anachronistic. There was not even an accounts section. Once a year someone called Molly Lochnane descended from the Treasury, the next year's financial allocation was argued over and settled, and that was it.

———

In order to get anywhere, I needed to make a mark. The first exhibition with which I was ever involved carried the somewhat deadening title *Some Portraits of Charles II*; this was cobbled together in 1959 for the three-hundredth anniversary of the Restoration in 1960. David Piper

assembled the paintings, which included the beautiful group portrait of
the king dancing with his sister from the Royal Collection. Not everything, however, went according to plan: when the Gallery van arrived at
Parham to collect a portrait it was found not to fit, so the warders, much
to Mrs Tritton's horror, suggested tying it on to the roof. My task was
to assemble the engravings and medals to demonstrate the projection
of the king within the idiom of the baroque. There was a private view
but no one came. I was galled.

So far I have not mentioned Benedict Nicolson, who enters my life
at this point. Eldest son of Vita and Harold, his upbringing ticked all
the establishment boxes: Eton, Balliol, the friendship of Isaiah Berlin,
John Pope-Hennessy, Philip Toynbee and Bernard Berenson. Ben had
been Deputy Surveyor of the King's Pictures under Anthony Blunt
and in 1947 became editor of *The Burlington Magazine.* Under his
inspired editorship it gained an unassailable status as the vehicle for
art-historical discourse. His editorials were magisterial and he saw
that the magazine's contents were of the highest order and written in
English of a kind which was readable by any educated person. His was
a shambling, benign presence like an old dog moving around nudging
people. He was particularly encouraging to the young. Although a small
article of mine on the miniaturist Nicholas Hilliard had appeared in
1959, it was 1963 that was to be my *annus mirabilis* in the magazine and
that began with my article 'Holbein's Cartoon for the Barber-Surgeons
Rediscovered' in January.

This was my first opportunity to shine at the NPG, and it came my
way quite by chance when a set of X-rays taken by a member of the
Royal College of Surgeons landed on my desk. They had already sat
around for some months when David Piper, who was off to the United

States, pushed them my way. They were X-rays of what, until then, was thought to be a seventeenth-century copy of Holbein's group painting of Henry VIII bestowing the charter on the Company of Barber-Surgeons. The X-rays revealed, however, that the paint was over paper which was pin-pricked, so the question arose of whether there was a Holbein cartoon underneath it, like the one of Henry VIII which was by then on display in the Tudor Gallery.

In the October of the previous year I had written to Jan:

Did I tell you about this? There are two version of Holbein's famous group of the Barber-Surgeons, that in the possession of the Barbers Company and what has always been thought to be a seventeenth-century copy in the possession of the Royal College of Surgeons. The latter has been x-rayed and reveals a lost Holbein cartoon beneath. As you can imagine such a find is sensational in the extreme even though for the present there seems no likelihood of getting the layers of paint off the top to get back to the original drawing. The only thing which is certainly Holbein visible in the x-rays are the pin-pricks, thousands of them (the x-ray would go straight through the original carbon drawing). This has meant screwing my eyes up over a magnifying glass and joining all the dots up with white paint and reconstructing the Cartoon. As David Piper has gone off to the States and the exhibition is scheduled for late December the whole thing has been thrust onto me to prepare. I have been working like a slave as I have promised to produce an article or preliminary report on it for *The Burlington Magazine* by mid-November so that it can appear in the January issue simultaneously with the opening of the exhibition and thus give it a little publicity as we as a gallery are too poor to afford a poster [I in fact got one]. I have worked non-stop at this which has meant a mass of reading up on Holbein and a lot of messing around with pots of glue and paint and rushing around with technical experts taking paint samples for chemical analysis. I have finished however the first draft of the article and expect to be out of

the wood by the end of next week. This means I shall have articles
appearing four months running in the *Burlington.*

The story continues on 30 December:

> The Holbein has driven me mad and will continue to do so until
> it opens. From the moment I get into that Gallery to the moment
> I leave it is an unending battle over curtains, lighting, wallpaper,
> captions and so on. A turning up while B doesn't only to find that
> C hadn't brought the necessary tools anyway. Forays for invitation
> cards, for posters, for a gorgeous *mise-en-scène* of yards of rich
> damask and rich wallpapers, for good lighting, for scaffolds and
> screens to be built to take the exhibits. Added to this the actual
> object has been a worry as the wretched man [Stephen Rees-Jones
> of the Courtauld] who has been cleaning a piece of it wouldn't make
> up his mind until the Friday before Christmas as to whether or not it
> was the lost Cartoon. Now the pin-pricks fit and he has established
> that the first layer of colour is repaint (i.e. it goes over the pin-
> pricks) he believes it is.

And the finale on 11 January:

> I wish you had been here to share in the triumph. No one quite real-
> ized that this was the cartoon until it was launched and now it is out
> it has of course caused a sensation. 'X-rays reveal hidden Art Riches'
> chorused the papers and £300,000 was a mooted price. After going
> nearly mad in the last-minute preparations for the exhibition it
> opened with everything perfect, the carpet going down an hour
> before it opened. I'd fought and it came off. No more soul-destroying
> private views with 10 people turning up but one lured some of the
> rank and fashion ... I feel a sense of achievement both personally and
> for the Gallery.

For the first time ever the Ministry of Works had carried out the
installation I wanted, with the final painting, the Cartoon and the
mounted X-rays exhibited side by side. The result was that the exhibition

was extended a month and during January and February the NPG attracted some nineteen thousand more visitors than for the same period the previous year.

The first letter to Jan mentions several more articles to appear in the *Burlington*:

> The three articles on Robert Peake, Hieronimo Custodis and Marcus Gheeraerts the Younger have all been finished and checked and sent off to the *Burlington* to appear from next February onwards. The editor [Ben Nicolson] was most flattering about them, even though I must admit (with modesty) that they are a major breakthrough in a field over which an impenetrable fog has hung for far too long.

At that period Elizabethan painting was a complete mystery. A large number of pictures existed and there was a list of painters known, but the two were never brought together. There were occasional signed paintings but they were very, very few. So what was this breakthrough?

Strangely, it went back to a paper given by Frances Yates at the Warburg Institute. These lectures were called 'internals' – or, more generally, 'infernals'. Frances had tried to link the famous portrait of Elizabeth I known as the Ditchley Portrait with another depicting a lady attired as a Persian virgin crowning a weeping stag. Setting that to one side, what she did point out was that both pictures had cartouches with poems within them, which, I noted, were in an identical script. As she projected these images, it crossed my mind that I must investigate further.

The Gallery photographic archive, as I have said, was a hugely underused resource, so I began to pull out photographs of Elizabethan portraits and group them by the calligraphy of their inscriptions. Until then there were only two pictures known certainly to be by Robert Peake but one of those included a quite idiosyncratic way of adding the date

A breakthrough into a forgotten era of English painting: the discovery that certain painters repeated a formula for inscribing the date and age of their sitters, thereby enabling their *œuvre* to be reconstituted.

and the age of the sitter. I quickly assembled thirteen other pictures, all with an identical form of inscription and all in the same style. The same happened in the case of an exiled Antwerp painter, Hieronimo Custodis. In his case there were three signed portraits but his script was so idiosyncratic that once again a little bouquet of portraits was speedily assembled. And lastly, applying the same technique, seven more portraits by Marcus Gheeraerts could be added to his œuvre. And so 'Elizabethan Painting: An Approach through Inscriptions' appeared running through the February to April issues of the *Burlington Magazine*. I had art-historically arrived and these were to be the foundation stones of my book *The English Icon: Elizabethan and Jacobean Portraiture* six years later, by which time much else had happened.

Frances Yates had no interest in scholarly work of this kind and once somewhat dismissively told me that I had an 'eye' as though it were some flaw in one's make-up. Nor did she warm to any form of cataloguing, regarded by her as work fit only for antiquarian drudges. But that had been the prime reason for my recruitment to the NPG, to catalogue its early portrait collection. Indeed, I was put on to this formidable task very shortly after I arrived. In retrospect it is interesting to note David Piper's recollections of his work on the seventeenth-century collection, as it was radically affected by the era of hierarchy and forelock-touching that still lingered at the Gallery. Pete had modelled his entries on those by Sir Martin Davies cataloguing the National Gallery's early Netherlandish pictures. He produced a series of specimen entries, which were then butchered by Sir Henry Hake and the Chairman, Lord Ilchester. Davies, of course, had taken it for granted that he could set any National Gallery picture within the context of other versions of the same picture and discuss their status as being wholly by the master, the studio or a later copy. Pete realized that it was essential to deal with the NPG's portraits in exactly the same way, recording various versions and setting each portrait within the sitter's total iconography. Ilchester and Hake saw this as a horrendous and impertinent infringement of private property rights and ruled that Pete could only ever refer to portraits in public collections. To write that a portrait in a private collection was a copy was seen as an intrusion into someone's privacy. Neither the identity nor the attribution of any portrait in a private collection was ever to be questioned.

Interestingly, when I embarked on the Tudor and Jacobean catalogue I was never told this; however, it did resonate a little when the prickly Viscount De L'Isle was far from pleased when, this same year, in my *Portraits of Queen Elizabeth I*, I pointed out that the painting purportedly showing Elizabeth dancing the volta with the Earl of Leicester depicted a ball at the Valois court. By 1959 the Courtauld Institute had begun its photographic survey of pictures in country houses and, as a consequence, hundreds of photographs of portraits began to pour into the reference collection. In writing my catalogue it never occurred to me that I should not refer to them. It was equally clear from the outset that each sitter's entire iconography would have to be considered and key items not in the Gallery's possession also reproduced. I rapidly learnt that cataloguing was not a discipline to be despised and was reaching new levels of sophistication. When *Tudor and Jacobean Portraits* finally appeared in 1969, it was rightly regarded as a landmark. It had absorbed a decade of my life, my enthusiasm for it ebbing and flowing along the way. What is satisfying is that a catalogue, as it were, grows in the dark, each entry being a self-contained study. And so they pile up until, one day, hey presto, it is there.

Such cataloguing at this stage in the NPG's post-war history was not easy. Every picture had to be examined out of its frame, which only made me realize how most of them were sunk under repaint and discoloured varnish; but there was nothing to be done about it. No one visiting the Tudor gallery today, where so many of the pictures sparkle, would realize how deadening some of these looked. But Adams subscribed to Hake's anti-cleaning principles. As the NPG had no technical department, we had to rely on the charity of the National Gallery. Joyce Plesters was a generous and charming colleague but only a mere handful of our pictures were ever subject to her examination. And only towards the final stages of writing my catalogue did I meet Dr John Fletcher, one of the early pioneers of dendrochronology, the dating of panel pictures based on the tree-ring growth establishing the date of felling and hence the likely date of the object.

What can be said in favour of the catalogue at this point in my life is that so little happened at the NPG that I could just get on with it. And that I benefited so enormously from an accumulation of material stretching back a century to Scharf's brilliant pencil sketches of portraits he had seen in collections long since dispersed. Then there were photographs, sometimes whole boxes of them, of portraits of a particular sitter, not to mention envelopes containing what were called 'Icon Notes'. All of this was waiting to be exploited, put in order, synthesized and made available to the public.

I find it fascinating that it was my final rift with Frances Yates in March 1966 that spurred me on to finish:

> The result of the disturbance caused by her was to throw myself into a final paralysing paroxysm of labour on the Catalogue – I FINISHED IT – (fell ill the day after). Can it really be true after seven years? I

cannot grasp the fact yet. It is an immense achievement and I feel a vague glow and thrill about it all. In the form I have devised it will be a unique, new form of reference book. Why the Dutch haven't done it some years ago seemed to David Piper and I very strange. The labour of creation and accumulation has ended – now the introduction and indexes which can be written when the catalogue is in galley [those were the days!]. How I long to see those three volumes on the shelf.

In fact it turned out to be two volumes, one of 450 pages of text and the other with 700 pages of plates. And, of course – unlike today – it was to take three years to grind its way through Hake's monster, the HMSO.

I have digressed somewhat to complete the tale of the catalogue, taking us three years on from what was for me the *annus mirabilis* of 1963. That had as its finale the first exhibition I ever staged on my own, *The Winter Queen: Elizabeth, Queen of Bohemia and Her Family*. This also came my way by chance. It was the consequence of a huge exhibition mounted in the castle in Heidelberg on England and the Palatinate in the seventeenth century, to which large numbers of pictures from Britain had been lent, above all from the collection of the Earls of Craven, direct descendants of the Winter Queen's admirer. The opportunity presented itself for the British loans to be displayed at the NPG before being dispersed back to their various collections. I organized this virtually single-handed, with the help of the Gallery's art-school-trained library assistant, Caroline Brown. A letter to Jan van Dorsten captures something of the exhilaration I felt. I had just returned from my first visit to the United States:

I tottered off the plane to sleep for two days and into the NPG to find pictures arriving from Heidelberg for *The Winter Queen*, the

Innovative biographical collage. A showcase in *The Winter Queen* exhibition, 1963, in which books, drawings, miniatures and photographs were arranged to tell a story, in this case that of Elizabeth, Queen of Bohemia's childhood at Combe Abbey in the charge of Lord Harington.

whole place crawling with Works people putting up curtains, lights, moving in showcases. Every day I seemed to stand in that gallery watching everything done by those workmen or else disaster. The hanging required so much thought and the layout of the cases with their juxtaposition of manuscripts, miniatures, drawings, jewels, etc. I found the latter very exciting and I think we managed to evolve a quite new way of display.

I had learnt earlier that year how to harness the resources of the Ministry of Works and I was determined to give vent to all my frustrated urges for proper design and display. Here was an opportunity to be seized. Looking back, it was done with a frenzy of amateurism, getting the walls painted or covered with yards of pleated butter muslin, persuading the carpenter to up-end old Victorian showcases, which we lined with wallpaper imitating watered silk, and arranged miniatures, books and other objects like a still life, ordering blow-ups of contemporary engravings which told the story of the Queen's journey to the Palatinate. The aim was to present something quite new in exhibition terms: the biographical exhibition. The anonymous *Times* critic succinctly understood what I was attempting to do, writing that the exhibition,

> [which] tells the story of the Princess Elizabeth, daughter of James I, in portraiture and in a variety of paintings, drawings, engravings, and documents, is the first of its kind and a highly successful experiment in historical story-telling which suggests that many other historical characters and themes may find similar graphic illustration.

It was to be the fount of my rearrangement of the public galleries under Piper, as we shall see, and of later exhibitions on Samuel Pepys, Richard III and Sir Thomas More.

Other aspects were also new to the NPG. It was the first exhibition ever to have something resembling a proper illustrated catalogue, although the Director had reservations about whether such an innovation would have to be priced beyond what the visitor could afford. I seem to recall that it cost two shillings and sixpence and 3,779 were sold. It was a modest affair but had some plates and, another great breakthrough, the cover reproduced a portrait of the Winter Queen that was in the Royal Collection. Never but never, I was told, under any circumstances, could any Royal Collection item be used for a poster or a cover. As far as I am aware this was the first occasion when this was allowed. The exhibition opened on 22 November 1963, with a proper invitation to a proper private view and a proper poster. A lunch was also given by the German ambassador, attended by the Prince of Prussia.

During the exhibition's run it attracted 10,000 more visitors than usual to the NPG. And through the post came a letter of congratulation, written in his own hand, from the Director of the V&A, Sir Trenchard Cox. I was touched at such thoughtfulness. The initial response to the exhibition was slow but bit by bit it gained momentum, and I prepared a script for the television programme *Monitor.* As I wrote to Jan, I also received 'many letters of appreciation from the public. The latter makes the whole thing worthwhile just to get a letter from someone one has never met but who must write to say Thank You.'

These were the years during which I made my somewhat hesitant debut as a lecturer. I gave my first public lecture at the V&A on 15 January 1959, just seven months before I joined the National Portrait Gallery. That I must have owed to Frances Yates's friendship with Renée Marcousé of the Museum's Education Department, in whose employ also was the formidable Helen Lowenthal. I was later to fall out dramatically with Lowenthal when she greeted me, on being appointed Director of the V&A, with the words: 'You should never have been made Director.' But all that lay fifteen years off when I took the stage and delivered my lecture entitled 'Pageantry and Ceremonial in the Elizabethan Court Year'. The occasion terrified me, as I then feared speaking in public (much made up for later in life!); but as it was illustrated with slides, from the moment I began the house lights went down and I became unconscious of the scattered audience. And, of course, I was in love with the topic, which certainly fired the audience so much so that one elderly couple came down and thanked me profusely for the pleasure I had given them. I always remember that moment, for it was one of life's turning points. Until then it had never occurred to me that I was capable of giving people information and delight. I recall thinking how wonderful it was to have such an ability, to be able to reach out to ordinary people and enlighten them about the past.

Two years later the two people who thanked me after that event asked me to deliver the first of what was to be an annual lecture which they endowed for something called The Barnet Society. I was pleased to accept, and wrote to Jan van Dorsten:

> The two people who endowed the lecture heard me give the first lecture I ever gave ... over two years ago at the V&A and were apparently so pleased with it that they tracked me to the Gallery and asked me for a repeat performance. This sort of thing makes it really worthwhile. One always hopes that the listeners enjoy the material as much as oneself. I was curiously moved.

That ability to speak in public had been tested to the full the previous year, 1960, when I was asked to deliver a lecture to the Chelsea Society at its annual general meeting. This was the year in which I was involved in the NPG's somewhat disappointing gathering of Charles II's portraits. The subject I chose was the King's state entry into London and I wrote an account of this occasion to Jan:

> The Society is completely mad I may now observe and the meeting which preceded my lecture instead of being a genteel pat-on-the-back affair developed into a free-for-all. This largely arose out of the fact that the Annual Report had said that Lord Cadogan was pulling down beautiful Georgian houses in order to erect a monstrosity of a hotel which would bring 'foreigners' into the sacred precincts of Chelsea. His lordship turned out to be President of the Society and demanded an apology. Worse followed because the Annual Report insinuated that Chelsea Old Church was deliberately wrecking some of its sixteenth-century monuments by leaving them out in the churchyard to face the rigours of the English weather. This the vicar

got up and denounced amidst wild cheers from his supporters. The meeting continued with a violent quarrel about the colour of the lampposts in Chelsea. Meanwhile I was sitting on the platform with the rest of the would-be council of the Society not knowing whether to laugh, look shocked or smile enigmatically (which is not an easy thing to do).

The meeting, which was scheduled to last twenty minutes at the most, dragged on for over an hour and by the time that it came for my lecture there was a hasty stampede for the exits which was only counteracted by a friend of mine who cleverly secured all the doors, so that no more could flee the place. After ten to fifteen minutes with the most hostile audience I have ever coped with I succeeded to some extent in pacifying the storm and getting them interested in Charles II's pageants, in spite of the fact that the acoustics were appalling and I had almost to shout to be heard (which was odd considering that the Society had said that this room had the best acoustics in the whole of Chelsea and therefore, for them, in the whole of England).

Let this stand as an instance of the hazards of lecturing during these years. From time to time I was called upon to perform in horrendous venues across the country to minimal audiences: projectors exploded, slides melted, the sound system broke down and one was often lucky to get so much as a sandwich under a glass dome.

It was through this event that two characters entered my life who would figure quite largely, Margot Eates and E.H. Ramsden. In retrospect I would categorize ours as a threshold friendship, introducing me as it did to another world. Theirs was an unspoken lesbian partnership. Margot was large, somewhat florid of face and flamboyant of dress and with more than a liking for the bottle. When I kissed her in salutation

Curious but interesting couple: Hartley Ramsden and Margot Eates, 1987.

the make-up was so thick that I slid across her cheek. She had a deep, plummy voice and laid down the law on most things. Hartley was a diminutive dandy lifted straight out of the pages of the *Gazette du Bon Ton* from between the wars, who dressed as a man with an elegance a man can rarely if ever achieve with a stock, waistcoat and flared jacket. Her wavy hair was worn in an Eton crop, there was a degree of make-up and she affected a masculine angularity of movement.

Every year they went to Florence, staying at the Pensione Quisisana, and one year I joined them there. During the day we made stately visits to see the masterpieces they revered, and we even journeyed as far as Ravenna to see the mosaics. Margot would be her usual bossy self, exhorting Hartley from time to time to appreciate this or that feature in a work of art, exhorting her, 'Hartley, Hartley, notice how graciously the Madonna is gesturing to the donor'; Hartley's most memorable comment to me was: 'Why can't they say to one man to man?' Needless to say, we excited great curiosity wherever we went.

The extraordinary fact about them was that their unconventionality was coupled with such extreme conservatism. Things had never been the same, Hartley always averred, since carriages had vanished from Hyde Park. Margot had at one period worked in the Museum of London. During the period I knew them in the 1960s they both lived on limited means in a studio house in Mallord Street in Chelsea. The main feature of the house was a large studio room with a gallery. Its walls were cream and the paintwork a 1930s shade of blue. A large refectory table stood at its centre and nearby, over a chest, hung a superb Paul Nash of sunflowers. They had known Nash and both had been on the fringes of the Modernist movement, Hartley writing *An Introduction to Modern Art* in 1940. But in the period I knew her an obsession with Michelangelo had set in and in 1963 her translation of his letters was published. Their circle included the painter Eric de Maistre, the Italian actress Isa Miranda and the English actors Michael Denison and his wife Dulcie Gray (sometimes wickedly referred to as Gracie Dull). In 1960 there was an excitement about knowing such a couple, who were enthusiastic about the arts and generous to the young making their way. Unfortunately Julia found them repulsive, so that friendship went more or less into abeyance when we married.

I was twenty-four when I entered the NPG, an age by which many men are not only married, but fathers. By then friends from my research days were pairing off and marrying. The signals were there that this was what was expected to happen next. Both my brothers had already left home, Derek to a happy marriage and raising a family, Brian to a childless and less than happy one which ended in divorce and disaster. The path to marriage had not been a particularly happy one in either instance, thanks to my mother's obsessive hold over 'her boys': Derek's wife had to wait until she was twenty-one before they could proceed, and Brian married, to my mother's horror, an Irish Roman Catholic without telling her. I was to do something similar.

There I was, still stuck in that terrace house, albeit with more space thanks to the exit of two brothers, having a room upstairs which I could decorate and in which I could bring together those things that were precious to me, odd pieces from junk and antique shops along with the absurdity of a life-size plaster bust of the Emperor Marcus Aurelius from the British Museum – and, of course, books. 'Roy's far too sensible to marry', my mother always said as she continued within the wreckage of her own. Twice I seriously considered asking two very different women to marry me but I fell back from the resolution on contemplating the social gulf between their families and my own. In the case of the second I was beaten to it by someone who later became a colleague at the V&A. There, with tact, let it rest. But in the long run I was to be a very lucky man.

Socially I was still far from accomplished and this was a period of life when dinner parties began to figure, although the giving of one was not possible. I cannot remember how, but it somehow came back to me that I was considered a humourless bore. It came as quite

a shock, but it was one to which I responded. I therefore deliber-
ately set out to transform myself, if not into a delight at least into an
amusing companion at table. What I had to learn was that the English
distrust any exhibition of intellect: only those with a foreign name
like Bronowski or Gombrich could get away with it. I once wrote an
article in *The Times* which opened by saying that if my name had been
Strongski my whole life would have been different (shortly afterwards
George Steiner wrote a letter to me saying that in his case having a
foreign name had wrecked his). The English hide their intellect and
the fact that they might after all be serious beneath a froth of wit,
repartee and charm of manner. And this is what I set out to achieve,
albeit at a price, occasionally later being considered something of a
social butterfly.

By 1963 I had begun to put down roots and make friends within the
world of museums and galleries. Two were to be of lasting duration
and importance: one was Sir Oliver Millar, Surveyor of the Queen's
Pictures, and the other Dr John Hayes, my successor as Director of the
NPG. Oliver was the perfect courtier, gently deferential without being
obsequious, as one must be in any position in the Royal Household. He
had been trained at the Courtauld and his work cataloguing the English
pictures in the Royal Collection was to set new standards in terms of
thoroughness and scholarship. With his wife, Delia, an art historian in
her own right, they were a kind of double act that, thanks to the office
Oliver held, guaranteed entry into virtually every private collection in
the country. Delia would hold the torch while Oliver would make notes
on what he saw. The serious exploration of English art was new and

exciting in the late 1950s and early 1960s, and it was that which drew us together. I was deeply touched when he presented me with his magisterial two volumes on *Tudor, Stuart and Early Georgian Pictures in the Royal Collection* inscribed 'Roy Strong with gratitude and diffidence from Oliver 25 June 1963'. I treasure it still.

Oliver's passion was the seventeenth century, more especially Van Dyck's English period, of which he was to stage a memorable exhibition at the NPG. But his approach belonged very much to the connoisseur era, focusing on provenance and attribution. The placing of a work of art within its wider political, social and cultural context was not part of his make-up. Indeed, later in life, when we lunched either at the Garrick Club or at Brooks's, there was often a lament for the 'good old days' before British art had been colonized by Marxist art historians. Oliver had the virtue of seeing no one other than in a good light, which certainly accounts for the shattering effect on him of the unveiling of Anthony Blunt, for whom he had worked for so long, as a spy. That possibility had been doing the rounds of the fashionable chattering classes for years. But during the 1960s Oliver and I stood side by side as we worked to open up the field of English portraiture and its masters. It was Oliver with his ginger-tinged hair, his kindly smile and his enthusiasm who guided me through what were then the arcana of the Royal Collection.

John Hayes became a much closer friend as he was not, like Oliver, a husband and a father. He was unmarried and, in addition, had a car, which was to lead to us making country house tours together. John was six years older than me and in 1959 was an Assistant Keeper at the old Museum of London in Kensington Palace. He too was Courtauld trained and his whole life was to be dedicated to the art of Thomas

Gainsborough. As I developed my social skills I acted as the foil to this private, shy, reserved and, at times, awkward man. Bespectacled, he was endowed with features that gave him a look of perpetual surprise. He was never the master of any occasion and during his long (too long) directorship of the NPG, 1974 to 1994, would disappear into the corner of a room at any opening. We were, however, good company for each other in the pursuit of British painting. He became Director of the Museum of London in 1970, to be made redundant, shortly after, when the new museum was amalgamated with the Guildhall Museum and Art Gallery. Like Oliver Millar, Hayes was strangely unobservant of people, always telling me of his huge effect on women and of his happy relationship with his chairman, Lord Harcourt, who in fact couldn't stand him. But John was lucky as my move to the V&A opened up my post, into which he neatly slotted, solving a problem on both sides, for John had fought his redundancy via the Civil Service Union.

His end was awful, felled by a stroke which paralysed him down one side so that he was unable to speak, read or write. I visited him several times that autumn of 2005 but it was a living death; mercifully, he died on Christmas Day. As usual I wrote an account of him, prompted by his memorial service at St James's, Piccadilly, on Thursday 23 March:

> Suddenly spring arrived after a drear winter with bitter cold and never-ending leaden skies. This was the day of John Hayes's Service of Thanksgiving at St James's Piccadilly. It all went far better than I thought, although, frankly, as so often these days it was essentially a secular event. I never witnessed one flicker of faith in John. I noted that, as the words of so little of the service were printed, when it came to the Lord's Prayer how few people knew it any more. However, the centre of the church was full to the back so that was a relief. It was a plain and unadorned occasion, a few hymns, a piece

of Chopin, a little of Verdi's *Requiem,* a reading from Reynolds's
Discourses ... and two addresses, one by Derek Watson, former Dean
of Salisbury, and the other by me.

John remains, however, a person one never really knew, an
enigma, so buttoned up, so evasive, so locked within himself. I was
never asked to either of his houses, nor, it seems, was anyone else.
And yet he was thoughtful, kind, generous and devoid of malice.
He stayed too long at the NPG, wickedly getting an extension till
sixty-five out of Owen Chadwick, chairman of Trustees, between
meetings. The Board was not pleased. He was also too much in
America and much that happened was the work of Malcom Rogers,
now at Boston. He also made the NPG too like Tate Britain. But the
place never went back and innovations were consolidated.

For half a century he was obsessed by nothing but Gainsborough,
through whom he led a surrogate life, the painter, I suppose, being
what John would have liked to have been. He did not take kindly
to being challenged. When Adrienne Corri unearthed documents
which radically changed the accepted version of Gainsborough's life
he refused to accept them. He had that academic failing of 'owning'
a bit of the past upon which no one else had any right to impinge.

There was a moment in 1989 when I had quite a lot to do with
John when, as a consultant to Olympia & York and the Canary Wharf
Development, there was a proposal that the NPG should go there, but
it never happened. I wrote a little cameo of him on the day we voyaged
downriver, which depicts him as I shall always remember him:

John Hayes was late, which made things awkward, although he
was, as usual, oblivious of the fact. He flashed his teeth in his
accustomed manner as though they would somehow dispel the frosty
atmosphere. John Hayes is now sixty. The suit he had on must have
been at least twenty years old and was buttoned around him with
difficulty. His overcoat, which was of the same date, was buttoned

with even greater difficulty and I noticed that it had leather binding to cover up the frayed cuffs.

He needed a woman or partner of some kind to sort him out, but he never found one.

———

There was also at this period of my life annual travel for the first time. There's a bit of me that, like John Betjeman, is less than keen about 'abroad'; but in 1961, as the reader will already have discovered, there was a major tour of Italy and that country became a fixture from then on in my life. But 1962 and 1963 brought two other travel experiences, one which took me to Trebizond on the Black Sea and the other – far more relevant – to the museums and galleries of the east coast of the United States.

The trip to Trebizond was entirely the consequence of feeling that youth was slipping away fast and that I had never done anything so adventurous, so that if I was ever going to it must be now or never. The inspiration had come from Rose Macaulay's novel *The Towers of Trebizond*, with its unforgettable opening line, '"Take my camel, dear", said my Aunt Dot...' It was only on my return to England that I discovered that she had in fact never been and had spent her time pestering the great travel writer Freya Stark over details of the place. My companions were Sula Pfingst, who had got a First the same year as myself and was working for a doctorate under Charles Mitchell; John Olley, an architectural student who was shortly to become her husband; and Joy Winterbottom, who responded to an advertisement for a fourth person. I had just learned to drive that year and the four of us set off in a hired Dormobile for a trip which, in retrospect, seems wildly out of character for me.

The whole story of this disastrous expedition is told in a letter to Jan dated 13 September 1962:

let me tell you something about the tour. I'll start with the less cheering end, which in itself in retrospect was amusing. The accident happened last Saturday week, September 1st, when we were motoring on the way back home towards Ankara. I was driving. The road was unspeakable. I pulled over just that bit too much onto the rubble and sand to the right. In a moment the steering had gone and after a split second of swerves we were flying through the air off the road and into a ravine some ten to fifteen feet below the road surface. The luggage rack came off the vehicle and ended up under the front wheels, the windscreen was smashed, the windows broken, the bonnet and bodywork badly dented on all sides and the inside ripped away. We struggled out still conscious and, thank heaven; an American was passing by who helped us. The Turks stood by and looked. There is a law in Turkey, we subsequently discovered, saying that if you helped someone to a hospital you were liable for their bills.

We were all badly shaken up, cut and very bruised. One of the girls, Joy, had blood streaming all over the place from a cut over the eye. I had what proved to be a fractured clavicle for which I am receiving treatment here in England and still have my arm in a sling. In this condition we were carted off to the nearest hospital at a little mud town called Sungurlu. The hospital had no resident doctor, no x-ray equipment and no one could speak any other language than Turkish. After the binding up of wounds we were all put to be in one room (a mixed ward, the last one that I shall ever probably be in) and pumped full of hyperdermic syringes. I had six injections in the stomach in five minutes – never again. We had to keep our wits about us or the car would have been sacked. By dint of sign language we established a watchman on the car, had all movables transported to the local police station where Sula (minus broken spectacles) struggled down to make an independent inventory in English. We were all determined to get the hell out of

The vehicle

The crash

I leave the crash

I leave the hospital

BLAME ROSE MACAULAY: THE ROAD TO TREBIZOND

that hospital as soon as possible and put a brave face on it, with the consequence that we were allowed to travel to Ankara the next day by bus...

At any rate this in abridged form (it would take a book to describe all the complexities) was the miserable part of the saga. Up until then we had had a riotous time for most of the trip. As you know we travelled down through Belgium and Germany (we stopped off to see the Tiepolo frescoes at Wurzburg), on through Austria and over the Grosslockner Pass. The latter is one of the three highest in Europe and I was inveigled into going over it. If I had known what it was going to be like I would have put my foot down. It was hair-raising, nothing but sheer drops down of thousands of feet and what was worse the car kept on breaking down, once on a hairpin bend with myself and John controlling the traffic while the girls boiled up water for the radiator...

From Istanbul we crossed the Bosphorus onto the mainland and travelled via Ankara to Kayseri. The land is very hilly, almost mountainous, parched and barren. Ankara is a brand new capital city plonked down in the middle of this wilderness. As little as twenty miles from it people were living in villages much as they had been for the past thousand years, a hard life, mud houses, the women veiled and doing all the work while the men sat in cafes and played cards. We created a sensation wherever we went with our caravan car with its sink, gas stove, curtains, etc.

On we travelled through Kayseri and Tokat, both with wondrous Seljuk architecture, and up through the mountains via Nixa to the coast of the Black Sea (the sand really is black, the water warm and blue to bathe in). We drove along the most ghastly road for two hundred miles to Trebizond...

I forgot to mention our visit inland to Goreme and Urgup, the famous site of the rock churches of Cappadocia, utterly fantastic rock formations out of which whole Byzantine churches had been carved, all bedecked with frescoes. This, for me, was the real highlight of the trip.

The aftermath of this was a long and complex legal action and bills to pay, leaving me with a hefty overdraft.

————

Never again was I to be so adventurous or to look at so much, at that period, irrelevant material. But the Museums Association trip to the East Coast of the United States the following year was far more of a professional eye-opener. It lasted seven days and cost £142, and David Piper had decided that both John Kerslake and myself should go. It is surprising that I wrote no detailed account of this jaunt to Jan van Dorsten. The only reference reads: 'America was utterly exhausting – up at 7am and to bed at 2am the following morning with so much to take in, so much travelling, so many new people to cope with.' The tour took in Boston, New York, Philadelphia, Baltimore and Washington. The members of the Museums Association were so impoverished that it was difficult to fill the plane, so the offer was extended to the art trade. And so it was on this trip that I first met another old friend, the critic Brian Sewell.

Everything about Brian is extraordinary and he remains by far the most informed art critic in the country, fearless in his judgements both on the art he reviews and on the actions of those who present it. On this expedition he always had the guts to say the one thing everyone was thinking but did not have the nerve to articulate. Why we ended up in a tour of the strip clubs of Baltimore I cannot imagine, but my favourite cameo of Brian is when we found ourselves in an elevator in the company of a large-breasted woman festooned with garlands of flowers. Brian stared straight at her as we ascended many floors and then, fixing her with his gaze, said 'Are those flowers false?' The lady, somewhat taken aback, assented, to which Brian then added, 'I hope that's the only thing that's false.' At which point the lift doors opened and the poor woman fell out.

How can I describe him? In a way that is summed up in a drawing by a mutual friend, the painter Michael Leonard, one of whose talents is to draw people in the guise of other historical periods. In 1981 he depicted me in the manner of a drawing by Ingres. Thirty years later he revisited me as a drawing by François Clouet. Brian he envisioned as a French aristocrat on the eve of the Revolution, *en profile*, proud and disdainful. His voice alone seems designed for summoning an army of servants. Brian has ebbed and flowed in my life, not without a swipe or two, but when I finally resigned the V&A he wrote half a page imploring me to stay.

What most excited me about the trip was everything that had happened in American museums that made those back home the epitome of the dowdy. The gap has narrowed so dramatically since then that it is difficult to grasp the enormous culture shock. Everywhere we went there was a huge emphasis on appearance, the galleries elegant, the works of art beautifully lit, the pictures clean. The entrance to any museum or gallery was welcoming, with vases of flowers and a friends' desk providing information. Every museum had an ongoing education and exhibition programme, a shop crammed with books, postcards and facsimiles, a restaurant serving good food and coffee. It rendered the National Portrait Gallery gloomy and primeval by contrast. What I had seen and learnt was to contribute hugely to the dossier I drew up for myself when I applied for the Directorship.

But what was I really like during this period of my life? We are in the years before I discovered that I was photogenic and became the subject of every photographer from Cecil Beaton to Bill Brandt. Everything I had so far done had buried me in the security of the past and the Portrait Gallery only extended the years of escape.

But things were beginning to stir in my life. I had already decided that if ever I became Director of the NPG, I would change it. What I was not to know was that the opportunity would come so early. The autumn of 1963 finds me on the brink of what were to be major changes in my life, many of them precipitated by a doubling in income. It had been a year of successes: the Holbein Cartoon, *The Winter Queen*, the book on the portraits of Elizabeth I and the groundbreaking articles on Elizabethan painting. The fact that I could write in March to my Dutch friend in the hope of a few hundred pounds in royalties that 'it would be pleasant to use it as a deposit as one can now get 95% mortgages... All rather a pipe dream at the moment but pleasant', little did I know that I was not far off escaping from suburbia, which had become to me less a home than a detention centre.

SIX

LET THE SUN SHINE THROUGH

1964 to 1967

THIS chapter opens with a visual flourish, an overt flirtation with what we now call self-fashioning. The year is 1965 and the setting is an exhibition at the National Portrait Gallery of the portraits I had gathered for *The Shakespeare Exhibition* at Stratford-upon-Avon the previous year, which marked the playwright's quatercentenary. I am perching beneath Astrid Zydower's over-life-size statue of Shakespeare as a brooding youth. My suit is of a fashionable cut, as indeed is my hair, which has taken on a life of its own, reflecting the incipient locks of the peacock era which was arriving fast. The photograph, by Peter Amsden, also exudes a certain prosperity: the previous year I had been upgraded to an Assistant Keeper I and, even more important, I had at long last escaped from suburbia. The occasion of the picture? A commission to stage an exhibition in 1967 celebrating the Canadian Centennial at the National Gallery of Canada. They wanted a photograph of me and this was one of the ones that, much to their astonishment, I sent them.

The three years leading up to my appointment to the directorate were some of the most extraordinary in my life. Suddenly everything came rushing at me in a way where I had either to sink or swim. I was in demand as an exhibition organizer; British painting became the 'in' subject in academe; the public galleries of the NPG were given over to me to redesign and hang; requests to mount exhibitions at both the National Gallery of Canada and the Tate Gallery arrived; *The Times*, *Country Life* and the *Spectator* wanted me to write for them; involvement in *The Shakespeare Exhibition* brought a whole new world of creative people into my life; and, last but not least, I left the suburbs and moved into my first flat, which I shared with a museum friend, and so, belatedly, I could begin to have a social life of my own. How I handled all of this assailing me at such a speed and in such a short space of time I do not know, but youth aligned with ambition is a more than useful asset. But where to begin?

Within the institution the turning point came with the appointment of David Piper as Director in 1964. Suddenly the revolutionary fervour bottled up in me for so long was released. This is vividly captured in a letter I wrote to Joan Henderson on 23 December 1965:

> Now everything is changing fast ... thanks to David Piper letting
> me have my head and do what I like. It is a *super* job and the place is
> small enough for one to make a decided personal impact. As a team
> we are making inroads and people ask what is happening to the
> old NPG – new publications under way, theatre designers let loose
> in the rooms, outrageous exhibitions, super sound guide by David
> Piper, education programme being launched. It is all vital and alive
> – Kingsley Adams was a dear and one misses him but I could not
> have another 5 years of creative repression.

I owe an enormous debt to Pete for letting this ambitious thirty-year-old loose in every direction, as the reader will discover in this chapter capturing what was in effect a rebirth.

Perhaps this is an apposite moment at which to pause and ask what else was going on outside the closed worlds of the Warburg Institute and the National Portrait Gallery. Was there a wider context into which we can fit the decision in 1967 to appoint someone still aged only thirty-one to be director of a venerable national institution? Hake had been thirty-five when he was appointed, Adams fifty-two and Piper forty-four. In that context it is Hake who is the surprise, made more extraordinary by the fact that he died in harness at fifty-nine. If he had gone on to the retirement age of sixty-five he would have been Director for some three decades. There was, I recall, a pride in the fact that so few directors separated us from Sir George Scharf.

But what happened in 1967 must be set I think within a much wider context. There was a change of mood and an expansiveness to the 1960s. This was the era of the New Britain of Harold Wilson, which celebrated modernity, innovation and youth. Optimism was in the air. The wave of those who, like me, rose by way of the 1944 Education Act came of age. They wanted anything that was contemporary, revered the up-to-date in living style and fashion, and embraced expendability as a new norm. All of this was built, as we were bitterly to discover in the following decade, on a mirage. It was a move away from the 'You've never had it so good' years of increasing affluence expressed in the acquisition of useful domestic artefacts such as washing machines, televisions and refrigerators to one not connected with the practicalities of living. The focus moved to interior decoration, eating out, pop music, censor-free theatre, the new wave of Op and Pop and, above all, fashion.

My earliest awareness of style and glamour: Barbara Goalen in a New Look dress as photographed by John French, 1952, for the *Daily Express*.

For men nothing epitomized this more than clothes, for which I have always had a fascination. The dress historian Geoffrey Aquilina Ross summed it up brilliantly in the title of his book *The Day of the Peacock: Style for Men 1963–1973*. When I picked this up and opened it, my eye fell on many familiar faces of my generation, like that of the art dealer Christopher Gibbs and the photographer Patrick Lichfield, from that period. And there was I, who responded fully to this phenomenon. Some of what I wore then is in the V&A Dress Collection but the majority is in the Fashion Museum in Bath, to which I handed over virtually everything I ever wore between 1965 and 2005. But I was a civil servant and such plumage was reserved initially for out of office hours – although, after I became Director, that gradually changed.

My interest in clothes went back to my formative years. It began with the advent of the New Look in women's clothes, my reaction to which I recorded years later when the V&A acquired the John French archive of photographs. My mother read the *Daily Express*. As far as I can remember that paper had the formidable team of Anne Edwards, the journalist; Robb, the draughtsman; and John French as photographer. One item in particular sticks in the mind, a photograph of Barbara Goalen standing by a table, immaculately attired, one arm extended with a champagne glass in her hand. Through the camera's eye it opened up for me, after the years of bombing and evacuation, a world of style and glamour. I cut the picture out and kept it.

That was in 1952 when I was in the sixth form. But at the same time I was aware of the neo-Edwardian revival in men's clothes, with immaculately cut suits with flared jackets, discreetly patterned silk waistcoats and short covert coats with velvet collars. As a research student I blew part of my grant on just such a coat.

But that phase was as nothing compared with the explosion from 1965 onwards. I must have patronized every shop up- and downmarket selling the peacock's feathers. The first shop that sold evening shirts with frills down the front and at the wrists was called Hung on You in Cale Street, Chelsea. It was opened in 1965 by Michael Rainey. Earlier than that came Vince, famous, as George Melly was later jokingly to recall, for being the only man's shop for which seemingly your inner leg measurement was taken even if you only wished to buy a tie. Its catalogues paraded muscle-bound men in stretch fabric hipsters and much else that even I would not have had the nerve to wear. John Stephen had started his career there but soon opened shop after shop in Carnaby Street with affordable men's fashion, narrow flowered shirts with enormous collars, ever-expanding ties later known as 'kipper', and Regency-style jackets in patterned damask and velvet. I had and wore them all. And then hair got longer and longer and the barber gave way to the hairdresser and the unisex salon. This revolution in appearance then spread upwards, with Mr Fish in Clifford Street and a brief flowering of Turnbull & Asser in Jermyn Street as the male peacock's paradise. Turnbull & Asser made me a wonderful frock coat in brown velvet and long silk cravats to wind round my neck in emulation of Beau Brummell. The best suit I had from that era was my tight-fitting double-breasted one from Blades at the bottom of Savile Row, in which I was photographed for *Tatler* in 1968. Further up Savile Row was Tommy Nutter, another mecca for the dedicated follower of fashion. None of this would have passed without critical comment if I had still lived in N21 but by 1964 I had left it behind me. The era known as the Swinging Sixties coincided exactly with my exit from suburbia.

Myself as a male peacock in a Blades suit, 1968, now in the Museum of Fashion, Bath. Behind me the House of Commons listens to William Pitt.

Fashion was to be a leitmotiv in my life. For a time, later, I was an unlisted contributing editor to *Vogue*, then in its 1960s and '70s heyday under the legendary Beatrix Miller, who was one of the first to salute the arrival of this young lion in 1967 when she sent Cecil Beaton to photograph me. I must be the only museum director to figure in fashion shoots, one by John Swannell for *The Telegraph*, the other by Snowdon for Italian men's *Vogue*. The latter was a memorable image with me clad in a Versace black leather blouson and riding boots with my garden secateurs tucked into them in the manner of Vita Sackville-West. I was flanked by two topiary trees. During the shoot Tony kept on yelling, 'Give me more cleavage!' and his assistant yelling back, 'You can't do that to Roy!' The sixties were a legendary era in the annals of British fashion, when London became the mecca of innovation. I knew so many of those who were part of this generation of trendsetters, but two in particular became friends, whose loss I mourn.

The first was Jean Muir, whom I met shortly after I became Director of the V&A, when fashion came within my orbit. I had hoped to know and love Jean into old age but, alas, that was not to be. There was an electricity between us from when we first met. Here was another original, this tiny, bird-like, puckish figure with jerky, marionette movements, immaculate, with straight-cut hair, kohl-rimmed eyes and lips outlined firmly in brown. As I once wrote of her, she dressed like a Neapolitan widow while the swoops of her voice resembled those of a demented corncrake. Her handwriting was so idiosyncratic that any written communication required pinning up on a wall, standing back and deciphering. But she had energy, edge and an iron-disciplined work ethic. She was also a hugely ambitious woman who had come far from where she had begun her life in Bedford. Her creative genius framed minimalist clothes for the new woman of the 1970s; but it also fashioned Jean herself.

Her husband, Harry Leuckert, was German and had started his life as an actor but later became manager of the business. They had married as long ago as 1955 and as far as any marriage to such an exotic could ever work, this one did. Harry had a commercial art gallery in Germany and a place in Portugal to which he went to shoot. In November 1989 Julia and I went to spend a magical weekend with them at Lorbottle Hall, up beyond Newcastle, not far from Alnwick Castle. Theirs was a large neoclassical house decorated with an amiable clutter and in no sense interior-decorated. Whatever Jean's attributes, running a household was not one of them, so we were never sure when meals would appear; if they did, that was owed to Harry, who that weekend was into the mysteries of a bread-making machine. But there was an inspired zaniness about everything, which included the best fish and chips at Craster and wandering along the sands at Dunstanburgh, which Julia had last trodden in 1939 as war broke out. In the evening operetta music, which I love, would fill the house and I would sing along with Jean. The house reflected a magpie side to her make-up, caught again when she once said: 'I love travelling, Elizabethan music, Persian carpets, Provence, Man Ray, Danny La Rue, Coral Browne, Mozart, Richard Strauss, Tommy Steele, Alec Douglas-Home, Lord Harlech, the Victoria and Albert Museum' – and so the list continued. Typically, the logic of this eclectic collection is elusive.

Of all the English fashion designers, Jean was the one who should have been made a Dame, but she died too soon. The last time I saw her was in 1995, at a lunch given by Tony Snowdon at the Dorchester, in the suite designed by his uncle, Oliver Messel. These annual events were hand-picked assemblies of notables. On that occasion I recall the writer John Mortimer, the actor Alan Bates and the rock star Eric Clapton, next to whom I sat. As I left, Jean grabbed me by the arm and said, 'Let's go and have some champagne, darling.' So there we sat, laughing our way through a post-mortem on the lunch. How could I have known that she had had both breasts off and was dying of cancer? She kept those facts firmly hidden, so when the news came at the end of May it was a horrendous shock.

> We arrived back from lunch at Wenlock Abbey and turned on the ansaphone. It was a message from Beatrix Miller, who never leaves messages on such machines, saying that Jean Muir had died and apologizing for being so abrupt. I rang Beatrix at once. I couldn't believe it. She had been rung by Mary Henderson in floods of tears. Beatrix was in tears. Jean had died of cancer. She had had it for two years and had told no one ... She will be a great loss in my life. I didn't know until the obits came out that she was as much as sixty-six but even then it was all so tragic and far too early. She was always on my list of originals, self-created from little, exacting in her standards and puritanical *au fond*, epitomized in work, discipline, quality and no compromise. But we had always laughed so much together and were always *en rapport*.

The only person who was not upset about Jean's death was Hardy Amies, who, when I said to him, 'Wasn't it tragic about Jean?' snapped back 'No, it wasn't', much to my horror. But I record that because it captures the contrary nature of the man who was endowed with as many good and thoughtful attributes as waspish and bitchy ones. Hardy was the only other couturier whom I knew well, although we did regularly receive a gem-encrusted Christmas card from Norman Hartnell, whom I last encountered slightly the worst for drink, swaying down Bond Street.

But to return to Hardy... I first met him at a fancy-dress ball at Christie's in 1970, to which he went as Richard II, although one wearing glasses. Hardy epitomized the standards of a vanished generation, one which believed in hard work, exact attention to detail and the observation of social niceties. He embodied a certain type of Englishness whose essence was restraint mingled with splendour. He was a stickler for what he considered correct dress. One of the last occasions at which we saw him was a lunch party in the Cotswolds, for which I was perfectly correctly attired, according to the current code, in an open-necked shirt. Hardy had in tow a good-looking Australian who had initially dressed like me, in elegant casual clothes, until Hardy forced him to put on a collar and tie and jacket as no gentleman, in his estimation, should ever be seen at luncheon in the country attired in any other way.

In this and in several other ways Hardy never moved on, inhabiting a world in which women were still ladies and in which to be seen to exist without servants was anathema. The irony was that he had never been born to any of it. He firmly believed in the old hierarchy of class, which permitted the ascent into its upper ranks of those who, like himself, were talented and deemed worthy of admission. He had impeccable, understated taste, superb elegance of bearing and perfect manners. He was a brilliant tennis player, a skilled yachtsman, an avid opera-goer, a pretty good gardener and a wow with the needle. For some weird reason he had a passion for James I's daughter Elizabeth, Queen of Bohemia, the Winter Queen, and would embroider seat covers with patterns from the knots in her garden at Heidelberg.

He was, of course, wickedly funny and the master of the put-down. I recall having to follow him when he made a speech during which he suddenly sighed and said: 'Mary Quant, Mary Quant, what a shame no one taught her how to put a sleeve into an armhole.' Or, in my case, he wickedly defined The Laskett garden as 'Mr Pooter goes to Versailles'. My wife was ticked off for decking her re-creation of a room in the diarist Samuel Pepys's house in an exhibition at the National Portrait Gallery with dried hydrangeas. 'They didn't arrive before the eighteenth century' was the withering snub, to which Julia replied: 'Well they should have done as they look right.' His final put-down in my case was at a dinner given at the Garrick Club for the eightieth birthday of the gardener Rosemary Verey (who was later a major figure in my gardening life). I went to greet Hardy, saying that I was busy arranging the 'placement', to which came the stentorian reply: 'Dear boy, never use that expression. It's the word the French use for what they do with their money. The correct term is *place à table*.'

Hardy belonged to another lost world, too, that of the reticent homosexual. He never flaunted it. We have forgotten that in that era everyone who needed to know knew what a particular set-up was but it was just never referred to. The loser here was the man who was in effect his partner for so many years, the thoughtful and delightful Ken Fleetwood, for years the mainstay of the firm, whom Hardy would sometimes produce but often as not not. Hardy also had the old-fashioned virtues of discretion and maintaining a stiff upper lip. Although he could be quite funny about the Queen's taste in clothes he was never in fact indiscreet but always totally loyal. When the part he played in wartime intelligence came to light, his lips were sealed. When Hardy died, a bit of Old England went.

David Freeman, who had looked after him for those final years when he was over ninety, rang me about giving the address at his funeral, beginning by listing those who had turned down the chance, including the Dowager Duchess of Devonshire. But I accepted. The following passage is from my diary account of that day in March 2003:

> David Freeman had organized everything perfectly. The coffin was draped with the carpet Hardy had worked with all his favourite flowers acting as a hearse cloth. On top of it was placed his KCVO and swathes of more favourite flowers. Inside had been tucked a sprig of rosemary from his own garden and, at the last minute, a sprig was plucked from his sister Rosemary's garden to join the other flowers. The church was very near and I brought up the rear of the procession. Inside it was crammed and outside there was a sprinkling of press photographers which would have pleased him.
>
> The coffin sat on trestles before the chancel arch, on one side of which stood two clergy and on the other singers. The service was a simple sequence of communal hymns, readings and prayers. Ian Garlant read the piece Hardy wrote for *Interiors* when he was ninety-two about his love for his house and village, charming. I ascended the pulpit and gave my address and made them laugh, for he was both a wonder and a wicked old thing. But it was all perfect for him as he ended his life as a country gent in rockery nook Jacobean making his exit via the parish church.

Even now as I write in my seventy-sixth year I am still fascinated by fashion and its mutation, working out what would be a good look for a senior citizen.

———

Moving to a place of one's own is always a turning point in life. In that sense 14 Lancaster Gate stood for liberation, the ability to be able for the first time to express oneself in terms of decor and furnishings, even if only on a modest scale; liberation also to come and go without comment as to when and why and with whom; liberation, finally, to invite friends into one's own domain. I have always by nature been a homemaker, perfectly content to see a place in order and well run. To that can be added the excitement I got from interior decoration involving the deployment of colours and things within space.

The search for a flat began with a basement in Elgin Crescent, Notting Hill, which I almost bought. It brought with it a garden and the first mention I ever made to the possibilities offered by a garden, in a letter to Jan in May 1963: 'What I most liked was that the garden was mine. At the moment it is a nasty patch of earth with wild shrubs and a heap of rusty tins in the middle but with a little labour and love could be very nice and in summer another room.' That, however, came to nothing and silence descends until the January of the following year when I wrote that I was moving into a flat Michael Borrie had found: 'a very nice flat in Lancaster Gate with bedroom and living room each so as not to get under each others' feet.' That was to be the prelude to five extremely happy and carefree bachelor years.

Lancaster Gate is one of those 'north of the Park', vaguely neoclassical terraces of large late Victorian town houses which, after 1945, had been split up into flats. Next door to number 14 there was the Football Association and also what we thought was a brothel. On the other side was a hotel. In 1964 these terraces were a monument to post-war peeling paint and crumbling, faded grandeur. The terrace was a block away from Hyde Park and looking to the right on leaving the building one could see the Gothic silhouette of Christ Church, not that I ever went there. The flat, being on the *piano nobile*, had high ceilings and large sash windows. Each of us had one large room and a bedroom; we shared the kitchen and bathroom.

This was the first large room I had ever had to decorate. We had, of course, to do it ourselves. Mine was painted in the then fashionable

My £60 Elizabethan portrait, Sir Francis Hynde
of Madingley Hall, 1590.

shade of ginger. The green curtains I had had at home were lengthened
and I cut out buckram pelmets like a valance on a Regency pavilion,
edging the fabric with green cord. An off-white Indian carpet lightened
the room, in which I arranged items from my room in Colne Road,
soon amplified by ones from the nearby Portobello Road. Alas, the
chimneypiece was post-war tile so all I could do was paint it and hang
over it an early purchase, an Elizabethan portrait of Sir Francis Hynde
of Madingley Hall by Hieronimo Custodis. This I had bought for £60,
paid for in two tranches of £30, a few years before. Opposite were my
two bookcases, drawn slightly apart to admit a white marble bust circa

1825 of a lady called Susan Kinnear, which sat on a scagliola column. That was a Portobello Road trophy. And there were others: a small full-length of Joseph Leeson, 1st Earl of Milltown, by a little-known Irish painter called Anthony Lee, together with a half-length of one of his sisters, both rescued from an antique-cum-junk shop in Wood Green. Soon there was added an Italian giltwood side table from a down-the-line dealer in Endell Street in Covent Garden, to whom I was introduced by John Cornforth (of whom more to come). There were Victorian punch-back chairs and sofas and an assortment of other period chairs picked up as and when. And, of course, there were other bits and pieces. It was not exactly John Fowler but it was an attempt at something resembling what became the country house look.

14 Lancaster Gate fulfilled a whole raft of hitherto unfulfilled urges. And I was fortunate in the friend with whom I shared it. Michael Borrie had been a postgraduate student with me at the Institute of Historical research. He was a medievalist but never finished his thesis, not that this was to impair his steady ascent. Just as I had begun in the junior ranks of the museum profession so he entered it in a different way, as a member of the British Museum's Department of Manuscripts (now part of the British Library). He was to end up its Keeper, a prestigious post in the world of libraries. We had an overlapping circle of friends and worked to the same time schedule. It couldn't have been better. Tasks were shared: I cast myself as the cook and Michael was the shopper. As there were some fifty steps up to the flat, I perhaps got the better of the deal. This was the era when I worked through much of Elizabeth David's cookbooks. The rent, if I remember rightly, was £350 per annum. We were within walking distance of the Underground and, at a pinch, of Oxford Street. From the moment I arrived I knew that if I

Line-up of friends on the Front in Brighton, about 1970: myself,
Michael Borrie, the writer David Plante, and the poet and editor Nikos
Stangos. I had just purchased a tiny Gothick house there.

had to live in London I could only henceforth live in the centre, or not
at all. Twenty-eight years of between-the-wars suburbia had not left any
lingering longing for a return to its leafy streets. Quite the reverse.

What is striking in retrospect is that, apart from the colour of the
walls (very mid-1960s), the look I created was so locked into the past.
Part of that can be explained by cost: it was simply cheaper to buy old
rather than new. But it was also a natural instinct nurtured during these
years by someone who was to be a kindly and inspiring influence on me
in the years leading up to my marriage in 1971. I have already mentioned
his name: John Cornforth. Although he hated life in the country and

Knowledgeable, kindly but old-fashioned:
John Cornforth in the early 1960s.

could not drive, John was to spend his life as a major campaigner for the preservation of the country house as a uniquely English contribution to European civilization. John's interest in the visual arts had been fired by the teaching of Michael Jaffe, later a distinguished director of the Fitz-william Museum, Cambridge. In 1961 John joined the staff of *Country Life*, in which capacity he first entered my life in 1963 when he penned a few lines on *The Winter Queen* exhibition. Within a couple of years, as we shall see, I began writing for the magazine, which I still do half a century on. At that time John had a flat, an eyrie really, in the Belgrave Road opposite Warwick Square. He was a great entertainer and bringer together of kindred souls of a generation, forerunners, I suppose, of the Young Fogeys. We were all passionate about England's past, its art and architecture. That flat was full of 'things' which he picked up here and there. John taught me that you do not have to have a fortune to afford the elegance and flavour of the past. Eighteenth-century blue-and-white china, admittedly often slightly chipped, could be acquired for a modest sum. A harlequin set of coffee cups could be purchased and married to modern white saucers; if you could not afford a set of period dining chairs, make up a harlequin set. It was John who introduced me to the small-time dealer in Endell Street whom he nicknamed Wicked Uncle and from which I purchased items I still have.

Sadly I did not begin my diary in earnest until late in 1967 and then it was only patchy. But in January 2004 John re-entered my life three months after my wife's death. He and I had drifted apart after my marriage and my life by then had taken another turn, establishing a house and garden in the country followed by a decade and a half of non-stop dramas directing the V&A. But I think that what I wrote in my diary of that supper together so many decades on catches my experience and observation of the man:

> it was all so well meant, a kindly rescuing job of me, although at times I felt that it was he who was in need of rescuing! This was a life lived as though nothing had changed, one sustained by shutting out the real world, and where we'd got now in terms of email and the internet. I think that he thought my life and diary were blank whereas, on the contrary, my problem is how to get through it all. Old bachelors like this must have existed in Victorian times, shuffling around their littered apartments.

John's contribution to the survival of English country houses was seminal. In 1965 he joined the National Trust's Historic Buildings Committee and nine years later produced his landmark report, *Country*

Houses in Britain: Can they Survive? (1974). That was the year in which I became Director of the V&A and it was John Harris, the distinguished architectural historian, who came to me and urged that I should put on an exhibition on this topic to take the problem out to a wider public. The result was *The Destruction of the Country House*, one of the landmark exhibitions of the second half of the century. By then there was a network of scholars dedicated to the cause but John Cornforth was its *fons et origo*.

That renewed friendship was to be as dust because John was dead within months, at the age of sixty-six. I went to his Anglo-Catholic requiem High Mass at St Mary's, Bourne Street. Once again, amidst the doffing of birettas, I reflected on him:

> He was a strange man, a benign balloon really. He'd written 150 articles for *Country Life* and was greatly loved by the chatelaines. He had a great interest in Irish art and in interior decoration and the history of textiles and their use. All these were pioneer topics and he encouraged many.

John represented one aspect of my new life in Lancaster Gate. Another aspect, however, he wouldn't at all have approved of – but to me it was perhaps even more important.

———

There is no doubt but that my involvement in *The Shakespeare Exhibition* at Stratford-upon-Avon in 1964 was one of my life's great turning points. It first appears in my letters to Jan on 11 November 1963:

> Have you heard about the huge Shakespeare Exhibition they are going to do here in 1964? £100,000 is to be spent on it. It is being

run by Richard Buckle who did the Diaghilev exhibition so that we can expect merry madrigal music spouting forth at all angles from concealed loud-speakers. What fun. I wish I had a finger in the pie...

Amazingly, my wish was to be granted almost immediately. As with so much else, my association with it came about purely by accident, the falling by the wayside of the Keeper of Art at the City of Birmingham Museum and Art Gallery, John Woodward. He had been employed to deal with the portrait side of the exhibition but alas had entered the terminally inebriated phase of his life, a tragic drunk to whom one handed a fiver. A replacement was urgently needed. At the time I was cataloguing the NPG's holdings on that period and *Portraits of Queen Elizabeth I* had just been published. So an approach was made as to whether I could be involved. Sanction obtained, as a consequence I found myself entering another world.

The exhibition had been masterminded by the ballet critic Richard Buckle. On my bookshelves rests volume two of his autobiography, entitled *In the Wake of Diaghilev*. Within it is inscribed: 'To dearest Roy, with whom I have worked so often and so happily. Love, Dicky, January 1983.' I can pinpoint that gift for it related to a television piece in which I had to choose someone who had been a great inspiration to me early in life. I selected Dicky, then living in secluded retirement in Wiltshire in the aftermath of two ghastly breakdowns in the 1970s. In the 1950s and 1960s this man was the powerhouse of exhibition-making, above all through his revolutionary one on Diaghilev and the Ballets Russes, which I saw at Forbes House in 1954. This was one of the landmark exhibitions of the post-war era, not only for the celebration of its hero and the artistic achievements of the Ballets Russes, but also for its revolutionary exhibition technique.

Dicky died in his eighty-fifth year, one year into the present century. In my obituary of him for the *Guardian* I recalled the revolutionary effect he had on exhibition design – which in turn had a profound effect on me:

> As a schoolboy [not quite true as I was in my first year at QMC!] in the drab world of the early 1950s, I remember being swept away by the glamour of it all. From the moment one entered the now Forbes House, the visitor trod a pathway of fantasy: passed a tableau of grand ladies at the ballet before 1914, then the beach at Deauville in the 1920s, on through tented rooms hung with chandeliers, each with its separate theme, ending up ascending a huge staircase on which brooded statues of sentries embowered with greenery leading up to the palace of the Sleeping Beauty. One's ears were filled with the music of the ballet and the air was scented with Diaghilev's favourite perfume. This was magic of a high order, even if Ninette de Valois thought it was like Madame Tussaud's.
>
> Within 20 years, what was done here for the first time, had become clichés of exhibition making: the use of re-creations, of tableaux, of props, music and lighting effects, above all the one-way-round system which controlled the visitor's visual experience as the story was unfolded ... Their eventual impact on the staid world of art exhibitions and indeed on permanent museum display was considerable, even if never really acknowledged. Buckle was the first person to raise exhibition making of this kind to the level of an art form in its own right.

This was, of course, partly the inspiration behind what I had attempted to do with *The Winter Queen*.

I had never encountered anyone quite like Richard Buckle before. Indeed, coming from a suburban background and in the repressed world of post-war England I really had little idea what a homosexual was, let alone what he did. Poor Ros Lyons, wife of one of the major financial

Culture shock: the ballet critic and exhibition maestro Richard Buckle in the
Beaton Portraits exhibition, 1968, with me hovering in the background with
Buckle's assistant, Joe Predera.

backers of *The Shakespeare Exhibition*, would virtually keel over in
horror as Dicky would describe his preferred route to Stratford as being
the one with a lay-by where he could have sex with lorry drivers. One of
my other memories of him is slumped back in a car, slightly the worse
for drink, chanting 'Come to Western-super-Mare / All the prettiest
boys are there!' He lived in Henrietta Street in Covent Garden in a
large top-floor flat hung with family portraits but also, more excitingly,
covered with items, posters, designs and other memorabilia connected
with the Ballets Russes. That flat acted as a kind of office, with Dicky
as a disorganized whirlwind of energy whipping up a small army of

artists and designers who were engaged in what was to turn out to be
a financial disaster. It had begun with Lord Harewood and Jack Lyons
each backing the exhibition to the tune of £50,000, but, as Dicky had
no sense of financial restraint or control, costs quickly rocketed up to
a quarter of a million.

Coming from the cloistered worlds of academe and the museum, I
did not know what had hit me. 'I could write a book about the people
I've met', I scribbled excitedly to Jan. 'Dicky Buckle is straight out of
Evelyn Waugh. Deciding on the illustrations to the catalogue in the
intervals of *Swan Lake* is an experience.' And that was not to be the only
experience, as I visited a succession of scenic studios and workshops
scattered across London in which a small army of sculptors, painters
and designers, together with their assistants, were working away on
what was conceived as an imaginative panorama of Shakespeare's life
and England. My involvement was with the portraits that were to hang
in a Long Gallery designed by Alan Tagg, whose whispery voice and
fluttering hand movements I still can see in my mind's eye, but the
main body of whose work was with George Devine at the Royal Court
and with Alan Ayckbourn. I described this gallery in the exhibition in
a letter to Jan:

> Any relation to Shakespeare's life in this exhibition seems to me
> to be almost irrelevant and yet it does in parts have a strange
> fascination. My old theatrical yearnings well up to the surface
> when handed a long gallery 90 feet long to fill with portraits of the
> great in Gloriana's reign ... Portraits on one side with leaded bay
> windows to the ground on the other looking out over the Thames
> at dawn with London Bridge, Whitehall and the great noblemen's
> houses silvery white in the mist. Ships moored below in the river.
> At the far end there are the screens with a minstrels' gallery and

music playing and between the doors a marvellous Armada Portrait of Elizabeth flanked by royal beasts and surmounted by the royal coat of arms [I rescued the maquette for this and gave it to the University of Bristol Theatre Collection]. Beyond this one comes into the Gold Room – inspired by the room at Greenwich in which everything was of gold, silver or some precious gem. In this will sit the miniatures and jewels and a little fountain with an obelisk and golden popinjays.

The organization was chaotic, the show being staged in what was a vast temporary exhibition complex on the banks of the Avon opposite the Memorial Theatre. Most of the time one or other wall of the structure was missing, to my horror, as I trundled to and from the safekeeping of Barclays Bank, flanked by police and dogs as I brought the jewels and miniatures to place them in showcases that were never ready. Somehow I managed to gather some twenty-six portraits for the Long Gallery and fourteen miniatures for the Gold Room, to which were added some magnificent jewels, including some on loan from the Royal Collection. Dicky was caught screaming down the telephone to George Harewood: 'And you can tell your cousin from me I want those jewels!'

I spent most of my time standing around aghast at the scene while Dicky, acting like a Renaissance prince, guided the famous and fashionable around the unfinished exhibition. In front of me floated a number of people, like Cecil Beaton, Lady Pamela Berry and Diana Cooper, who were in a few years to become part of my life. Other excitements included Picasso producing an amazing five-minute scribble of the playwright, and Alan Tagg's evocation of the Globe Theatre with a *son et lumière* that included a cast that was a roll call of the great in the theatre: Redgrave, Ashcroft, Gielgud, Olivier, Edith Evans and Judi Dench, to name but a few. When it opened on 23 April 1964 it was still unfinished but I walked in the procession next to Leslie Caron, then married to Peter Hall, and laid my posy at Shakespeare's grave. The Duke of Edinburgh opened the exhibition and there was a grand luncheon that was ruined by someone handing me a piece of paper that read: 'We have mislaid Shakespeare's will.'

By the time it was up and running, the notion of the exhibition travelling to Edinburgh, let alone to London, had to be abandoned. It had already cost twice the initial budget. Only part of the show went to Scotland and the portraits alone came to London, for a short period in the National Portrait Gallery, while the rest of the exhibition, by then somewhat tired, was revived for a second season at Stratford the following year. But it was a disaster and ended in a welter of debt and recrimination, with the artists suing the organizers.

I have none of my letters to Jan for 1964, which I regret; they only resume in the autumn of 1965, by which time the exhibition had run its catastrophic course. It finally closed 2 October that year, when, as I wrote to Jan, 'there is a buffet lunch in the Long Gallery and Sotheby's flog everything (know anyone who wants to buy a Globe Theatre or a Long Gallery? Now is the time to snap these useful items up cheap!)'. I was at the sale and recall Ed Gilbert (the fabric designer, billed by Dicky as the new William Morris), who had created the pearl and gold encrusted tablecloth in the Gold Room, saying that he intended to have it even if he had to secure it pearl by pearl. Lincoln Kirstein rescued several pieces by Astrid Zydower, which were to find a home at Stratford, Connecticut.

Thanks to the exhibition, for the first time in my life I came into contact with contemporary artists and designers and it excited me hugely. Dicky had gathered an amazing assemblage of artists, some of whom were or were to become immensely important. He had commissioned large canvases from Peter Blake, Leonard Rosoman, Frank Bowling and Ceri Richards. When I was later approached, as Director of the National Portrait Gallery, to recommend someone to paint Miss Pears (subject of one of Millais's most famous canvases) I suggested Peter; the result was to be the soap manufacturer's most important picture for decades. When Robert Runcie as Archbishop of Canterbury asked me to recommend a painter to decorate the ceiling of the chapel at Lambeth Palace I suggested Leonard Rosoman.

After the exhibition debacle Dicky remained unrepentant, uncontrollable, and continued to drink far too much. He remained a friend nonetheless, and barely three years later was my link to Cecil Beaton and the famous 1968 exhibition, which Dicky designed and which took London by storm – and put the NPG back on the cultural map again. But in 1971 Dicky was to have a breakdown, moving items from his Henrietta Street flat into St Paul's Church, Covent Garden, as an 'exhibition' about himself and issuing a newspaper called *The Dicky Buckle Star*. He then got into deeper water when he decided that he must organize a charity gala at the Coliseum to help save the Harewood Titian for the National Gallery. I saw bankruptcy looming so I went behind the scenes in an attempt to get the event cancelled, but to no avail. Dicky was unsinkable and was to enter my life again when he began a campaign for a Museum of the Performing Arts, which, in turn, was to lead on to the saga of the Theatre Museum that was to blight my directorship of the Victoria and Albert Museum. In the end Dicky retreated to Wiltshire, not far from Beaton, where he added a gallery and a tower to his cottage and, thanks to bequests by endless aunts, managed to survive.

In addition to Dicky Buckle and Alan Tagg a number of other friend-ships and connections came out of the Shakespeare exhibition. Pauline Whitehouse, a brilliant scenic artist, I first met enlarging the French painter Jean Hugo's vast canvases depicting Shakespeare's journey across the Cotswolds to London. I was to call on her talents for a series of exhibitions: *A Pageant of Canada*, *Hans Eworth* and *The Eliza-bethan Image*. Tim O'Brien, who was to design no fewer than thirty-one productions for the Royal Shakespeare Company, I commissioned to design rooms at the NPG that in the end never happened. To these I can add Nicholas Georgiadis, one of the greatest of late-twentieth-century theatre designers, best remembered for his productions with Kenneth Macmillan and Nureyev. Dicky took me to the second night of Nico's *Romeo and Juliet* (1965), one of his masterpieces, at Covent Garden with Lynn Seymour dancing the role Macmillan had created for her and not for Margot Fonteyn, whom Ninette de Valois insisted must dance the first night. After I married a theatre designer, these friendships sadly fell away!

What so much of this represented was a burgeoning of connection outside my narrow world of academe and museums. Inevitably those in the creative arts are generally more interesting that those bent over a book and I remember peering into a looking glass and thinking 'God, you're dreary' and going out and having my hair cut 'back to front' in what might be described as the Henry V look. In the case of the sculptors I met through the exhibition, two in particular, Angela Conner and Astrid Zydower, were to become lifelong friends. Astrid had executed a mass of sculpture for the exhibition, including an amazing tableau of Queen Elizabeth and the Earl of Essex watching the first night of *A Midsummer Night's Dream*, glimpsed through the legs of

Astrid Zydower's vast over-life-size tableau of Elizabeth I and the Earl of Essex watching the first performance of *A Midsummer Night's Dream*, in *The Shakespeare Exhibition*, Stratford-upon-Avon, 1964.

gargantuan Yeomen of the Guard some sixty feet high. Perhaps Astrid is best described through what I wrote shortly after her death.

Astrid Zydower died in her sleep over three months ago. I would have written an obituary of her but, no, her family wanted everything under wraps, understandable in retrospect as, on the day she died, someone stole the Gaudier Brzeka drawing Dicky Buckle had left her and her maquette [of Orpheus] for the Harewood House fountain was missing. But I'd been rung up by her sister, Anita, in many ways her double, a small, smiling delightful lady. Would I like to come and choose an etching by Astrid or one of the models left in her studio...

I was presented with the modello for Essex for the great tableau in the Shakespeare Exhibition. Alas, Gloriana had vanished or fallen to bits ... It needs a bit of repair but I really would like this, a memorial of my past, my emancipation into the world of the living arts. Astrid's etchings were then produced. She was always very secretive about them and kept them hidden under her bed. One of a fierce-looking cat I was told that I had to have and one of a vase of flowers but the one I could choose myself was of a mysterious beach-marine scene of nude figures on the shore or in the water. These and a few drawings were quite unlike anything we'd ever seen her do. Her early drawings [including one of me] always used fifty lines where one would have done. These, in contrast, were sparse line etchings reminiscent of Matisse and Marie Laurencin. The marine etching on the back had 'For LK', I assume Lincoln Kirstein.

Astrid was a considerable artist sculptor, out of tune with the times, someone who could never produce on time and whose life was one long saga of being put upon. The house was falling apart, with a crack indicating that a wall would fall off. It needed a fortune spending on it. Dicky Buckle made her and ruined her. She had a long friendship with Lincoln Kirstein. Somehow Astrid was always there but now she's gone.

The maquette of Essex arrived virtually in bits beyond recall but later the one for the Queen was found and I had a cast made, which now presides over an anteroom at The Laskett, side by side with an impression of Nicholas Hilliard's Great Seal of Elizabeth. Astrid was extraordinarily talented but had a tragic history. She was a brilliant student at the Royal College of Art but with the appearance of a little girl, arriving there on the first day in a pixie hood and a coat with a Peter Pan collar. Her background was traumatic, having been one of a family of three who had been got out of Germany and brought to England in 1939, the rest of her family perishing in concentration camps. One evening she told us her memories, of how bit by bit they had been caged in until, with labels tied round their necks, they left for England. A Mrs Freeman was in charge of finding homes for such refugees but had failed to find anyone who would take on a family of three, so she took them in herself. Astrid's earliest memory of Mrs Freeman was of her standing on Sheffield station, her arms outstretched to embrace them. Astrid was so traumatized that at first she could not speak; this wise woman gave her plasticine to play with, thus starting her on her life's work.

Astrid occupies the role of the doomed artist in my life because, although she had exceptional talent, she attracted disaster. You knew that wherever she lived there was bound to be someone peculiar next door (whether they actually were or not never came into it) and that whatever work she undertook it would never be ready (the Harewood House Orpheus rumbled on for a decade) or, if it was, would be too big to get out through the front door. Life was a perpetual naïve surprise, which at times was maddening, as when she still, after decades, stared at the menu of an Italian restaurant in puzzlement. Buckle used her for exhibition after exhibition, as did the British Council, for which she was awarded an MBE for her work; typically, when asked by the Queen what she had done she replied that she really was not sure. Later in life she was kept going by commissions from the Harewoods and from Charlie Watts of the Rolling Stones. She also became a close friend of one of the great pioneers of ballet in this country, Marie Rambert. Both were Jews from the same area of Eastern Europe and Astrid was to sculpt a fine head of her while I was Director of the NPG. They were close, like mother and daughter in a way, and I recall Astrid reading Shakespeare's sonnets to Rambert on her deathbed.

Angela Conner was quite different: a dazzling redhead at the start of her career as a sculptor, having studied under Barbara Hepworth. Angela was a woman who had many men in her life until she eventually married the brilliant photographer and film-maker John Bulmer. Among these were the sculptor Robert Clatworthy, who at that time taught sculpture at the Royal College of Art, and the late Duke of Devonshire. Andrew Devonshire became a major patron and collected virtually anything Angela sculpted, including a head of me, the first she ever essayed, shortly after I became Director of the NPG. Reports came back of friends who went on the tour of Chatsworth and found me at the bottom of a flight of stairs. Angela was to go on and have a hugely successful public career, with commissions across the globe – a startling contrast to Astrid in her lair in Kentish Town.

———

So all of this forms one long thread from the autumn of 1963, in what was in effect a new life. A parallel thread was the revolution in British art studies. My passion for sixteenth- and early-seventeenth-century English painting could hardly have occurred at a more fortuitous moment, for the multimillionaire philanthropist and collector Paul Mellon was persuaded to turn his patronage in the direction of scholarship on the history of British art. That Mellon began to seriously collect British art from 1959 onwards was owed to the influence of Basil Taylor, a now largely forgotten figure but then Librarian at the Royal College of Art and more than anyone else the person most responsible for establishing George Stubbs as an artist of European stature. It was his interest in Stubbs that had drawn him into the Mellon orbit because, of course, Mellon owned racehorses. There was a touch of genius about Basil, but he was unstable and in the end committed suicide. My wife remembered him lecturing at the Royal College, edging closer and closer to the wall until the students were convinced that he would eventually climb up it.

As a result of his friendship with Paul Mellon, Basil became the Director of the Paul Mellon Foundation for British Art, an institution set up to publish scholarly works in the field. I was to write two books for it, *Holbein and Henry VIII* (1967) and *The English Icon: Elizabethan and Jacobean Portraiture* (1969). Both books were designed and produced in a manner that was revolutionary: large in format, lavish in layout and with elegantly designed plates. These early publications, as a consequence, were accorded an unprecedented degree of critical attention. But in 1965 this new foundation was to impinge on my life in another way. In an article in the *Contemporary Review* Basil Taylor outlined the objectives of the new foundation in terms of supporting the publication of scholarly books and exhibitions; he then went on to outline the endowment by Mellon of two lectureships, one in British Medieval Art at the University of York and the other in Post-Medieval British Art at the University of Leicester. The latter was offered to me early in 1965. Its main objective, I was told, was to create a major photographic archive. Otherwise it was to be primarily a research post with some postgraduate teaching attached to it. On 3 February 1965 I had written 'the general feeling all round is "Yes"', but, as such a move would have entailed a drop in salary, with conditions: the archive called for support staff and equipment and, Francis Wormald insisted, a guarantee of £7,000 per annum for at least ten to fourteen years. I also wanted to live in London and commute to Leicester three days a week. Basil was no master of decision and the letter I wrote outlining the situation went unanswered until May, when I saw him at the University of Yale for the first Mellon-sponsored conference on British Art studies. I wrote afterwards: 'I arrived a day early and pronto cornered Basil Taylor re the Leicester job. I really said that I could not go on any longer without knowing. Poor Basil looked blanched and haggard.' None of the conditions I had laid down could be met. 'I think', I later wrote, 'he wanted to meet my needs and was clearly paralysed at the idea of my not going for it.' On my return to England I went up to Leicester on 12 June to look the place over. I was far from enchanted.

By then the Foundation was beginning to run into difficulties and in 1966 Mellon was to set in motion the building of the handsome Yale Center for British Art at New Haven by the great architect Louis Khan. That had as its Director someone who was to become a close friend, Professor Jules Prown. But these were awkward years, as the initial foundation was closed down and a new one, the Paul Mellon Foundation for British Art, was established in 1970 with an initial advisory council that included Sir Anthony Blunt, Sir John Pope-Hennessy, Sir Oliver Millar and myself. The Director of the new foundation was to be that doyen of British art studies, Sir Ellis Waterhouse. The Foundation has since never quite vanished from my life: I came on and off its council and, in 1999, crossed the Atlantic to deliver a set of lectures at the Center in New Haven; these became a book, *The Artist and the Garden* (2000). In alliance with Yale University Press, the Paul Mellon Foundation, now in Bedford Square, has been responsible for publishing a series of groundbreaking studies of this country's art and architecture.

In December 1965 my diary records a shift in the emphasis of this ever-widening circle of people:

> I find myself drifting very much away from academic circles and finding museum-art world-practising designers more congenial and alive. I find myself impatient with the dreariness and stodginess that often goes with academic life and get appalled by friends who let themselves drift into a rut.

A year later, in October, I noted that as my social circle had enlarged – which was good – the number of academic people I now saw was practically nil.

The Shakespeare Exhibition had brought a network of artists and designers into my life, while the friendship of John Cornforth signalled something else: the emergence of a journalistic career. *Country Life* began to commission pieces from me in 1966 on topics such as the great Queen Christina exhibition in Stockholm and the Elizabethan portraits at Cowdray Park and Parham. *The Times* art pages followed in the same year, with occasional essays in a series entitled 'Things Seen' in which I wrote about subjects like the Juvenile Drama and Madame Tussaud's. And then the brilliant young arts editor of the *Spectator*, Hilary Spurling, asked me to become a regular contributor to its pages. Hilary was at the start of a career as a major biographer but in the mid-1960s that lay ahead – we were all at the start of our careers. I was commissioned to produce a piece once a fortnight, one of 1,500 words and the second half that length. Thus I entered the forbidden pastures about which Frances Yates had issued such dire warnings. I have no regrets, for I learnt much: firstly to write to order and length; secondly to look and articulate in words the appreciation and criticism of an exhibition; and thirdly to master gradually and polish some kind of prose style. Nonetheless, I felt pretty defensive about the path I had chosen to tread. 'I am keeping a check that I do not write too much journalism', I was to write to Jan in August 1966, with more than a hint of an apology to an academic, 'but the *Spectator* is a very highly respectable literary weekly and all sorts of top people write for it. I would aim not to write more than one lead article a month. I am amazed at my blossoming into a writer with a switched-on, way-out wit.' Later that year I was to add: 'I really enjoy it when not too rushed and I never knew I could be so funny.'

Simultaneously the NPG changed when David Piper took over as Director in 1964. The place ceased to be stuck in a rut. The *Annual Report*, the bane of my life, changed in style, opening with statements about the dire financial plight of the Gallery with a purchase grant of a miserable £8,000 per annum. The acquisitions exhibition in 1966 opened with items worth £200,000 on the walls, including a Gainsborough self-portrait and two outstanding portraits by Reynolds of Warren Hastings and James Boswell. The Chairman's opening, penned by Pete, was now addressed to the Secretary of State for Education and Science and no longer to the Lords Commissioners of Her Majesty's Treasury. That brought a plea to the government that a central fund be set up to meet such crises (it never was). Gallery attendances began to rise. In the calendar year 1965 the figure was 231,713, the highest in the Gallery's history. 'The increase it seems', the *Report* records, 'is due less to temporary exhibitions than to the general improvement in the display and presentation of the collection which has been widely appreciated.'

When Pete became Director he said to me, 'The galleries are yours', and I responded with alacrity and enthusiasm. That huge change in the public face of the Gallery has been the subject of an excellent article by a present member of the NPG's staff, Dr Peter Funnell. My entire directorate passed without issuing a single *Annual Report* but what happened from the autumn of 1964 onwards is caught in a retrospective account in a *Report* covering my directorship, the years 1967 to 1975. This records an aim to 'provide a visual history of Britain, from the Tudor period onwards' by establishing within each room 'a theme or mood', which could include additional material such as prints, furniture and objects 'to create a stimulating and imaginative effect'. 'The aim', it concludes, 'is to provide a revealing historical background to the portraits and to set them firmly in the context of their time.'

Funnell points out that, unbeknown to me, this approach had been anticipated by C.J. Holmes when he had been Director (1908–16) but it had been reversed by his successors. As a result the NPG became a gallery catering only for connoisseurs and antiquarians and attendances between 1918 and 1939 consequently collapsed. The 1964-5 *Annual Report* announces the reversion, which owed more than a little to the V&A's post-war division of the collections into primary and reference galleries. The plans outlined in that *Report* envisaged a three-tier system, the traditional format of the picture gallery, related to it 'a series of thematic, story-telling, and changeable displays' and, finally, reference portraits 'in areas adjacent to the primary galleries'.

All of this coincided with the arrival of Jennie Lee as the first Minister for the Arts, the thrust of whose policy was education and children through the opening up of the country's museums and galleries to a far wider public. In the first-ever White Paper on the Arts, entitled 'A Policy for the Arts: The First Steps' (1965), she pilloried 'those of our museums ... that had failed to move with the times, retaining a cheerless unwelcoming air that alienates all but the specialist and the dedicated'. What I attempted to do to the NPG galleries was coincidental but entirely accidental, although of course it worked in my favour. Later, when I became Director, I was to deliver the speech to the Museums Association advocating 'Martinis with the Bellinis'. And so it has all but come to pass.

The 1960s witnessed a boom in popular history publishing, epitomized by the advent of the 'coffee-table book', lavishly illustrated history made possible through the advent of cheap colour printing. Funnell traced my approach to the Gallery's reinstallation to my childhood delight in Victorian history pictures. He concluded that I had a 'deep sympathy for popular and pictorial types of history', which expressed itself through this revolutionary deployment of the collections. All display has a time limit, a sell-by date, and the rooms I arranged with energy and passion began to be dismantled in the 1980s and 1990s.

———

As a consequence of the 1960s boom I found myself in increasing demand as an organizer of exhibitions. As early as March 1963, when my articles on Elizabethan painting were still appearing in the *Burlington*

Magazine, I wrote to Jan: 'There are hints that the Tate might sponsor an exhibition of Elizabethan art in which yours truly would, I think, be largely in the limelight.' In January of the following year I reported: 'out of the blue came a letter from Sir John Rothenstein asking me to stage an exhibition at the Tate of English painting from the death of Holbein to the arrival of Van Dyck. I hope that this will lead to a complete reassessment of this period in English painting.' It did. It was to open two years into my directorship in 1969 with the title *The Elizabethan Image*. It was a thumping success, a revelation and, as an exhibition, very, very beautiful.

The precursor to this was an exhibition on the mid-Tudor artist Hans Eworth. It was the idea of John Morley, then Director of the City of Leicester Museum and Art Gallery, and it opened at the NPG in mid-December 1965. This was the first exhibition ever devoted to a single Tudor artist other than Holbein. Over twenty works by or attributed to Eworth were gathered and the project was supported by the recently founded Mellon Foundation. By then the impact of *The Shakespeare Exhibition* was making itself felt in the addition to the decor of hangings and cloths of estate. The show was dramatically lit so that these precious panel paintings floated as jewels in the darkness. 'Eworth was a triumphant opening', I wrote to Jan, 'after an annihilating amount of work. Very elaborate decor, lots of gold fringe and drapes.' By then I was getting a bit above my station and David Piper was not exactly pleased to see my face on the cover of the *Illustrated London News*, with further pictures inside of this young museum lion directing the hanging. In retrospect I think I probably had overstepped the mark. But it was a period when I was bursting with energy and drive – and filled with more than a touch of egomania.

Early the previous year I had been asked to mount an exhibition at the V&A entitled *The Growth of London*. It was staged on the occasion of the Twentieth International Geographical Congress being held in the city. I had permission to moonlight but only in my own time, so that meant using leave, working on it at weekends and in the evenings. This came my way in January 1964, opening in the summer. The budget was a shoestring one. It had a one-way route, starting, as I wrote to Jan, 'with Mithras and the legionaries and finishing at the other end with sky-scrapers'. John Hayes was responsible for the objects and Ann Saunders for the catalogue. This had more than a touch of *The Shakespeare Exhibition*, with Pauline Whitehouse executing vast banners of the City's twelve great livery companies, which I had suspended floating above the exhibition. The entrance was a re-creation of Holbein's pageant arch for the coronation of Anne Boleyn. Cases were arranged as still lifes and whole lamp posts and park benches were brought in.

It is interesting to read half a century on how much of an impact *The Growth of London* made. The *Sunday Times* wrote: 'those interested in presentation will be impressed by the skill and excitement of the installation designed by Dr Strong ... he has evolved an exciting two-dimensional technique of display.' Terence Mullaly in the *Daily Telegraph* wrote that 'the exhibition is crowded, but its arrangement is extremely ingenious. Everyday objects are suddenly seen for the first time. Above all the past is made to seem as real as the present.' Frank Davis in the *Illustrated London News* found it on first encounter 'a trifle bewildering' but was 'then vastly intrigued by the ingenuity with which [the exhibits] have been arranged'. The exhibition had huge coverage but oddly the most perceptive analysis of what I was attempting to do came in the *Liverpool Daily Post*: 'it is very different from most shows of

Exhibition making as spectacle: a glimpse of *The Growth of London*
exhibition at the Victoria and Albert Museum, 1964, in which pictures,
photographs, artefacts and theatrical props were mingled to produce
a panorama through time.

this kind. It's scholarly and accurate, yes, but it's refreshingly free from
museum conventions.' The reviewer goes on to say of me: 'he represents
the young idea that contemporary exhibition techniques can and should
be used in our museums and galleries; that a display of this kind must
be handled imaginatively to attract the public.' I cannot conceal that I
was anything other than punch-drunk with it all.

'All right I know I may know little about the history of Canada but I *do* know how to put on a damn good exhibition.' These were my words to Jan in a letter dated 16 October 1965. By then I had been commissioned by the Chief Curator of the National Gallery of Canada, Robert Hubbard, to stage what I titled *A Pageant of Canada*. The exhibition was to mark the Canadian Centennial in 1967 and would be staged in the as yet unseen and deeply depressing office block which then served as the gallery. 'I have done a marvellous scenario for the exhibition!!!' (note the three exclamation marks); this included revolving globes and multi-film projection. I conclude the letter with these words signalling my mood: 'Life is a ruddy great cake and it is no use sitting and looking at it – when one can cut a great chunk of it. I have never worked so hard or enjoyed myself so much as in the past two years.'

I am struck reading these letters to Jan van Dorsten that I seem suddenly to have grown up. *A Pageant of Canada* opened in the autumn of 1967, after I had become Director of the National Portrait Gallery. It was an exhibition of a type that originated with *The Winter Queen* in 1963 and, therefore, was quite unlike anything seen in Canada before. It involved me in visits to collectors of Canadiana, to France to negotiate loans from the Marquis de Montcalm and to Scotland for those from the present Lord Elgin. Through it two new people entered my life, for both of whom I have huge respect. One was Jean Sutherland Boggs, who became Director of the National Gallery of Canada the same year that I did of the NPG. She was to be an outstanding Director and was to see through the erection of a new building. The second person was Janine Smiter, in charge of public relations and press, from whom I learnt a huge amount about directorial presentation to the media. Janine prepared me for becoming what was surely the country's first media museum director. She stressed the importance and the handling of availability, the role of press interviews, exhibition promotion and the part played by photography. This ran clean against the NPG's attitudes when I arrived: that the phone should be put down on any journalist. In the long run, this of course had its downside, summed up in an art critic screaming down the telephone to the V&A's Press Office during a turbulent period: 'We made Roy Strong. Now we're going to destroy him.'

———

On 17 May 1965 I wrote an account to Jan of my first long visit and tour of American museums and galleries, occasioned by the staging of a conference on the future of British art studies to be held at Yale. I began the tour with four days in Montreal, which was bitterly cold, followed by Ottawa, Toronto, Detroit, Toledo, Cleveland and Indianopolis:

> Practically without exception the hospitality has been marvellous ... But very wearing. There is nothing so *utterly* exhausting as a continuous stream of new wavelengths on which to tune. It is more exhausting being a guest than a host every time on these tours! Believe me I was glad to have a free evening and sleep for fifteen hours to recover. And so to *St Louis* which I liked. Here the Director is Charles Buckley, who is working with Ben Nicolson on a Wright of Derby book. Very nice man. We had a riotous time whooping it round St Louis ending in the jazz clubs. I think that he is one of my most valuable contacts and he will be at the [Yale] Conference.

I then travelled on to Kansas City, Chicago and, finally, Boston, at the end of three very exhausting weeks. From there trips were made to Providence, Rhode Island, to Worcester and then on to Yale for the great conference held under the auspices of the new Foundation. There follows another long, diary-style letter:

The conference sessions went well and I presided for two and a half
hours, really a minor triumph as I was an unknown quantity. The
general scholastic level is low but when they are brilliant they are *very*
brilliant ... There were cocktail parties, buffet suppers, receptions,
etc., ending in a visit to the W.S. Lewis shrine to Horace Walpole
– filled with books, pictures and furniture from Strawberry Hill – at
Farmington, Connecticut. The lectures on the last day were awful,
either wrong, bad or just dull. I was glad, however, for the Yale contacts and meeting again my old teacher, a marvellous man, Charles
Mitchell, who used to be at the Warburg. He is the salt of the earth
and absolutely brilliant and devastating. 'What have you done to your
hair?' was his opening gambit! And so on to New York. I LOVE New
York. It is classic, lyrical, beautiful, liberating and just everything
... [I] rushed round, saw people at the Frick, Metropolitan, Hispanic
Society and so on. A week was far too short. The Frick lecture went
reasonably well. The audience stayed. It tends to be *grandes dames*
with hats. That at the Metropolitan was my most successful. I
worked frantically at the Folger [Shakespeare Library] ... It was 91 in
Washington and the heat was killing. After four days I made the flight
to San Francisco, a wonderful journey almost 3,000 miles across via
Dallas, Texas, where I changed planes (a frontier civilization still.
All the magazines on the bookstands were on shooting and everyone
was still wearing those large hats). Then over the Grand Canyon, a
nightmare landscape as though some gigantic rodent had gnawed
chunks out of the earth's surface. And so I arrived in San Francisco.
This is one of the world's *most* beautiful cities. It is breathtaking. It is
built on hills jutting out into a peninsula surrounded by blue water on
almost every side and, in the distance, hills. The streets are very steep
and the houses, very distinctive architecturally, are painted every
pastel shade imaginable and cascade down the hillsides. The light is
clear and beautiful and the temperature never sinks below 45 or rises
above 75. And there are two great bridges, the most marvellous being
the Golden Gate Bridge. I was astounded and amazed and loved the
place. The vegetation is lush and luxuriant, palm trees and exotic

flowers. I was royally entertained by both the curators of both the town's museums ... And so to Los Angeles by plane. Another wonderful flight on a clear day looking down on the Pacific and the green coastal shoreline, hills, mountains, desert and the inland plateau...

And so I ramble on. But pertinent is my general conclusion about America after having made the twentieth-century equivalent of the Grand Tour:

> Wild horses would never get me here ... As a visitor one has the best. One makes money to take home and can be warmly accepted as a visitor and not as a competitor. The whole museum and university set-up is cankered and rotten. Staff is bid for like cattle and one can use offers from outside to lever promotion and salary rises. It's sordid. A friend of mine in the Metropolitan was offered a contract by Sotheby's. She put it in an envelope to the Director and he had one way or the other to outbid to hold her ... Everyone is charming and one's life-long friend in five minutes flat and one is wafted everywhere and wined and dined. But what does it mean? NOTHING for the most part whereas if an English person asks someone home it really does mean something. This so far sounds a scathing indictment and it is, yet I have several people who will remain long and faithful friends, but one has to keep one's wits constantly sharpened. You are useful to them, they are useful to you. Play the game to mutual advantage and leave it at that. Most of all I fear the sort of person one could so easily become if one settled here. I have learnt a lot about human nature and a lot about myself on this trip. You will obviously come here sooner or later and be treated, like me, as visiting royalty. Bear in mind what I have said and always penetrate the veneer. The pastures are lush but remember the mud beneath.

This was the most intensively American period of my life but in the 1960s there was so much to learn there. Almost half a century on Yale still remains for me a loved and respected connection, particularly a friendship with the former first Director of the Yale Center, Professor Jules Prown. After I resigned from the V&A in 1987 I was offered an American museum post but, as can be seen from this letter, I had already reached my own conclusions and declined it.

⸻

With a flat to furnish and a burgeoning lifestyle, money was a constant incentive to hit the American trail. Twice I undertook a summer school at Burlington, Vermont, in August. What follows is an account written to Jan of one of these that, in 1966, is not without interest:

> Well the great thing was the Burlington Vermont trip. It was a rave success and I had such a good time. I was thrilled and got so much out of it. After a hair-raising flight from Boston to Burlington in a thunderstorm, the worst I have ever experienced (I was terrified) I touched down at Burlington, of course not to be recognized by Professor Pappoutsakis and wife who expected someone aged ninety with Oxford bags and white hair. When they eventually concluded that the Beatle boy was actually their costly little Elizabethan art expert they tried hard not to show surprise. The set-up was this. It was an MA summer school, 1,500 people had applied and sixty were accepted. They came from all over the States. They ranged in age from 20 to 50 and from the very good to the, let's face it, dim. Nearly all of us, including me, lived in a hall of residence and the sex life which went on was just no one's business. The man who played Hamlet wafted his girls into the fall-out shelter.

Each day morning lectures were followed by post-lunch discussion groups and then it all came to a close at three o'clock every afternoon:

> I generally went down to the pub in Burlington called Conrad's and played American shuffle-board. Evenings: there were several nights

of new productions by the Champlain Shakespeare Festival Troupe. They massacred three plays in an arena theatre. I presided for seven one-hour lectures. I opened with the festivals which knocked them flat and, at the last lecture, bless their hearts, they all rose to their feet and clapped me and wouldn't let me go. I was very touched. They all clubbed round and presented me with a sweat-shirt inscribed Conrad's which I wore at my last lecture. They were really fun as people and as a group were so responsive and excited. I can think of so many little incidents that brought home what I had done and it made it all seem alive and glittering to me once more. The students as such fall mentally into two groups, the Germanic-Catholic education group [who] wanted me to lay down the law and for them just to scribble in submissive silence and group two, the group I cherished, those who wouldn't accept a word anyone said at face value, that questioned well and intelligently and had a quick and ready wit and sense of humour.

These two summer schools were to be my last appearance as a university lecturer/teacher. Later I was twice to be a visiting lecturer at Yale for short periods delivering a series of lectures but that was it.

The mileage covered in these three years, the people I met and the exhibitions I staged convey something of the frenzy of activity of my life from the moment I left home. There was so much catching up to be done! At the NPG David Piper was proving to be a fine Director. Everything seemed settled for the next few years, with Pete doing the political-managerial cut-and-thrust and myself re-presenting the galleries and staging exhibitions to wow the public. And then suddenly, like lightning striking, in December 1966, when he had been in office barely two years, came the news that he had accepted the directorship of the Fitzwilliam Museum, Cambridge. I was shattered.

EPILOGUE

J UST A FEW WEEKS into my directorship the formidable former editor
of *Vogue* and now much-valued friend, Beatrix Miller, decided that
something was stirring down in St Martin's Place and commissioned
Cecil Beaton to record this new phenomenon. I was to be one of what
Beatrix called her 'firsts', reflecting her remarkable ability to spot those
who were to be the new stars in the sixties firmament. Beatrix estimated
that Cecil's photograph of me was one of the best he had taken for some
time. Inevitably I was nervous at being photographed by someone
who was to me a legend. Cecil snapped away as, under his direction,
I assumed a variety of poses but I can claim that the definitive image,
which appeared as a double-page spread in the September issue, was
my idea. This was me as I was when I achieved the first of my life's two
great ambitions, to be Director of the National Portrait Gallery.

The news that the directorship was up for grabs electrified me. I descended into gloom as initially I found it inconceivable that they would appoint a thirty-one-year-old. There would be pressure for someone over forty to be appointed. There would also be the problem of me leapfrogging over John Kerslake, who was senior to me and within memory the directorship had never been anything other than dead men's shoes, everyone moving up one. Logically David Piper should have been appointed Director when Hake died, for he was to be an outstanding Director of both the Fitzwilliam and Ashmolean Museums. However, I recall him saying to me in respect of the NPG: 'You can change it. I can't.' This was an admission that he had been there just too long to shift it.

So the wheels of the Civil Service appointment machine were set in motion. The job at least for the first time was to be advertised. That was to be in February and the interviews were to take place in March. There was, however, a minor glitch, for initially applicants had to be at least thirty-five to apply. But the new Chairman of Trustees, Lord Kenyon, and Pete saw that reduced to thirty. Naturally I was seized by tides of contrary emotions, the strongest being that so much of the recent public success of the NPG was owed to my initiatives and hard work, so 'why the hell should I slave transforming this place for someone else like I have done for David Piper?' There is no doubt but that he wanted me to succeed him, and for that I revere his memory.

But I had to recruit my referees. Pete, of course, was one as I was a member of his staff. Francis Wormald, by now President of the Society of Antiquaries, was a second, joined by Sir Oliver Millar, Surveyor of the Queen's Pictures, and Frances Yates. This was a pretty formidable line-up but I knew that I needed more than that in my armoury. I needed to go into that interview with a plan. I still have the strategy document I wrote, written in longhand. Here is how it opens:

THE NATIONAL PORTRAIT GALLERY
The Next Ten Years

The National Portrait Gallery, as is well known, houses the nation's collection of famous British men and women of the past. It was founded in 1856 for this purpose, but also embodies a reflection of Victorian attitudes to portraiture, i.e. moral didacticism. The latter attitude can no longer be sustained and is compensated today by the Gallery's role as a centre for the science of portrait iconography. On the scholastic side the Gallery should aim to be the fountainhead of portrait studies or at least be recognized as an institute of historical research in its own right. This will depend on the intellectual calibre and activity of its staff in the next two decades.

As a public institution it should aim to present English history in the form of its personalities in a way both delightful and informative. We have passed the period when to be instructive was to be dreary. As in the Victorian period, education and entertainment are once more compatible...

There then follow several pages going section by section through the Gallery's structure as to what needed to be done. And it concludes with what I thought of the existing staff.

There are also forceful paragraphs about promotion and publicity and the need for both. There is recognition of the 'rudimentary stage' of the NPG's publications: 'There appears to have been little or no effort by the staff to produce any range of publications in the past. It will require an enormous effort to catch up even with some of the provincial galleries, but we must.' There are laments as to the quality of the warding staff, who also hung the galleries: 'The difficulty lies in the failure to obtain any except the aged and decrepit.' Education had already come on the agenda under David Piper and the task fell to Richard Ormond: 'We have got over pre-conceived attitudes', I wrote, 'and seen that there is a huge potential.'

Under exhibitions there is a strong statement that one on contemporary portraiture was badly needed, mentioning Graham Sutherland, a retrospective of whose portraits eventually happened under my successor, John Hayes. More surprisingly (unless a page is missing), I can find no reference to photography, which was to be a major policy shift when I took over. I may have regarded it as dangerous waters into which to wade in respect of the Trustees. It amuses me now to read under the role of Director: 'Must be the major social envoy of the gallery on the London scene and abroad...' And then comes the comment which nearly cost me the job: 'There would be a good case for obtaining a country house near London to take major items in the reserve collection.'

On 14 March I reported to Jan that I was to be interviewed two days later, on 16 March at 2.35 p.m. What an extraordinary time! By then I knew of only three people who were in for it: John Jacob, Deputy Director of the Walker Art Gallery, Liverpool, John Kerslake and myself. The interviewing board was to consist of Lord Kenyon, the new Chairman, Sir Gyles Isham as a second Trustee, a Civil Service Commissioner, Professor E.H. Gombrich, by then Director of the Warburg Institute, and Professor E.K. Waterhouse, doyen of British art historians.

All I can remember about the interview is that I left knowing that I could not have done it better. I had worked up to it for three months and I had mastered, as far as I could, every detail of an ongoing programme. Only the proposal, as yet undeveloped, that the NPG should have a relationship with the National Trust and decentralize some of its huge collections nearly cost me the job. In the eyes of the Trustees, nothing should ever leave the sacred precincts of St Martin's Place. It makes me smile now in retrospect to see Lord Kenyon cite those outposts as one of the Gallery's greatest achievements under his chairmanship.

Both my private and gallery appointment diaries have inscribed in them on 17 March, in capital letters: 'THE DAY I HEARD'. Lloyd Kenyon took me out to dinner to celebrate. The news, however, had to remain under wraps until it was officially announced on the Court Circular page of *The Times*, so it was not until 25 March that I was able to write to Jan:

> GOT IT [*underlined twice*]. I feel humbled in exultation as it is a fantastic achievement at 31, beaten only by Sir Kenneth Clark at the National. The short list was hot and fantastic and included star-bright boy Michael Levey from the National [where he became a fine Director]. I apparently swept the board. But the tasks ahead are terrific and daunting and exhilarating.

The news that this relatively unknown, bespectacled young man had become the National Portrait Gallery's new Director duly appeared on a Saturday when I was in the Gallery and feeling a trifle lonely and unloved. The phone rang and it was Dicky Buckle: 'Come over and have some lunch.' So I made my way to the Henrietta Street flat and he plied me with champagne and smoked salmon before going off to review a matinée at the Opera House. I will always remember that gesture of kindness.

Both diaries have inscribed, again in capital letters, on 1 June: 'I TAKE OVER AS DIRECTOR'. Already on 25 May, thanks to Dicky, I had been to lunch with Cecil Beaton in Pelham Place, and the exhibition which was to change the public's perception of the NPG forever began its journey to realization. On 3 June I wrote to Jan:

Things are moving: one great triumph scored already. Via Dicky
Buckle I went to lunch with Cecil Beaton and he has agreed to
present prints of any of his portrait photographs we want, 1928–67.
They are ravishing and brilliant and of all the greats. To mark this
Buckle will design us a Beaton show in the autumn of 68, which
ought to cause a furore!!

It did. Meanwhile, the letters of congratulation poured in from people
as varied as the musician Thurston Dart to the writer Elizabeth Jenkins,
and from a whole gamut of national museum directors – although not
from Sir Philip Hendy, Director of next door. Lincoln Kirstein wrote:
'I'm so happy for ENGLAND'. Joe Trapp saluted me as 'the first Warburg
Old Boy to become Director of the NPG – as indeed of anything besides
the Warburg Institute'. And a touching one from E.H. Gombrich read:
'I have not forgotten the silly letter I wrote to you years ago trying to
dissuade you from taking up an academic career. I have rarely been
happier at being so utterly wrong.' And there let it lie.

Ahead of me lay over twenty years directing and changing two of
the nation's greatest institutions, for the V&A came my way in 1974,
when I was thirty-eight. In the case of the NPG my challenge involved
re-presenting the public galleries, setting in motion a programme of
cleaning and restoring the collection, giving status to photography,
establishing an education programme, staging innovative exhibitions
and getting the Trustees to agree to collect portraits of living sitters.
In the case of the V&A it was to be a bloodier saga involving getting
the museum out of government hands by Act of Parliament, setting up
the Friends, starting what was in effect a development office, forcing
the curatorial staff to collect the present and establishing a course with
the Royal College of Art which would ginger up the smug antiquarian

attitudes of the staff. None of that was easy or happy during an era of swingeing cuts to staff and militant union power. And beyond stretched yet more, a life as a writer, diarist and gardener, little of which could have been foreseen in those heady days in 1967.

———

So what are we to conclude, if anything from this journey, as I wrote of it at the opening of this memoir, of 'a young man from nowhere who went somewhere'? Firstly I think of it as an act of reconciliation. I feel penitent about those relationships and events which went wrong, wishing that they had not happened. That has to be balanced by the fact that in so many instances those frissons enabled me to develop and cut loose and make what contribution I could. Also, I am struck by the good fortune that came my way. Minus the legislation which put in place what was in fact a social revolution, none of this would have happened. Luck came also in the form of a passion for portraits during a period when they were despised. Luck also came into being the right person in the right place at the right time. Although I was to have powerful allies, all of it was achieved by someone who was totally devoid of any connection that brought advantage through either wealth or family. Later in life people assumed that I had had a privileged upbringing. Aspiration and dogged determination were there in abundance, and relentless application. If parts of this narrative have struck the reader as tedious, that would be right, for much was dull. Several of the virtues we were brought up on – duty, patriotic pride, obedience, service to others, living within one's means and competitiveness – have vanished or been held up to ridicule. But when friends of my generation start bemoaning the new generation – *O tempora! O mores!* – I always reply: 'No, it wasn't better then; it was just different.'

INDEX

I get a B+? for the European paper and B (I was told I would have got B+ if I had finished the paper) for the English history to 1815. I came fifth in the general knowledge paper thanks to my essay on art and economics. So you can see I have not done too badly. I suppose next year will be spent in eliminating the question mark elements in my papers.

For my optional subject next session I have chosen the Civilisation of the Renaissance in Italy with a view to doing Florence and the Renaissance as my special subject. As you know long essays are my stumbling block and I have had a sorry year of Italian evening classes. My Italian is lamentably weak so I have yet to get to grips with it during the vacation or else the outlook will be a bit grim.

Q.M.C. is not exactly one's ideal of a college (what a dreadful building! what awful surroundings!) and I must admit the journey through the not very salubrious parts of the East End is extremely dreary, tiring, expensive and time wasting. I also have periodical yearnings for the Courtauld Institute ever since I was told by a friend of mine about the contents of the course. I do hope to be able to go on to the Warburg — that is if the grant continues or I can get a scholarship. I realise that one degree is not really of much use — interesting jobs are so difficult to get. All I want